Publications in Librarianship No. 58

Centers for Learning: Writing Centers and Libraries in Collaboration

James K. Elmborg and Sheril Hook

Association of College and Research Libraries
A division of the American Library Association
Chicago, 2005

The paper used in this publication meets the minimum requirements of American National Standard for Information Sciences-Permanence of Paper for Printed Library Materials, ANSI Z39.48-1992.?

Library of Congress Cataloging in Publication Data

Centers for learning : writing centers and libraries in collaboration
 / edited by James K. Elmborg and Sheril Hook.
   p. cm.   (Publications in librarianship ; no. 58)
  Includes bibliographical references and index.
  ISBN 0 8389 8335 9 (alk. paper)
  1. Academic libraries Relations with faculty and curriculum.
2. Writing centers. 3. Academic libraries United States Case
studies. 4. Libraries and colleges United States Case studies.
5. Writing centers United States Case studies. 6. English
language Rhetoric Study and teaching. 7. Report writing
  Study and teaching (Higher) 8. Interdisciplinary approach in
education. 9. Information literacy.   I. Elmborg, James K.,
1953   . II. Hook, Sheril. III. Series: ACRL publications in
librarianship ; no. 58.
Z674.A75 no. 58
[Z675.U5]
020 s dc22
[027.7]

                                              2005013806

Printed in the United States of America.

07 08 09 06 05   5 4 3 2 1

Table Of Contents

Acknowledgments

James Elmborg

I am happy to take this opportunity to thank the many friends and colleagues who have shared in the journey toward this book. For my collaborator, Sheril Hook, I am extremely grateful. To have worked through a project of such complexity and to emerge with mutual respect and strengthened friendship is no small feat. I continue to be thankful for the fine graduate education I received in the English Department at The University of Kansas. The ten years I spent at KU teaching undergraduate composition continue to inform every aspect of my work. I am also grateful to the many colleagues over the years who have shared my interest in the intersections between writing and information literacy, a group that includes both librarians and writing professionals. From Washington State University, special thanks go to Amy Beasley, Dennis Bennett, Alison Walker-Manning, Paula Elliot, Alice Spitzer, Nancy Baker, Bill Condon, Sue McLeod, and Victor Villanueva—an absolutely remarkable collection of educators from whom I learned much; from Wofford College, I especially thank Shelly Sperka, Ellen Tillett, Deno Trakas, Oakley Coburn, and Adam Lamkin; from Furman University, I thank James Inman,, Janis Bandelin, John Payne, and Hayden Porter. I am especially indebted to the Andrew W. Mellon Foundation for supporting my interests in Information Literacy and emerging technologies. And most of all, I am grateful to my wife Ann, who supports me, argues with me, and helps me grow in every way.

James Elmborg
The University of Iowa
Iowa City, Iowa

Sheril Hook

First, I thank Jim Elmborg for his collaboration on this project and for our many fruitful conversations on the subject of writing and research. I would also like to thank Pat Promis at the University of Arizona Libraries, who supported the project by granting me research time to prepare the manuscript. I especially appreciate those librarians and writing professionals who worked with me to develop collaborations and implement programs on several campuses. They are Goodie Bhullar and Sally Foster at the University of Missouri-Columbia; John Van Balen and Jill Tyler at the University of South Dakota; Carla Stoffle, Donna Rabuck, and Pat Youngdahl at the Unviersity of Arizona. Finally, I especially thank my husband Brian and our children Talitha, Naomi, and Zachary Niall for their patience, wisdom, and love.

Sheril Hook
University of Toronto at Mississauga

v

Introduction

James K. Elmborg and Sheril Hook

This is a book about collaboration. It reflects the work of many people who have reached out across institutional boundaries, believing that by doing so they can do more effective and more meaningful work. Such an approach is difficult. Academic culture is conservative, and creative new approaches to work sometimes arouse suspicion or meet resistance for a variety of reasons. Sometimes the participants in collaborations encounter difficulties internally as they attempt to understand each other and learn to work together. All these difficulties are reflected in this collection. In addition to the difficulties, however, the excitement and sense of new possibility that arises from collaboration also are reflected here. As people learn to work together toward a common and important goal, they learn exciting new things about themselves and about the people who share their institutions. In preparing the book, we have endeavored above all to allow the reality of the collaborations to emerge and to encourage the voice of each collaborator.

The book itself began with a collaboration—or at least a shared idea. We met in Iowa City, Iowa, at, fittingly enough, the Powerful Teaching, Powerful Partnerships conference (November 1999), at which we were encouraged to get out of our "academic silos" by considering partnerships that could benefit students. Sheril attended Jim's presentation on creating scope and sequence in information literacy by using composition as a model. Later at the conference, we met for lunch to talk about writing and researching as shared processes with shared agendas. We both lamented that both writing program staff and information literacy librarians seemed stuck in their respective "silos," and we wondered how we might encourage them to work together. We vowed to "keep in touch." Two years later, we met again at the Association of College & Research Libraries (ACRL) conference in Denver (April 2001). Jim attended Sheril's presentation on a library, writing center, and speech communication collaboration. In a discussion after the session, the idea for this book was born. We have since worked together on other projects, most notably, the Best Practices in Information Literacy advisory panel. We both have changed jobs since our first meeting, with Jim changing roles entirely from academic librarian to library and information science faculty. We have had our own silos to overcome in producing this book, and that, too, is part of this tale of collaborations.

In assembling this book, we have tried to weave the collaborations into the structure of the book. We asked for coauthored chapters. We wanted each pair of writers to consist of a writing center director and a librarian, though in some cases we accepted single authors with a particularly important voice. One such voice comes from Southwest Missouri State student Casey Reid. Reid was an undergraduate writing tutor and student reference assistant. She reflects on her growing sense that in providing reference service and in tutoring writers, she was involved in a single synergistic process. She also provides an important student perspective on collaboration, as she discusses the potentials and barriers to work in "the trenches." Judy Arzt at St. Joseph College provides a longitudinal discussion by narrating the institutional history of collaboration between the writing center and the library. Speaking from the writing center perspective, she surveys several generations of the collaboration, giving an invaluable overview of the ebbs and flows of a partnership.

We strove with the authors to find the balance of interest between writing centers and librarians, and we encouraged what we called a "warts-and-all" analysis of the work these institutional partners were doing. We wanted to know about both the successes and the "challenges" of the work. Some of the case studies we solicited seemed to roll off the press with little to no urging from us. Others were more difficult, but in these cases we encouraged the writers to make the difficulty part of the story. Some of the case studies surprised us and stretched our own conception of our topic. We did not expect to receive a proposal from a writing center director and a university archivist discussing the assembling of a university writing archive, yet this study became one of the most intriguing chapters in the book. Indeed, the story of the University of New Hampshire-Durham archive has much to teach librarians about how to approach their own history and how they might study the evolution of information literacy as an academic movement.

Although our intent in this book is to discuss a collaboration between two particular campus units in order to illustrate common practices and shared theories that can bring us to appreciate and support each other's work, we acknowledge that many units on campus have the potential for collaboration and that academic libraries and writing centers themselves have other potential partners. Surely, some readers will identify different or additional units in collaboration. We hope this book will provide them with ways to begin those campus discussions. A model for such discussions is provided in the case study from The

University of Kansas. Eodice and Curry provide their observations on a meeting they had with the campus leadership. Their goal is to examine the nature of collaboration and where the institutional incentives and impediments to collaboration lie. The current climate on most campuses welcomes such discussions that require reassessment of services and a consideration of isolated units partnering to combine facilities and resources, identifying common goals to contribute to student learning, creating and supporting learning environments that are intellectually challenging for students, and codeveloping and supporting curricula. Through these campus discussions, it is likely that new models for learning will emerge, models that are not tied to seat time and in which a variety of campus units play significant roles in creating, maintaining, and assessing their impact on student learning.

Several case studies in this collection describe such new models. Leadley and Rosenberg offer the story of their course-integrated project at the University of Washington-Bothel. They examine several generations of course development designed around bringing active learning strategies to an interdisciplinary course on research and writing. Particularly interesting is their analysis of faculty development workshops and what they have learned about working with faculty. Toth and Boff describe their pilot project at Bowling Green State University, in which they experimented with Term Paper Clinics for students held in the library. Pobywaijlo and White describe their program at University of New Hampshire-Manchester, with special emphasis on tutor training and "just-in-time" instruction. Giglio and Strickland consider the interpersonal aspects of collaboration: how two people at Wesley College have worked to keep their institutional partnership going through institutional and technological change. They remind us of the importance of personal commitment to the collaborative process. Hook and Rabuck provide an in-depth look at the dynamics that inform the tutor–tutee relationship. By focusing on the risks that writers and researchers take in their work, they explore the importance of building trust between learners and tutors. This case study examines the support that graduate students need as they work toward producing independent scholarship. In total, these case studies give us a dynamic picture of many multifacted collaborations and the many ways the case study writers found to approach and describe their work signals the creative, intellectual energy involved in their work.

Even though libraries and writing centers have different missions and roles in their institutions, we think we'll be the wiser if we follow rhetorician Rolf Norgaard's timely advice:

> With our disciplinary territories marked and our professional identities protected, we could easily share our stories of teach-

ing and service and content ourselves with a bit of friendly theory-swapping between our intellectual neighborhoods. We could commiserate, offer nods of support, pick up a tip or two, jot down that interesting reference to recent work, and be on our merry ways. And be poorer for it.[1]

Our choice of topic represents our own academic trajectory as former teachers of writing who found our way to librarianship and information literacy. We have prepared this book primarily for writing center directors, writing tutors, and librarians, and secondarily for those interested in teaching writing, whether in a composition program or part of a writing-across-the-curriculum effort. We hope that those reading it, and the students with whom they work, will be the richer for it.

James K. Elmborg
Iowa City, Iowa,

Sheril Hook
Tucson, Arizona
August 2004

Note

1. Rolf Norgaard, "Writing Information Literacy in the Classroom: Pedagogical Enactments and Implications," *Reference and User Services Quarterly* 43, no. 3 (2004): 225.

Chapter one

Libraries and Writing Centers in Collaboration: A Basis in Theory

James K. Elmborg

For at least the past twenty years, writing centers and libraries have been living parallel lives, confronting many of the same problems and working out similar solutions, each in their own institutional contexts. During that time, they both have established a new kind of instructional practice within the context of a sometimes resistant academic culture and, in many cases, have become change agents on campuses, advocates for the importance of teaching and learning and for improving the educational experiences for students. If politics is "the art of the possible," libraries and writing centers have been politically successful at expanding the boundaries to stretch what has been possible in their respective worlds. By all counts, the work has been challenging and rewarding, and from the current vantage point, it is tempting to conclude that both information literacy instruction and writing centers have "arrived" in institutional terms. Both have established credible academic practice along with a new kind of research and theory base that connects daily instruction with an increasingly rigorous inquiry into student learning and the production of student work. What is remarkable, as Barbara Fister has noted, is that the two have done so with almost no formal interaction in either theory or practice.[1]

Indeed, the underlying thesis of this book is that both writing centers and information literacy instruction have grown to a point where formal collaborative partnerships might be the best way to open new lines of development. In doing so, we contend that more powerful, more dynamic, and more effective instructional practice can be achieved than either has been able to achieve alone. Although this collaboration may seem logical, it is clearly not easy. Collaboration depends on many factors—timing, personalities, institutional context, to name a few. Having achieved a level of maturity and confidence, writing centers and libraries now are able to strike more coherent institutional partnerships. Having the maturity to stand effectively alone, both instructional librarians and writing center staff can leverage their strengths to explore a new kind of shared practice where research and writing can be treated as a single holistic process.[2] The logical points of collaboration are delineated throughout the case studies that comprise the second part of the book. General themes that emerged in the course of collecting the case studies are explored here, with the goal of articulating in broad terms the context for the collaboration and the theoretical assumptions that the case studies illustrate. What has emerged is a snapshot in time composed of a series of independent collaborative initiatives. The overarching sense one gets from these narratives is that collaboration continues to be difficult, requiring both an institutional commitment that transcends personalities and shared individual commitments by those actually doing the work. These commitments can only be expected when those involved share a vision of what becomes possible through their work.

Political Possibilities

We are obviously in the midst of major changes in the landscape of higher education. These changes—driven by (among other things) technology, the increasing diversity of American culture, a global economy, and a new accountability demanded by funding agencies and the workplace—require creative new approaches. Academic disciplines no longer hold absolute power in higher education, and new alliances bring the potential for new opportunities. As J. F. Lyotard argued in one of the first descriptions of this new, emergent climate, the questions of higher education increasingly would be approached through a series of "pragmatic" questions: "Who transmits learning? What is transmitted? To whom? Through what medium?" Lyotard argued that the "student is no longer a youth from the 'liberal elite,' more or less concerned with the great task of social progress." He wrote that today's students are simply "young people who have yet to become 'active'" in a practical sense, and higher education will become increasingly charged with transmitting the skills and concepts that students need to be "active" in the world they enter upon graduation. Lyotard concluded that the foundational pedagogy of the university is in transition. In the emergent model with knowledge, or "content," increasingly stored in databases,

> students ... still need to be taught something: not contents, but how to use the terminals. On the one hand, that means teaching new languages and on the other, a more refined ability to handle the language game of interrogation— where should the question be addressed, in other words, what is the relevant memory bank for what needs to be known? How should the question be formulated to avoid misunderstandings?[3]

Lyotard's educational model demanded a new pedagogy, one that would treat the teaching of content as less important than the process of inquiry and the mode of access to that content. This shift sees the student as "plugging in" to the network where knowledge is stored and interacting with that knowledge in a new way. No longer responsible for holding knowledge in his or her head, the new student needs the ability to access quickly and process efficiently the knowledge stored in databases and the parallel ability to synthesize that knowledge into something "active" in the world.

Evidence of the shift Lyotard described can be seen throughout the university today. Although little consensus has emerged about the nature of the "new student," what has emerged is an agreement that today's student is somehow different from past generations of students. Whether we label these young people as Generation X, Generation Y, "Millennials" (or some other name of the moment), speculation about how they will best learn and how schools should change in response to them abounds. Nearly all such speculation begins with the "plugged-in" nature of these students' learning and with consensus that a new "learning style" is evolving. Howard Gardner redrew the intellectual landscape, proposing that intelligence is a much more elastic concept than we have presumed. He argued that in addition to linguistic and logical–mathematical intelligence (those traditionally tested and rewarded in schools), people possess other kinds of intelligence, including musical intelligence, bodily–kinesthetic intelligence, spatial intelligence, interpersonal intelligence, and intrapersonal intelligence.[4] G. Kress and T. van Leeuwen argued that traditional literacy is not enough for today's students immersed in the modern academic landscape. They claimed that modern literacies are "multimodal" requiring students to process text, images, and sounds with the same kind of expertise traditionally required of print.[5] Donald Tapscot saw the new students as engaged, politically astute, highly loyal to friends and family, but very cynical about school and very turned-off when schools fail to capitalize on the possibilities of the new learning environment, rich with multimedia and information technology.[6] Although Tapscot emerged as a champion of the new student, others portray a much less rosy picture, emphasizing, instead, the propensity for sloppy thinking and shoddy research made possible by a cut-and-paste approach to research and writing.[7]

To reach these new students, new student services have been evolving outside the context of academic disciplines, the traditional power bases of higher education. These new models include freshman seminar programs, honors programs, service learning programs, women's studies, area studies, efforts to infuse writing, critical thinking, critical literacy, and media literacy across the curriculum. Studies such as the Boyer Report suggest that research universities need to reinvent undergraduate education, and foundations such as Mellon, Kellogg, and Carnegie pour money into projects that use technology and new teaching methods to reinvigorate the undergraduate experience.[8] The federal government, through programs such as the Fund for the Improvement of Post-secondary Education, funds projects to move higher education in new directions.

Key to understanding these new programs is to understand the ways they presuppose that higher education needs to be "fixed." There is general consensus that the traditional concept of knowledge as it is transmitted in disciplinary classrooms is inadequate for present and future student learning. Lyotard described a fundamental change in the relationship between teaching, learning, and academic content. Increasingly, knowledge itself is stored and handled by the computing network. Students are charged with learning to manipulate that network to retrieve knowledge. They also are charged with learning to integrate the knowledge they retrieve into their own writing and lives, to make it their own, and to convey it to others. These are skills students will need to become "active" upon graduation, an activeness they will need to maintain throughout their lives. This new process is not the result of choices made by teachers; rather, it is a reflection of the way the world now works.

A Collaborative Age

There is general consensus that the realignment of academic institutions currently under way raises new questions about collaboration, and we are clearly living in an age of experimentation and redefinition. D. Ward and D. Raspa saw the "collaborative imperative" as arising from fundamental social change:

> We know today that standard practices from the past do not suffice. They do not help much to deal with the complexities of contemporary life, nor with the realities of information. Old borders separating disciplines along departmental lines are blurring ... The old, fragmented view of disciplinary practice cannot deal with the complexity of social issues today.[9]

They concluded that collaboration provides the best means for libraries (and others) to explore solutions to problems and to explore new models.

Libraries are self-consciously redefining themselves, moving away from the warehousing definitions of the past and toward instructional models. The literacy metaphor adopted by librarians in defining their instructional services, information literacy, links them to new and critical literacies. These definitions of literacy, descended in large part from the work of Paulo Freire, reframe education as the process of developing empowered students who create personal knowledge.[10] Education is reconceived as the transformative power of creating that new knowledge. By moving away from tool-based approaches that focus on discrete skills, such as the construction of good search statements and the mechanics of bibliographic conventions (the grammar of information), information literacy emphasizes, instead, the role of information in the larger learning processes of students, helping them to make the shift from a world where mastering content constituted education to one in which navigating information systems and making new personal and public knowledge constitutes education.

Pragmatic Fields at Work

Of all the things librarians and compositionists (and, by extension, writing tutors) share, perhaps the most important is an essentially pragmatic orientation. Libraries and writing centers deal with real-world problems that involve a high volume of students doing work under time pressure. Both libraries and writing centers have found themselves on the front lines of technology implementation,[11] being among the first to explore online services[12] and online tutorials to allow students to do their work remotely. Librarians and writing center personnel regularly struggle to help students make sense of assignments that seem to work against the learning process or against the logical use of their resources. They must mediate between faculty members who assign the work and students who must do the work. Consequently, how they relate to faculty has been a primary concern of both librarians and writing center personnel.[13] They regularly deal with students who want to have their papers edited for them or have their sources found for them. They do so without the power of the grade to enforce their instruction and one could argue that, as a result, their relationships with students are more genuine and honest than those between students and their professors. Both librarians and writing center staff deal with an anomalous status in their institutions, often without full-faculty status or full-faculty prestige. In institutions that sometimes seem dominated by abstraction and intellectualization, librarians and writing center staff have practical concerns. This basis in reality does not imply, however, that the work lacks intellectual rigor. In fact, the constant testing of theory against practice demands a new kind of rigor. The strength of both the writing center literature and the information literacy research is its basis in reality.

Idealistic, experimental approaches to the work are part of the discourse of both fields, but, ultimately, if something fails the "reality test," it will be discarded. "Theory" can be valued, but only if it accurately correlates with what happens in the day-to-day activities of the work to be done. Theory interacts on a daily basis with practice, and the challenge to theory is to translate directly into practice. Eric Hobson persuasively argued for the legitimacy of such practice-based theory:

What is available to the writing center community is the radical idea (institutionally at least) of acknowledging and articulating the ways that writing center discourse as pragmatic and contextually aware as it is, creates knowledge that is valid. This understanding of knowledge can be used to replace the modernist/disciplinary, theory/practice dyads with a more flexible, pragmatic understanding of contradiction as acceptable and responsible.... [A] pragmatic perspective toward writing center knowledge accepts contradiction between theory and practice; we reject the "logic" of dialectics.... Instead, we must reshape theory to fit our particular needs in the particular historically located situations in which writing center practitioners find themselves.[14]

In effect, Hobson (and other writing center theorists) have turned their practitioner-grounded perspective into an academic virtue, a way of avoiding the irrelevant abstractions that result from sterile, self-referential theorizing.

Library instruction has been much slower to develop a strong practitioner theory base to inform its work, and the bridge between learning theory and information literacy theory has yet to be completely built. The reasons are complex and involve (at least in part) the differences between how writing programs and libraries have evolved in the academy. Every major university in the United States has a composition program that teaches thousands of students every semester. Such programs employ a faculty of graduate students to teach the students, many of whom take course work in writing theory and pursue Ph.D. degrees in rhetoric and composition. Many such programs are freestanding academic units with tenure-track faculty who both teach in and supervise the writing programs, creating a tight link between the research and the practice of teaching. This arrangement constitutes a powerful research engine with a coherent focus on classroom practice.

In contrast, library and information science (LIS) as an academic field is relatively fragmented and dispersed, distant from the daily practice of teaching librarians in colleges and universities. Those who teach in LIS programs also are dispersed among various specialties based on library types, various library functions, and various research methodologies. Indeed, many faculty in LIS have little concern with libraries at all, focusing, instead, on information as a discrete subject. Unlike composition programs, LIS programs exist on very few campuses, and within these programs, educational research competes with management research, historical research, and computer science (and other research traditions) for prestige and dwindling resources.

The consequent dispersion of energy has made it more difficult to develop critical and theoretical approaches to librarianship as a teaching profession. In LIS, a scientific, empirical research model has been predominant, as indicated by the dominance of the "information science" in the names of courses and departments. Such a model works against practice-based research into issues of teaching and learning. Tenure-track faculty in LIS rarely teach in information literacy programs for undergraduates, and as a consequence, much of the newer research into teaching and learning in academic librarianship has been driven by practicing professional librarians rather than by research faculty in LIS. Professional organizations such as ACRL continue to experiment with alternative models for professional education through offerings such as the extremely successful Information Literacy Immersion Institutes and the Instruction Section's research agenda, both powerful examples of new initiatives grounded in library practice that have evolved outside the context of schools of library and information science. For the above reasons, and many others, information literacy theory has matured much more slowly than writing theory and libraries can learn much from writing theory about how to develop a strong classroom research tradition.

Writing and Research as Processes

Both writing instruction and library instruction share a central belief in the importance of process. This belief is based on an understanding of student development and years of research that suggest that to improve student performance, instruction must engage learners in the context of their own efforts to do work that has meaning to them. It has become commonplace to say that library instruction and writing instruction are based on process, not product. In fact, issues that arise in both fields suggest that although process is the dominant model, it is increasingly important in these outcomes-based times to make sure students can actually do the things they need to do. Process means nothing if it fails to produce a product, and each field has its "skills" advocates—those who argue for the importance of grammatical skill in the writing process or the importance of searching skills in the research process.[15] Indeed, the healthy refusal of all teachers to fall into lockstep allegiance to one methodology or one point of view marks a healthy, dynamic field; and one of the most valuable outcomes of a collaboration between writing centers and librarians might be to enlarge this debate and to continue to challenge the assumptions each group makes about process–product dichotomies.

Both writing instruction and library instruction have grown toward a process-based model of instruction through an understanding of how students learn and work. The process model evolved through the interplay of constructivist learning theory and close observation of students at work. Constructivism is based on the argument that humans constructed knowledge as part of their effort to make sense of their environment. Therefore, knowledge is created (or built) by each individual through a scaffolding of concepts and activities. According to Lev Vygotsky, language is the key building block for knowledge. Language is the medium of thought, and the ability to externalize thought in language is a significant measure of concept mastery.[16] Jerome Bruner became a powerful advocate for constructivism in schools through the 1960s. He argued that instruction should be based on three key points: the "readiness" of the student to accept the instruction, the organization of the instruction so as to be accessible to the student, and the opening of exploratory space for the student to pursue further work.[17] In the mid-1970s, a series of landmark studies began to appear that applied constuctivist theories to student writing. Two works that stand out as key are James Britton's *Language and Learning*[18] and Janet Emig's "Writing as a Mode of Learning."[19] Together, these scholars and many others built a bridge from constructivism to writing instruction by suggesting that writing is more than a set of "skills." Rather, it is a key means by which people learn and express what they know. The teaching of the writing process was not merely old wine in new skins. It was a way of placing writing in the larger context of student learning. Following Vygotsky's logic, teaching a student to write well is tantamount to teaching a student to think well. The two go hand in glove.

The writing process is generally understood to include four major phases: brainstorming, drafting, revising, and editing.[20] Each phase has different demands and emphases, and writing process theorists are quick to suggest that these phases, though linear in nature, are really fluid and recursive. As students move from phase to phase, they are really doing all four phases simultaneously. They are drafting while brainstorming. They are brainstorming while revising. Instructors who understand this process can help students become better writers by helping them decide where to spend more energy. In librarianship, the process model was first articulated by Carol Kuhlthau, who identified six stages in the research process: task initiation, topic selection, exploring information, formulating a focus, collecting information, and closing the research process to begin the writing process.[21] She grounded her theory explicitly with the constructivist tradition. She also described the process in recursive terms, more like a "spiral of thoughts … than a neat step-by-step progression."[22] In addition to Kuhlthau's model, the ACRL's Information Literacy Competency Standards propose a simplified process model, as follows:

1.   Determine the extent of information needed.

2. Access the needed information needed effectively and efficiently.

3. Evaluate information and its sources critically.

4. Incorporate selected information into one's knowledge base.

5. Use information effectively to accomplish a specific purpose.

6. Understand the economic, legal, and social issues surrounding the use of information, and access and use information ethically and legally.[23]

Although these standards imply a research process and acknowledge that the information will be used to "accomplish a specific purpose," they make no effort to correlate the search process to the writing process.

One of the foundational principles in this study is that the writing process and the research process are so intimately intertwined in the academic work of students that any effort to separate the two compromises the effort to create an accurate model for working with students. Kuhlthau's initial process model was an important first step in recognizing that research is a process that depends on emotional readiness and timely intervention by teachers, but not nearly enough work has been done in the more than ten years since her initial study to explore the implication of the process model for information literacy. Her work opens large areas of research that still need further exploration to refine our understanding of student research processes and to test it against various academic contexts. For example, Kuhlthau made no distinction between the research process in the social sciences, the sciences, and the humanities. Given the major differences in how these fields define research (from laboratory to ethnographic fieldwork to survey interpretation to textual interpretation, etc.), it seems highly unlikely that one research process describes what all students do. Indeed, part of the problem centers on questions of definition. Kuhlthau described the research process as preceding the writing process, but in descriptions of the research process she included the activities of note taking and journaling (clearly writing activities). It would seem valuable to reconcile the discrepancies between these two versions of process by looking at writing and research as one holistic process, if only to send a more coherent message to students about how the process works.[24] Clearly, more work needs to be done to align what happens in the research and writing processes.

Perhaps a more pressing concern involves the way students engage with their own research. The student's research question derives from a specific assignment in a specific class and his or her level of commitment varies based how committed he or she is to the class or subject. The major models of information seeking (Dervin's "sense-making theory" and Kuhlthau's "seeking meaning" approach, both discussed in more detail later) assume the researcher's sincere best efforts to answer the research question. Kuhlthau's sample groups tend to come from high-achieving students. The first study was composed of students with "standardized test scores above 90 percent, using national percentiles and grade point averages." These students were selected "to investigate the search process of successful students and to observe the strategies they used to work through the process," a worthwhile goal, of course.[25] Kuhlthau described students in another study as having "positive attitudes toward research assignments and [who see] themselves as scholars who would be using libraries for this type of work in the future."[26] This ideal group of student researchers provided a model to be emulated by less successful students, but it tells us little about why some students with just as much academic ability refuse to commit to the research (indeed, to the entire academic) process. Kuhlthau expressed frustration at her lack of success in reaching these less successful students with the survey methodology, indicating at one point that "using a flexible tracking mechanism and perhaps a more qualitative approach is required to investigate the search process of this population."[27] It can be extremely difficult to study the processes of struggling students because they tend to lack the metacognitive ability to reflect on and critique their own efforts. Sometimes such students have the needed skills but refuse to commit to the academic task for social or cultural reasons. Much of the "reform of higher education is designed to reach precisely these students. In fact, critical literacy scholars argue that the ideology of school alienates many students and that we have a moral obligation to continue to try to make education work for these students. A growing body of literature explores the complex reasons why students resist their own educational success.[28] This problem seems to lie outside the methodology employed by Kuhlthau and clearly deserves much more attention from the academic library community.

In the final analysis, the ultimate product of student work is the written assignment and students are often not in a position to determine their information needs in relation to this task. They are learning what is expected of them as college writers and researchers, and they often think their information needs are met only to discover that their instructors think otherwise. In this sense, students often spend more energy figuring out what their professors want than learning to ask and answer genuine question for themselves. Librarians and writing tutors can begin to work with these students by looking for the key points in the writing and research processes where their shared expertise comes into play. During the writing process, students encounter a series of decision points that relate to information and its use. Kuhlthau suggested that there are two major decision points in the research process: topic selection and focus formation.[29] Both occur in the early stages of the writing process, and clearly other decision points occur elsewhere. During the brainstorming phase, students use many sources (the library, the Internet, their friends, their teachers) to try to figure out what is credible to write about and what approach to take. They might pick a good topic or approach and they might not, depending on how they evaluate their sources of information. During the drafting phase, students amass "proof," sometimes without entirely understanding the conventions of evidence and proof in the discipline (what will "count" as evidence). In revision, students are still seeking information to bolster their argument or prove their point. They are driven back to brainstorming/drafting from revision because they have what Brenda Dervin described as an "information gap."[30] They are trying to bridge gaps in their argument or their understanding, gaps that are often abstract or that they themselves fail to understand. In editing, they often require bibliographic information and are driven back to their sources. Sometimes students may think they need information when, in reality, they have a rhetorical problem with a point they are trying to make. Librarians and writing tutors can be very useful throughout this process by asking probing questions that represent the values and interests of the academic community. In most cases, writing tutors can refer students to librarians for information needs and librarians can refer students to writing centers for help with ideas, rhetoric, or presentation. Cross-training of tutors and librarians can help increase the likelihood that such referring will take place appropriately.

The recursiveness in the research/writing process is related at least in part to the recurring interplay between writing and information. By segregating the research process from the writing process, we have obscured this fact and thereby impoverished both the writing process and the research process. This segregation reflects institutional divisions, but not the reality of student work. Composition faculty see the "writing process," whereas librarians see the "research process." This bifurcated approach fails to explain the integrated, holistic experience of the student using information in the writing process. By working in collaboration, these two units can treat the research process and the writing process as a seamless whole. Both writing tutors and librarians can become more adept at recognizing these "decision points" when information moves the research in new directions. Engaging student writers in discussion about these decisions (at both the reference desk and in tutoring sessions) might be very productive, indeed.

The Social Nature of Academic Work

By creating formal, polished academic products, scholars create the sense that writing and research just "appear." In fact, nearly all writers of academic prose find both writing and research to be very difficult work, and their publications usually evolve through many drafts with multiple readers offering feedback. Students who read the published results of such work rarely get much insight into the process that went into the production of any given piece. Peers who read and aid in the revision of academic work are usually members of the academic discipline of the author or share some aspect of the author's research tradition. Academics tend to cluster into distinct (if loosely defined) learning communities. Indeed, finding a peer group is crucial to academic advancement and at the heart of the academic emphasis on peer review. The work of the undergraduate mirrors that of the mature professional academic. In the process of looking for an academic major, students are searching for a peer group that will endorse their efforts and bring them into a community with shared values and shared ways of knowing. Indeed, too little is done to help students understand this process and librarians and writing tutors are uniquely positioned to help meet this need. They can do so by providing students with mentorship and conversation about the academic choices they make.

Kenneth Bruffee argued that the idea of conversation is at the heart of the academic enterprise and at the heart of how people learn. His definition of learning and how it relates to collaboration were derived in large part from Vygotsky's work. Two key points from Vygotsky underlie Bruffee's work. First, learning is highly correlated to conversation. It is through conversation that people exchange ideas and share insights. Students who talk to each other about their academic work do considerably better in school than students who do not. This relatively simple observation holds tremendous power. "Conversation," Bruffee wrote, "is of such vital importance to learning that, with it, any of us has a shot at doing whatever we want to do. Without it, few of us stand a chance."[31] Conversation is at the heart of the learning community, and conversation is at the heart of the process model of instruction, as well.

The second major point that Bruffee derived from Vygotsky is the "zone of proximal development," which he described as "the distance between actual developmental level as determined by independent problem solving and the level of potential development as determined through problem solving under adult guidance or in collaboration with more capable peers."[32]

According to Bruffee, the zone of proximal development refers "to understanding what lies just beyond current knowledge and ability: what we cannot learn on our own at the moment, but can learn with a little help from our friends."[33] Kuhlthau renamed the "zone of proximal development," calling it the "zone of intervention," which she defined as "the area where a person can do with a little assistance what he or she cannot do alone."[34] For Kuhlthau, "identifying when intervention is needed and determining what mediation and education are appropriate is the professional's art, or the role of the reflective practitioner."[35] Indeed, in process-based instruction, an understanding of the student's developmental level (Bruner's "readiness") must come from conversation. Both Kuhlthau and Bruffee saw this conversation as central to the educational process.

According to Bruffee, "collaborative learning models the conversation by which communities of knowledgeable peers construct knowledge."[36] This definition merits examination. Knowledge, according to Bruffee, is "non-foundational." It is not a stable, concrete thing but, rather, something "constructed" by a "community of knowledgeable peers." Who are these peers? They could be college professors, those in the academy most recognized for knowledge creation. But they also could be any group of people who share a peer relationship and are invested in figuring something out. The key to collaborative learning, as Bruffee defined it, is to empower students in peer groups to "model" the conversation of the peer groups they want to join. If a peer group of students want to be biologists, for example, they should "model" the conversation of biologists—to "make believe" they are biologists, in effect. Their professors are ready role models for this game of make-believe. According to Bruffee, when the students have mastered the game of imitating biologists (or engineers, or philosophers, or economists, etc), they will actually be these things.

To help students make this transition, librarians and writing teachers need to become more like anthropologists or sociologists in their study of academic disciplines. Although the advanced knowledge of the disciplines or specialties may be out of reach for these teachers, a sociologist's understanding of the cultures of these departments is not. Bruffee argued,

> Every college and university classroom... is a community. Like all communities, each has its own set of mores, rules, values, and goals, all of them accepted, more or less, by all its members. These community conventions govern every member's language, deportment, relationships, and expectations. They inform the assumptions shared by every member of the community about human nature, the human mind, and the nature and authority of knowledge.[37]

Tony Becher has provided a useful overall framework for understanding how disciplines negotiate their values and structure their social orders. He has approached disciplines as social units, describing the ways they establish their boundaries and how they negotiate prestige and belonging. These factors represent sophisticated distinctions not always accessible to outsiders. In taking a sociological approach to disciplinary knowledge, writing teachers and librarians can be co-investigators with a shared agenda. Students need to understand two critical things in order to become fluent conversationalists in academic discourse. First, they need to understand the nature of academic proof valued in the discipline. Becher described two kinds of proof: empirical proof and theoretical proof. He labeled them "hard" and "soft" proof.[38] Students need to know which kind of proof will succeed in their disciplines, and librarians should be prepared to discuss these conventions with them. Second, students need to know the conventions of publication. These include the publication cycle (the normal purview of librarians) and the conventions of writing (the purview of composition). By collaborating together, librarians and writing instructors can create a powerful learning community with an overlapping zone of proximal development. They can learn from each other and inform each others' work.

Peer Tutoring and Counseling

Students need various kinds of conversation to succeed; they need conversation that is supportive and understanding, as well as conversation that is challenging and problem posing. In addition to conversation with authority figures who represent academic standards and audience (i.e., teachers and librarians), they need conversation with peers. Writing centers employ peer tutors who provide that conversation to students. The advantages to this arrangement are many. Students tend to see the academic environment differently than do those employed within it. Students sympathize with each other's plights as they attempt to navigate obscure assignments or arbitrary grading standards. They share each other's confusion over arcane systems and bureaucratic snafus. Ultimately, they share the desire to succeed in this environment, the desire to figure out how things work and why. Peer tutors in writing centers provide an important kind of conversation, a constructive conversation aimed at figuring out the conventions of academic discourse and what kinds of writing succeed in the academy. In the process, the tutors (already successful academic writers) have the opportunity to become more reflective about their own writing and the choices they are making as young academics.

Bruffee described peer tutoring as a "formula" that is "simple and familiar."

Working through an academic department or some designated structure such as a "writing center" or "learning center," the institution selects undergraduates to work one-on-one with other undergraduates. Tutors meet the students they tutor either individually or in small groups to talk through the academic problems that the tutees have brought to the session. The way they do it depends on the program's "philosophy" and how it is organized.[39]

Bruffee credited peer tutors with the power to act as change agents on campuses because they model a different educational paradigm, one based on conversation rather than lecture. He argued that "peer tutors work best when they do not regard students in the foundational way, as tablets waiting for imprint, but in a nonfoundational way, as members of a variety of nested and overlapping knowledge communities." The job of the tutor, in Bruffee's model, is to "help in translating the terms of the communities they are trying to enter—the academic and professional disciplines, people who read and write standard written English—into the terms of the communities they already belong to, and vice, versa."[40]

Indeed, the importance of tutors in the writing center model cannot be overstated. Peer tutors understand the student perspective because they live that perspective. If academic knowledge is negotiated in a community of "knowledgeable peers," peer tutors provide a readily available resource for students to learn to negotiate that identity. As Bruffee noted, different writing centers have different philosophies but, broadly speaking, share several concerns. All writing centers depend on tutors to do the bulk of the work. The general status of tutors in the scheme (e.g., their level of professionalism, academic training, and availability to walk-in traffic) depends on the philosophy of the center but in all cases is consciously managed by the writing center to provide tutors and their tutees in a coherent way that optimizes the chances for success. Tutors are often required to enroll in classes bearing academic credit that help them tutor more effectively. They manage a complex relationship that depends on their ability to negotiate their own academic expertise with a peer relationship with other writers. A host of interpersonal and academic issues come into play in this relationship—some ethical, some professional, some developmental.

Peer tutors have been used rarely in library instruction in ways that mirror their extensive use in writing centers, though the underlying principles of peer tutoring suggest they would be effective in a library setting. In their extremely useful overview of the role of peer tutors in library instruction, Susan Deese-Roberts and K. Keating outlined a model for hiring, training, and evaluating peer tutors that is largely based on the writing center approach. They suggested, first of all, that any program should be based on sound theoretical principles:

> The philosophy of a peer tutoring program is the basis for answers to overarching questions such as what are the goals of the program and what services are offered. It also creates the context for many implementation issues such as the expectations of tutors, the content of the training program, the methods and systems of tutors and program evaluation, and guidelines for tutee responsibilities.[41]

Deese-Roberts and Keating suggested that the move toward a peer-tutoring program should be part of a larger theoretical orientation based on learning theories and an understanding of the changing role of the library—away from the warehousing model and toward the instructional model. Finally, they argued that collaboration with other campus units that employ peer tutoring would provide many advantages. Indeed, they suggested that "before planning for [a Library Instruction Peer Tutoring Program], one important question regarding program structure must be answered: Should the program be established through collaboration with an existing campus learning center or should it be a library-based program?"[42] They noted many advantages that result from collaboration. Existing peer-tutoring programs have in place "mechanisms for hiring tutors, training tutors, and evaluating tutors." Indeed, they concluded that "numerous possibilities exist for collaboration when library and learning center missions, goals, and values are congruent."[43]

Having outlined the advantages of collaborating with other academic units that do peer tutoring, it might be useful to point to two areas of potential difficulty. These difficulties arise in large part because one of the units in the collaboration fails to understand the other's perspective. Deese-Roberts and Keating provided an extremely valuable overview of the peer-tutoring model in the library. Still, writing center personnel may well disagree with important ways the peer tutor is positioned in their version of the collaborative center. Ideally, the philosophy of the center and the philosophy of the library will be a product of a more overarching philosophy of the institution. In reality, such a sharing of philosophy may not occur without work.

The selection of peer tutors provides the first important occasion for communication. As Bruffee argued,

> the educational effects of peer tutoring, in the short and long run, depend on the degree to which tutors and their tutees are real peers.... In peer tutoring, this equality means, first of all,

that the students involved—peer tutor and tutee alike—believe that they both bring an important measure of ability, expertise, and information to the encounter and, second, that all the students involved believe that, as students, they are unequivocally institutionally status equals.[44]

This peership is, in reality, very difficult to manage. As tutors become more knowledgeable about the subject of their tutoring, they may naturally begin to assume authority over the material. If the tutee begins to perceive this authority and to defer to the knowledge of the tutor, the peer relationship is no longer based on peerness. Deese-Roberts and Keating noted that "peer tutors are recruited from those students who have been successful in courses or areas for which tutoring is provided."[45] They also argued that "tutors are hired with an assumption that they possess a certain level of subject area knowledge."[46] The delicate balance between understanding the subject and remaining a peer to students learning the subject can easily tilt toward an expert–novice relationship that might undermine the foundations of the tutoring relationship. Deese-Morris and Keating grounded their approach in principles of learning theory and described a tutoring philosophy compatible with general principles of writing center tutoring. Still, their presentation of peer tutoring implies an extensive knowledge of search strategies, including Boolean search techniques and knowledge of specific indexes. The line between reference librarianship and peer tutoring can easily blur given this emphasis on subject knowledge, and writing centers might question whether their tutors need this level of librarians' expertise. How knowledgeable should peer tutors be about the intricacies of searching? Are tutors "experts" in information-seeking strategies, or are they peer coaches who provide context for conversation about the library? Questions such as these will naturally arise during the cross-training of the peer tutors.

Peer tutoring is the hallmark of writing center pedagogy. It is based on the belief that students in conversation are effective in helping each other learn how to navigate the complex and unnatural constructions of the academic life. In the collaboration between libraries and writing centers, how peer tutors perceive their role may become increasingly complicated. If writing center and library personnel can come to some agreement about where authority resides and how tutors relate to it, the chances for a successful collaboration increase exponentially.

Conclusion

In the emergent educational environment, collaboration and conversation can create new opportunities and new directions. As Ward and Raspa noted,

The reformation of higher education is taking place in discussions on an interdisciplinary level. Our academic boxes keep us from seeing the big picture, keep us from participating in the broader discussions now taking place on our campuses. ... If we wait for the future, we may not be part of it. But through collaboration, we can participate in shaping the world.[47]

Writing centers and libraries have arrived simultaneously at a very similar position, one built on the credibility that comes from daily transactions with students driven by their own choice to use our services. Integrated as they are across the curriculum, libraries and writing centers can increase their influence tremendously by sharing their reputations and expertise, leveraging their strengths, and learning from each other. Opportunities are plentiful. From tutor training to faculty development, from coreferencing clients to facilitating new learning communities, each collaboration no doubt evolves according to the conversations and contexts of each campus and its particular politics.

Notes

1. Barbara Fister, "Common Ground: The Composition/Bibliographic Instruction Connection," in *Academic Libraries: Achieving Excellence in Higher Education*, ed. Thomas Kirk (Chicago: ACRL, 1992).
2. Dennis Isbell and D. Broaddus, "Teaching Writing and Research as Inseparable: A Faculty–Librarian Teaching Team," *Reference Services Review* 23, no. 4 (1995): 51–62.
3. J. F. Lyotard, *The Postmodern Condition: A Report on Knowledge* (Minneapolis: Univ. of Minnesota Pr., 1984), ix.
4. Howard Gardner, *Frames of Mind: The Theory of Multiple Intelligences* (New York: Basic Books, 1993).
5. G. Kress and T. Leeuwen, *Multimodal Discourse: The Modes and Media of Contemporary Communication* (London: Oxford University Pr., 2001).
6. Donald Tapscott, *Growing Up Digital: The Rise of the Net Generation* (New York: McGraw Hill, 1998).
7. For a thoughtful articulation of this position, see N. Postman, *Technopoly: The Surrender of Culture to Technology* (New York: Vintage Books, 1993).
8. Boyer Commission on Educating Undergraduates in the Research University. "Reinventing Undergraduate Education: A Blueprint for America's Research Universities." Stony Brook, NY: State University of New York, 1998. Online at http://naples.cc.sunysb.edu/Pres/boyer.nsf/.
9. D. Ward and D. Raspa, *The Collaborative Imperative: Librarians and Faculty Working Together in the Information Universe* (Chicago: ACRL, 2000), ix.
10. Paulo Freire, *Pedagogy of the Oppressed*, trans. M. Ramos (New York: Continuum, 2002).

11. E. H. Hobson, *Wiring the Writing Center* (Logan: Utah State University Pr., 1998).

12. J. Inman and D. Sewell, eds., *Taking Flight with OWLs: Examining Electronic Writing Center Work* (Mahwah, N.J.: Lawrence Erlbaum. 2000).

13. L. Hardesty, "Faculty Culture and Bibliographic Instruction: An Exploratory Analysis," *Library Trends* 44, no. 2 (1995): 339–67.

14. Eric Hobson, "Writing Center Practice Often Counters Its Theory. So What?" in *Intersections: Writing Theory and Practice* (Urbana, Ill.: National Council of Teachers of English, 1994), 8.

15. D. Mulroy, *The War against Grammar* (Portsmouth, N.H.: Heinemann, 2003).

16. Lev Vygotsky, *Thought and Language* (Boston: MIT Pr., 1962).

17. Jerome Bruner, *Toward a Theory of Instruction* (Cambridge, Mass.: Harvard University Pr., 1966).

18. James Britton, *Language and Learning* (Harmondsworth, Eng.: Penguin, 1970).

19. Janet Emig, "Writing as a Mode of Learning," *College Composition and Communication* 28 (1997): 122–28.

20. For a succinct and readable account of the rise of process in composition instruction, see J. Harris, *A Teaching Subject: Composition since 1966* (Upper Saddle River, N.J.: Prentice-Hall, 1996).

21. Carol C. Kuhlthau, *Seeking Meaning: A Process Approach to Library and Information Services* (Westport, Conn.: Libraries Unlimited, 2004).

22. Ibid., 79.

23. Available online at http://www.ala.org/ala/acrl/acrlstandards/informationliteracycompetency.htm.

24. The approach is advocated by B. Stotsky, *Connecting Civic Education and Language Education* (New York: Teachers College Pr., 1991), 107–15.

25. Kuhlthau, *Seeking Meaning*, 31.

26. Ibid., 77.

27. Ibid., 57.

28. See, for example, H. Kohl, *I Won't Learn from You: The Role of Assent in Learning* (Minneapolis: Milkweed, 1991); M. Rose, *Lives on the Boundary: The Struggles and Achievements of America's Underprepared* (New York: Free Press, 1989).

29. Kuhlthau, *Seeking Meaning*, 42.

30. Brenda Dervin and M. Voigt, "Communication Gaps and Inequities: Moving toward a Reconceptualization," in *Progress in Communication Studies* (Norwood, N.J.: Ablex, 1980).

31. Kenneth Bruffee, *Collaborative Learning: Higher Education, Interdependence, and the Authority of Knowledge* (Baltimore: Johns Hopkins University Pr., 1983), 14.

32. Vygotsky, *Thought and Language.*

33. Bruffee, *Collaborative Learning*, 37.

34. Kuhlthau, *Seeking Meaning*, 155.

35. Ibid., 155.

36. Bruffee, *Collaborative Learning*, 53.

37. Ibid., 63.

38. Tony Becher and P. R. Trowler, *Academic Tribes and Territories: intellectual enquiry and the culture of disciplines*. 2nd edition. Buckingham, England; Philadelphia, PA: Open University Press, 2001. (This work was copublished with The Society for Research into Higher Education.)

39. Ibid., 93.

40. Ibid., 94.

41. Susan Deese-Roberts and K. Keating, *Library Instruction: A Peer Tutoring Model* (Englewood, CO: Libraries Unlimited, 2000), 33.

42. Ibid., 49.

43. Ibid., 50.

44. Bruffee, *Collaborative Learning*, 95.

45. Deese-Roberts and Keating, *Library Instruction*, 37.

46. Ibid., 40.

47. Ward and Raspa, *The Collaborative Imperative*, 16–17.

Chapter two

Teaching Librarians and Writing Center Professionals in Collaboration: Complementary Practices

Sheril Hook

The theory outlined in chapter 1 provides a basis from which teaching librarians and writing center professionals can understand each other's work and discuss it on their campuses. Several such discussions are illustrated in the case studies section of this book. In this chapter, we move from examining the underlying theories that frame the work of writing professionals (including both writing tutors and teachers of composition courses) and teaching librarians (including both academic librarians with instruction responsibilities and those working at the reference desk) to describing and comparing their daily practices and to considering their combined potential to enhance student learning.

Writing center professionals and teaching librarians need to work more closely together because they are working with integrally related processes. Currently, writing professionals tend to assume that the research process is subordinate to the writing process and thus have not given enough attention to understanding the research process itself and teaching it to students. Teaching librarians have tended to underestimate or ignore the necessity to understand the writing process well enough to successfully integrate the research process with the formal teaching (i.e., composition classes) or tutoring of writing. And perhaps they also have tended to think of the writing process as subsequent to the research process. If these two groups understood each other's theories and practices, they could develop a more integrated model of writing as a mode of inquiry. An integrated model that promotes inquiry would help to create learning environments that encourage students to reflect on the choices they are making in ways that will enable them to generalize what they learn to new situations.

Others have addressed this disconnect between the teaching of writing and the teaching of research. The fully integrated model advocated here will not evolve if writing professionals and teaching librarians fail to investigate what we in this book and others have urged. Librarian Craig Gibson encouraged us especially to investigate "the commonalities in the process approach shared by both librarians and writing faculty."[1] More recently, as a guest columnist in *Reference*

& User Services Quarterly, rhetorician Rolf Norgaard urged us to "be in closer intellectual conversation."[2] Librarian Barbara Fister summarized how both groups have treated research and presses them to move beyond discrete approaches to doing research: "Librarians generally focus on the significance of information retrieval and evaluation. Course instructors [and writing center tutors by extension] are generally more interested in how information is interpreted and how the student works out that interpretation in a written or oral presentation."[3] Allan Luke and Chushla Kapitzke push us to help students in the "Use of information technology in dialogic, agentive ways that enable them to critique and create knowledge"[4] If writing professionals and teaching librarians model inquiry by coinvestigating these ideas, they will have begun a dialogue that can surely take them farther than either group could go alone in helping students develop critical thinking. Where do they start?

Pedagogical Intersections

Perhaps one way to learn from each other is to better understand the study of rhetoric and its relevance to the current pedagogical practices of writing and researching. While working with students, both writing professionals and teaching librarians model behaviors of invention (brainstorming or more significantly topical reasoning), inquiry (seeking information, reading), and reinvention (through discovery, discussion, writing, and collaboration) that are not always reiterated or reinforced in a traditional classroom, even in a composition classroom. We can understand the complementary nature of their activities (and by extension their processes) by developing our understanding of the Canons of Rhetoric. The Canons of Rhetoric are invention, arrangement, style, memory, and delivery. Reinventing memory as a dynamic art of invention exemplifies the significance of the research process and its relatedness to the writing process. Invention is not simply brainstorming; memory is not simply stored knowledge. Memory is "the 'treasury of things invented,' thus linking Memory with the first canon of rhetoric, Invention."[5] Although there are other relationships among the canons that are useful in developing an understanding of shared practices, here we will elaborate on only invention and memory.

Memory is significant to invention. Without considerable attention given to research instruction during writing instruction, most students are limited in their ability to invent. As Phyllis Reich has noted, "No one imagines for a moment that, on the basis of abstract reflection, someone decided to invent the wheel. Invention, like research, is related to observation and experience."[6] Observations or experiences can reside in our memories and be readily recalled when needed while writing or speaking, but they also are the stored memories that are physically housed in, or virtually accessed through, our academic libraries (or other gateways) in a variety of formats, including audio, video, electronic, and print. Access to and retrieval of such stored memory is essential to invention. Thus, when students do not know how (1) to access stored memory because they are unaware of the wide range of tertiary sources (fee-based or free indexes, databases, encyclopedia, etc.) or (2) to retrieve relevant information efficiently and effectively because they do not possess the skills to do so, they are limited in their ability to invent.[7]

When teaching librarians or writing professionals teach writing or research as independent of the other, processes that were once part of shared canon and learned holistically become bifurcated and thus offer a fractured learning activity. In the early twenty-first century, memory is primarily *stored* information (research, data, images, etc.). It is stored in complex information systems that require particular skills to locate relevant materials but also require knowledge of the arrangement of information (librarians use the term *organization*). The arrangement itself leads to discovery (invention). It is not surprising that we are seeing, once again, the importance of understanding the Canons of Rhetoric. However, teaching students to do research, although important to the development of an idea, is usually subordinate to the teaching of writing in composition classrooms and in tutoring sessions. Bringing as much attention to memory as it deserves means that teaching librarians will need to work with writing professionals to ensure that research and writing are both given considerable attention in curricula. To include memory or arrangement in any significant way in the composing process requires the exchange of skills and knowledge of conventions of writing and research held by teaching librarians and writing professionals.

Another way that writing centers and libraries might collaborate is through an understanding of shared processes. Teaching writing as a process is a well-developed idea and an accepted pedagogical strategy among writing professionals.[8] On the other hand, teaching research as process is a fairly recent concept for librarians. A proponent for teaching research as a process and a pioneer in conducting empirical research to understand the search process, Carol Kuhlthau in *In Seeking Meaning: A Process Approach to Library and Information Services* identifies six stages of the search process, which she has described as the information search process (ISP).[9] These are task initiation, topic selection, prefocus exploration, focus formulation, information selection, and search closure. With each of these stages, she describes the students' tasks and their associated thoughts, feelings, actions, and strategies when trying to complete them. A problem with her model (discussed more fully in chapter 1) is that she ignores the role of the writing process and its impact on the research process. In Kuhlthau's model, the ISP precedes the writing process: "The research process occurs prior to the writing process, essentially in preparation for writing and presenting ideas."[10] She does, however, acknowledge that students in the formative stages of task initiation and prefocus exploration should employ "exploratory strategies, such as listing important facts and interesting ideas or finding a few sources and settling in to read and reflect" before continuing to seek information.[11] Kuhlthau recognized that although the steps she outlines are sequential, they are not linear, but recursive. In fact, students not only read and reflect, but they also engage in the development stage of writing at this point in the research process. It is through writing and the articulation of an idea, argument, or theory that a writer clarifies his or her thoughts and begins to narrow or broaden the scope of the paper and thus will more naturally broaden or narrow the research needed to inform his or her thinking and support or challenge his or her ideas.

Even upon brief analysis, it can be seen that the writing process and the research process are inextricably linked such that each process enables the other in order for a student to construct new knowledge. Kuhlthau's model, as useful as it may be, particularly in describing the high anxiety levels that students face during the prefocus exploration stage, fails to represent the practical experiences of students who revisit information sources continually throughout the writing process. Indeed, in the revision stage of the writing process, students research intensively as they attempt to shape their arguments and support their positions. The research process is interwoven with the writing process, and information needs are driven by the needs of the writer. In practice, writing tutors typically focus on helping students in the following areas: invention, outlining, organization, development, revision, integration of sources, and documentation. These areas comprise the writing process, and although they may be sequential in nature, they are not linear. Students arrange as they invent; invent as they revise; integrate sources as they develop.

In practice, teaching librarians describe the research process using terms similar to those used by writing professionals and encourage some of the same activities as those used in the writing process. They especially emphasize the recursive nature of research. The research process involves brainstorming; narrowing or broadening the focus of the topic; searching for, evaluating, and synthesizing information; revising (i.e., finding more information as the topic changes) through writing, reading, and reflection. These practices are discussed in more detail later, but for now to develop an understanding of how these processes intersect, we can focus on a discussion of the practice of narrowing a topic. Choosing a topic and exploring it, whether through traditional brainstorming techniques taught in writing centers or topic exploration through library resources, is an essential step in both writing and research. Assistance from a librarian can help a student who does not have a research topic. Fister explained the work of a reference librarian as follows:

Brainstorming and invention techniques can be described; students can be shown how to search for possible topics as bibliographic tools are explored; strategies for "mapping out" the literature of a discipline or field can be discussed, including ways to locate controversial or cutting-edge issues by scanning annual reviews or current indexes, abstracts, or databases to find out what other scholars are exploring.[12]

Fister described both the strategies and the tools that teaching librarians use. These are often different from the tools and strategies used by writing professionals—clustering, mind-mapping, listing, asking the who, what, where, when, and how questions. Although the respective strategies serve similar purposes, they have different outcomes. In the writing process, they serve as an exercise in critical thinking and reflection before being exposed to published research; in the research process, they serve as an exercise in exploration of stored memory and some reinvention of that.

Although any attempt to separate writing from research fractures the learning experience, it also is equally important that both processes be recognized, rather than one being subsumed by the other. It is not useful to segregate the research process from the writing process, which would be simplistically following the model dictated by our respective academic units—the composition and rhetoric department on the one hand, and the library on the other (i.e., writing professionals understand the "writing process" whereas librarians understand the "research process"). This bifurcated theorizing fails to explain the integrated, holistic experience of the student using information in the writing process. Striking a balance between respecting the different processes and understanding their holistic nature allows them to pave the way for true collaboration. By working in collaboration, these two units can treat the research process and the writing process as a seamless whole, recognizing the commonalities in both and their respective differences.

Because librarians and writing professionals have integrally related processes, it should not be surprising that they also share terminology. The terminology used by each unit is similar, although under different circumstances for different processes. For example, they both consider audience, authority, and language use as important to their processes. Writing professionals teach students to consider their audience when writing. Is it a general audience, or an audience of professionals or scholars? Are the sources and evidence being used appropriate to the field of study and thus considered credible by the audience? Are sources located written by experts in the field and published in scholarly journals, by generalists writing for popular magazines such *Time* or *Psychology Today*, or by professionals writing for trade publications? Librarians ask the same kinds of questions, but within the context of the secondary or tertiary sources being used. Librarians discuss the audience to whom a database is geared. Is it geared to a general, multidiscipline audience? Does the database index a mix of sources, including popular, scholarly, and nonmainstream? Students learn through researching and writing to evaluate sources for authority and credibility, so considering who the audience is for a particular database or journal can help them determine the credibility of the types of sources they locate.

As for authority, students are learning how to engage in discourse communities and are encouraged by writing professionals to write like an authority in a selected field. To "try on" that authority, they are taught to use a research methodology appropriate to a discipline and learn what kinds of evidence or reasons are acceptable in supporting claims. To do so, they have to be able to locate acceptable evidence. During the research process, librarians teach students to evaluate the sources they find, not in the way that writing professionals, who are aware of the "rhetorical dimensions of texts—the implied audience, the argument, and above all the evidence used to support the argument" do, but in a different way.[13] Librarians bring to the evaluation process their experience with publishers (i.e., the quality of content in books and journals and determining whether to add titles to the collection). They understand the structure of databases, the importance of specificity in subject indexing, and how journals are selected for indexing in those databases. From this understanding, librarians determine which subject databases to use for each field of study. Additionally, they work with faculty to determine reputable journals and have access to a variety of tools that provide information on issues related to authority, such as the impact factor (level of circulation) of journals in each discipline. This experience plays a significant role in the way they teach students to evaluate information. Once again, we see that teaching librarians and writing professionals bring different, but complementary, approaches to the same concept.

Finally, both writing professionals and librarians are interested in seeing that students are capable of variations in their use of language.

Writing professionals encourage students to consider how language is used to convey authority or to appeal to a particular audience and then to apply that to their own writing. For example, considering her audience, a student might choose to use the word *adolescents* rather than *teenagers*, or vice versa. If she is writing as a scholar and her intended audience is sociologists, she probably will choose *adolescents*, but if her audience is a group of high school students, she might be more effective using *teenagers*. Similarly, when searching for information, students need to be able to think flexibly about language and make sophisticated choices about the terms they use when conducting searches in databases. They need to be able to generate keywords and synonyms for use in databases and other reference resources or they will significantly reduce the number of both primary and secondary sources they retrieve. The decisions students make about word choice are important in efficiently and effectively locating relevant materials. For example, if the majority of sociologists use the term *adolescents* in their published writing, but the student only searches for the word *teenagers*, she will severely limit her search results. Fister contends that students need to know "that search terms are contingent on who is speaking and that researchers, therefore, need to be flexible and creative in their use of language and aware of the clues offered in cross-references and subject tracings."[14] If students are guided to understand and use a variety of terminology when searching, and thus ultimately to develop a facility for language, one can imagine that this would also help them become more cognizant of "choosing" terms in their own writing (i.e., choosing terms appropriate to their audiences and that best present their positions).

Goal of Engaging Students

Detailing how and why writing professionals and teaching librarians use certain terms—*audience, authority,* and *language*—demonstrates that there is an overlap in the writing and research processes; by recognizing these shared terms and developing an understanding of how they are being used during these processes, teaching librarians and writing professionals have more potential to provide codeveloped learning activities for students. The case studies in this collection demonstrate the potential for such activities. By using similar terms when working independently with students and by having an ability to discuss both processes with them, teaching librarians and writing professionals reinforce writing and research as shared processes. Approaching the situation in such a way encourages students to construct knowledge about writing and research in a holistic way and view the two processes as interdependent.

The work that teaching librarians and writing professionals do with students has enough in common that one wonders why they do not collaborate more frequently. Their individual work could be the result of the artificial academic boundaries that have developed over time, perhaps resulting in each believing certain processes to be their turf, an attitude that is consistent with academic culture: Teaching librarians think of the research process as their territory; writing professionals think of the writing process as theirs with the research process subordinate to it and thus often overlook or do not understand the difficulties students have engaging in research. As librarian Craig Gibson noted,

> Writing teachers sometimes assume that learning to use the library is only a matter of hands-on practice, emphasizing narrow procedural skills, with on-line catalogs, CD-ROMS, and other tools. Although hands-on work with tools is essential for students to gain confidence with information systems, an overemphasis on this particular kind of skill, removed from a larger rhetorical or critical-thinking context, shortchanges real learning of the type many librarians have been espousing in recent years.[15]

This notion also may have been perpetuated by librarians who take a tool-based approach in their instructional sessions.

In recent years, there has been a transition in library instruction from a tool-based approach to a problem-solving and learning approach, which necessitates working closely with the writing center, as discussed in chapter 1. As Jennie Nelson pointed out, "while college freshman may need to learn how to take advantage of the range of resources available in university libraries, it seems that unless we change the limited goals that students bring to the research process in the first place, they may continue to be satisfied with a few easily located sources"[16] The need for teaching librarians to work with writing professionals emanates from the idea that students will only learn how to learn on their own if they are encouraged to "seek meaning, rather than a right answer, and view information as a way of learning and finding meaning or as a process of construction."[17] In order to seek meaning, they will have to develop higher-order thinking skills and locate, evaluate, synthesize, and analyze information. Writing professionals are in positions to see students' efforts in these areas. However, if writing professionals are focusing on the writing and not questioning the research, students are likely missing a crucial process that has the potential to develop their ability to think critically about their topic. Writing professionals could examine bibliographies, ask about research conducted for the paper, facilitate the search process, and make referrals to the library. These efforts would help students develop some of the critical competencies of writing, reading, and researching that are important to academic success.

Peer Instruction

Clearly, peer writing tutors are at the heart of any collaboration between libraries and writing centers and are key to brokering any relationship the two may develop. Because they are models for writing as a mode of learning, insofar as they are not experts and are themselves engaged in a learning process, they challenge us to think creatively about expertise and inquiry. How peer writing tutors function at the intersection of writing and research will determine in large part the nature of the collaboration that takes place. Librarians will have to let go of territory, encouraging others to be lifelong learners (i.e., competent researchers such as writing tutors) who can teach others the process of research. In the most aggressive scenario, peer tutors would be extensively co-trained to provide both writing support and research support. They would be able to discuss with their peers both the way their writing is evolving and the way their research choices are shaping that writing. This is an intriguing model, but it puts a heavy burden on the tutors and on the training they receive, perhaps too heavy a burden. It also calls the entire expert–novice relationship into question. If writing tutors are trained to provide expert writing support, by extension, they also should be trained to provide expert research support. On the other hand, if the philosophy of a writing center emphasizes the peer relationship between tutor and tutee, that philosophy should extend to all aspects of the tutoring relationship.

Ideally, a peer writing tutor would be able to assist a writer in locating more relevant sources in a manner similar to library reference provision (usually based on a teaching model rather than a service model), rather than make a referral to a librarian who may be housed in another building. This type of assistance takes considerable training and knowledge because the tutors could encounter complex topics from a wide range of subject areas. The most useful sort of collaboration is one in which students encounter a seamless experience during the research writing process by providing peer writing tutors with the necessary skills to be successful in assisting students with both the writing process and the research process (and online searching) when research is needed before the writing can continue or before it can begin. Ideally, this would become a learning environment for students that refocuses our instruction (both library and writing center instruction) to provide both writing and research assistance with the goal of developing higher-order thinking skills in students in a collaborative learning environment that demonstrates a convergence of facilities, instruction, and philosophies.

This is a two-way collaboration, however, and teaching librarians, too, would have to expect some changes in their provision of reference by supporting and training peer writing tutors to be successful in their research tutoring. This may be a difficult transition for some teaching librarians, but necessary if libraries are to move toward creating a learner-centered environment, in either their current facilities or a space elsewhere on campus, and if they are to become more actively involved in student learning. Librarians have to trust that tutors can provide adequate (and even excellent) reference instruction and also will know when a referral to a librarian with subject expertise is warranted. Such a collaboration between writing centers and libraries is inherent in the concept of information literacy that "speaks to fundamental processes of inquiry, and the expression of that inquiry in communicative endeavors."[18] When writing professionals and teaching librarians explore the concept of research and writing as intertwined and acknowledge that perhaps both processes require similar (and substantial) attention, they can open up avenues of conversation, sharing their practices in order to move beyond the artificial boundaries (budgets, departments, etc) they have maintained for too long and which have nothing to do with engaging students in critical thinking.

Although librarians and writing professionals work with integrally related processes, they have ignored the overlap and thereby weakened students' ability to think strategically about researched writing as a mode of inquiry. The collaborative model advocated in this book encourages teaching librarians and writing professionals to create a holistic experience for students. In such a model, the writing center and the library would think creatively about students' writing and research processes. If each unit shares its instruction and trains tutors and reference staff into a hybrid model, the line between resources and writing can be made ambiguous. This model more accurately reflects the natural, recursive flow between reading, thinking, and writing within the five-canon rhetorical framework mentioned earlier. It does not encourage gathering information in a single sitting, as research is so often described in writing handbooks or as Inman illustrated by commenting that writing tutors "send students upstairs for database searching."[19] A fully collaborative model anticipates that research writers will benefit from an experience with writing tutors and librarians and that, as a result, the research process will become entwined with the writing process such that they appear seamless. Students would be encouraged to refine topics, find additional sources to investigate and further their thinking at many different times during the writing process, grapple with difficult scholarly material and a wide range of sources, and consider the social or political impact of their work. Revised thinking results in revised writing *and* revised research.

Libraries and writing centers have many practical reasons for collaboration. First, simply understanding each other's pedagogical practices and processes can encourage referrals at appropriate times. An online writing center can become a conduit to a library's online gateway to resources as a starting point for finding materials for research projects. A library's gateway can link to the writing center site and post hours, locations, and tutoring sessions. Although this is the least desirable sort of collaboration, at least it is a beginning. Additionally, each unit offers online tutorials (e.g., OWLS, SearchPath, TILT, Colorado State OWCC) and online assistance in the form of both e-mail and live-chat. These services could be combined to demonstrate the interdependent relationship between the two processes. Writing center Web sites could be developed that show the interweaving of both processes.

Role of Course Instructors

Whatever combined efforts we make toward engaging students in learning, however, will be affected by the demands of the course instructors. Each unit has concerns about how assignments are written and given to students and how students interpret them. The way that instructors write assignments is at times in conflict with the professional work of teaching librarians and writing center professionals. Typically, writing centers offer help in developing both lower-order skills and higher-order skills, with more emphasis on the latter. Higher-order skills include evaluating, synthesizing, and analyzing information sources. The table below provides examples of these skills. The Writing Center at the University of Maryland articulates concerns over assignments, which seems indicative of writing center professionals' expectations of their work:

> A great deal of the writing that students are asked to do invites them simply to demonstrate knowledge. On exams and quizzes and in many out-of-class writing assignments, they are asked merely to recall and report what they know or have collected in research. In Bloom's *Taxonomy*, the acts of recalling and reporting knowledge are seen as less sophisticated than the alternatives of translating information into new forms, applying it to new contexts, analyzing, synthesizing, and evaluating it.

The chart below arranges Bloom's levels of cognitive activity in a grid moving (left to right) from simple to complex, and it lists a number of verbs describing its activities for each mode of thinking. The chart may thus offer suggestions to teachers for varying the level of sophistication in what they ask students to do in writing assignments.

Bloom's Ranking of Thinking Skills					
Knowledge	**Comprehension**	**Application**	**Analysis**	**Synthesis**	**Evaluation**
List	Summarize	Solve	Analyze	Design	Evaluate
Name	Explain	Illustrate	Organize	Hypothesize	Choose
Identify	Interpret	Calculate	Deduce	Support	Estimate
Show	Describe	Use	Contrast	Schematize	Judge
Define	Compare	Interpret	Compare	Write	Defend
Recognize	Paraphrase	Relate	Distinguish	Report	Criticize
Recall	Differentiate	Manipulate	Discuss	Justify	
State	Demonstrate	Apply	Plan		
Visualize	Classify	Modify	Devise		

Source: Effective Writing Program, University of Maryland University College, http://www.umuc.edu/ugp/ewp/bloomtax.html.

The list of terms from the University of Maryland is not inclusive, of course. We could add to it a student's need to develop skill in advocating, arguing, proposing, and so on. Although writing tutors have long been focused on higher-order skills, librarians did not clearly articulate an emphasis on teaching higher-order thinking until the last decade. They have frequently left that to the classroom instructor, choosing, instead, to focus on teaching tool use, which falls into Bloom's categories of knowledge, comprehension, and application.

Fister encouraged librarians to move away from teaching "library research as information retrieval through access tools" because this method of teaching:

valorizes information retrieval as the purpose of research—a misconception that puzzles students and frustrates teachers. Students who perceive their task to be one of merely locating, synthesizing, and presenting information found in library sources will not do well on research assignments because this approach to research will not yield what most college-level assignments demand—an idea that is developed, argued, and supported by evidence.[20]

Traditionally, librarians have been invited into courses to present a lecture (demonstration) on search tools to students, an activity that has likely contributed to this tool-based focus. However, as librarians begin to see the result of students not really understanding the high level of complexity in doing research, they are beginning to work more intensely across campus to create assignments that encourage students in more sophisticated research. Although teaching librarians' concerns have more to do with the implied activities, skills, and knowledge in assignments and making them explicit, they, like writing centers, must work with instructors to create assignments that reduce barriers to student learning and increase successful completion of assignments.

Librarians and writing tutors acknowledge that instructors currently have the responsibility of assessing a student's final work and will be assessing a student's ability to "translate information into new forms." However, librarians and tutors have the opportunity to encourage students "not to report on topics, but to engage in reflective thinking."[21] As they encourage, librarians and writing tutors become mediators in student learning and, as such, have the opportunity to shape the learning environment such that it facilitates higher-order thinking and encourages recursivity rather than linearity.

Libraries and writing centers have a long history of instructing students. Now this teaching is frequently available online as well as face-to-face. Staff from these units assist students in negotiating the practical, theoretical, and contextual aspects of assignments, "consciously unpack[ing] the institutional culture and its enigmas and invit[ing] students to learn the ropes of academic inquiry by participating as active members in a community of inquiry."[22] An example of such practical negotiation is when an instructor discourages students from using Internet sources and those students come to the reference desk for help in finding research. Reference librarians often interpret such a statement as meaning Internet information sources found through search engines, such as Google™, that have not gone through a vetting process. They assume that it does not rule out the use of peer-reviewed, online scholarly journals that are available through subscription databases. When students insist that they cannot use *anything* that is on the Internet for fear of failing the assignment, librarians encourage them to seek clarification from instructors about the use of scholarly, online material. We need to move beyond these practical issues that sometimes become barriers to assisting students in becoming "active agents in the production of knowledge."[23] The more intellectually challenging work of librarians and writing tutors is to encourage students to situate their work within the academy by discussing conventions, selecting secondary and primary sources, understanding the arrangement (or organization) of information, evaluating sources, considering audience, and encouraging revision.

We need to take a more active role on our campuses in the "critical practices of mentoring, teaching, and apprenticing others into engagements with technology, knowledge, and power."[24] The faculty development workshop has been a longtime mainstay of writing programs and libraries. Readers of this chapter will no doubt recognize the ways both units have worked to construct experiences for faculty to explore more effective ways to integrate research instruction, and an extensive literature exists in both fields to indicate points of emphasis. Sharing workshops has significant advantages. It broadens the base of advocacy, with libraries and writing centers able to lend credibility to each other's agenda, and by placing their work under a larger umbrella, librarians and writing centers are forced to think larger, be less provincial, and appear less self-interested. Sharing faculty workshops also lessens the demand on faculty time.

Among the most vexing issues librarians and writing center professionals face is their relationship with faculty. In providing support for students trying to do the assignments given by faculty, teaching librarians and writing tutors navigate the sometimes-incomprehensible tasks students are given by faculty. Sometimes such assignments display a troubling lack of awareness about the demands they place on the support system, and, more troubling, sometimes they display a lack of awareness about the educational methods they encourage. As librarian Larry Hardesty noted, "faculty members' academic background and training work against an understanding of the proper role of the college library. He has been trained as a scholar-researcher and is not really interested in how his students use the library; he, after all, learned to use it in his discipline and assumes students can also."[25] Indeed, librarians and writing centers share a number of concerns that need to be addressed to teaching faculty: "Both attempt to infiltrate the curriculum with basic academic and life-long learning skills and to embed those skills meaningfully in the disciplines."[26] These include concerns about plagiarism, assignment construction, and course development and curriculum design. Because they deal with the efforts of students who are doing the work assigned by faculty, librarians and writing professionals are in a position to report to faculty what works and what does not. Unfortunately, due in large part to differences in academic status and the tendency of faculty to see themselves as autonomous in the classroom, it can be difficult to find effective ways to communicate to faculty.[27] It is important to find those ways of communication or we are left working with frustrated students who do not have the skills necessary to complete an assignment successfully. As Fister points out that faculty frequently fail to clearly state their goals for research assignments, "assuming that students are familiar with the nature of academic writing" while librarians fill that void "with the notion that finding and presenting information is the goal of research. If librarians fail to place their advice to students in the rhetorical context of research, they may reinforce the misconception that the main point of research is to report on knowledge found elsewhere."[28] Both libraries and writing centers have developed a tradition of workshops for faculty to address these concerns. On campuses where both units offer workshops, they might well find themselves competing for faculty participation. One of the most promising trends in the collaboration of writing centers and libraries appears to be in the area of faculty development. Including faculty as active co-creators of learning situations, teaching librarians and writing professionals can help students develop the reflective modes of inquiry needed with new literacies by creating learning communities.

When students receive a writing assignment that involves research, they typically have much to interpret. The various tasks or skills students need to complete assignments successfully are not usually identified explicitly. Moreover, faculty often assume that their students have a more advanced level of knowledge, skills, and abilities than the students actually possess. Sometimes language itself is a barrier. For example, when the words *article*, *citation*, or *bibliography* are used, there is a good chance a student does not understand those terms. In a recent study by librarian Norman Hutcherson, 47 percent of freshman and sophomore survey respondents understood *article*, 51.7 percent understood *citation*, and 14.9 percent understood *bibliography*.[29] Students have more than terminology to understand, though, before they can complete an assignment. A scan through various writing guides, such as *The Craft of Research*, shows that students will need to understand *claims*, *reasons*, and *evidence*.[30] Students will have to understand their audiences and choose terminology and research methodologies that will situate them in a particular academic community (i.e., among scientists, social scientists, or humanists). Indeed, one of the many outcomes expected by faculty is that students will "Use conventions of format and structure appropriate to the rhetorical situation."[31] All of these, when unknown to the student, are potential barriers to successful completion of a research project. Students have to negotiate immediately when given an assignment. Their "task interpretations and choices—whether solitary or collaborative, reflective or unexamined—will help to determine whether [their] research assignments become valuable opportunities to extend their knowledge through critical inquiry or unchallenging exercises in gathering and reproducing information."[32] Writing tutors and librarians help students reflect on their work and develop the critical competencies they need to complete their assignments successfully.

Ultimately, if research and writing processes were taught simultaneously, students would be working in a learning environment that is more conducive to constructing knowledge than the current educational environment with its continued emphasis on lecture over active learning techniques that engage students in dialogue and inquiry and encourage independent thinking. Paulo Freire has maintained that "Knowledge emerges only through invention and re-invention, through the restless, impatient, continuing, hopeful inquiry human beings pursue in the world, with the world, and with each other."[33] Working collaboratively, the writing center and the library could provide students a physical and virtual space in which the research process and the writing process are understood as shared constructive processes from which knowledge can emerge. Some of this discussion would likely strike Freire as oppressive, such as the emphasis on conventions and genres and expectations of scholars in their respective fields. However, the intent in reaching out to the writing and library communities is to help cultivate an academic culture that is less oppressive and to take a more active role in student development and learning on our campuses. Why? Because daily librarians and writing tutors are faced with assisting students who are not engaged with the curriculum—students not engaged in their research and writing assignments, or why and how they are learning. The banking method of which Freire has written is alive and well in our campus classrooms, but students find their ways to oft-underfunded, oft-understaffed writing centers and libraries whose staff spend time engaging them in inquiry. Such a claim is not only supported by anecdotal evidence, however. Lack of student engagement with learning is supported by the Boyer Report[34]; the low retention rates among all, but the elite institutions of higher education; the persistent discussions of engaging students in their learning through dialog, peer learning, and collaboration[35]; and publications such as *Learning Outside the Lines* by students who have graduated by learning how to work a system that did not work for them and who advocate more active student engagement in learning.[36]

By engaging in such collaborations, we can rediscover the value of collaborative spaces or contact zones and model more engaged forms of active learning. A merged center is the logical place for that collaboration to occur. Teaching research and writing as shared processes will require a shared space in which teaching librarians and writing professionals can continue to share their knowledge with each other and provide a space for students that allows both processes to be practiced simultaneously.

Sharing Facilities and Resources

Carol Severino has argued that the writing center is a "contact zone." He described the writing center in terms that apply equally well to libraries. Writing centers are places "where diverse cultures, languages, literacies, and discourses 'meet, clash, and grapple with each other.' The center is a 'disciplinary borderland' where the rhetorics of the humanities, social sciences, and natural sciences meet—to both intersect and conflict."[37] Tutors and tutees work in a dynamic educational environment. Although not all writing centers employ undergraduate students as their tutors, some hire only undergraduates. These tutors are students with their own educational challenges, and as they work with other students on their writing, both students' identities and language practices are forming. In either situation, it is that contact among writers of different backgrounds, different skill levels, and different attitudes that makes the tutoring relationship so dynamic. Libraries are quite accustomed to managing space, but they have only recently begun to think of it as a dynamic "learning space."[38]

Awareness of the library as a "contact zone" has been limited. In fact, the creation of learning space requires a conscious effort. In order to co-manage a space that would facilitate holistic learning, both units must share a vision for engaging students in learning and with that be able to discuss the theoretical as well as the practical commonalities that unite their practices. Both units also must have a general respect for their differences. When shared goals around student learning or shared understanding of each other's theory and praxis are lacking, the result is simply the sharing of space. We can see these difficulties in the work of James Inman who manages a collaboration between a writing center and a library. He notes that in planning the Center for Collaborative Learning and Communication (CCLC) at Furman University, the group learned that "specific architecture could make a profound difference on the engaged learning activity that could take place in the space," so they designed their space with the idea that peer consultants would be able to move around comfortably in shared, flexible spaces that could meet a variety of consulting needs.[39] Inman recognizes the potential for learning in such a space and, in fact, in his description of the center, he collapses the writing and research processes into what he calls a process approach for engaged learning. He explains that:

> the current CCLC features a process approach for engaged learning much like the process approach writing studies scholars have developed, but also more general. We imagine that clients can begin their work in the Informal Gathering Areas, chatting with each other about ideas and helping to generate collaboratively the initial shape for whatever project they are developing. With this dialogic foundation, the project teams could then move to the Collaborative Workstations, where they could begin to shape the ideas collaboratively into a project draft.[40]

Although he does not specifically mention research as a process, it seems that he has embedded it in the engaged learning process that he describes. In fact, he later describes the student experiences as being holistic, but here we also begin to see that he has, in fact, separated the CCLC from the library by distinguishing the clients:

> Our collaboration with various library departments has been most often in terms of offering clients the best possible holistic experience, whether library clients or CCLC clients. We've held several workshops with library personnel, and each time we've emphasized ways we can support each other's work.[41]

Such a statement about clients indicates that in Inman's model, CCLC clients are distinguished from library clients. He also appears to have his own reservations about the arrangement of services:

> If someone comes to CCLC and asks about database searching, for instance, we explain that they may want to venture upstairs to the reference desk to ask one of the librarians for help, just as those librarians refer questions about writing, communication, and technology to us. I would be naïve to suggest such collaboration is always in the democratic spirit [John] Dewey sought, but I do believe the relationship is in good faith and that we all have good intentions.[42]

The tension between the goal for students to have a "holistic experience" described by Inman and the relatively bifurcated practice he later describes (i.e., sending students somewhere else to do the research) severely limits real educational collaboration.

Inman's efforts and similar ones across the country, however, have multiple advantages and do provide benefits to students. The benefits include a referral system that may not have been in place before the collaboration; a space in which the two elements of instruction (i.e., writing and research instruction) are in the same facility and relatively close to each other, making it easier for students to get the help they need; and consolidated technology that can be used for multiple purposes. Plus, the writing center can take advantage of the late hours that libraries typically provide without fearing for tutors' security and a move to the library usually entails a significant upgrade in writing center facilities. Inman and similar library–writing center collaborators have, in a sense, facilitated the work flow of students to create a seamless information/writing experience, allowing librarians and writing tutors to be experts in part of the larger process, co-referring students back and forth between research and writing, creating spaces for creative, yet disciplined, work and co-training each other, as In-man noted, in ways that each can support the other.[43] This is a better model than when a library and a writing center simply cohabitate in the spaces provided and no real educational collaboration occurs.

Conclusion

In establishing a collaborative relationship, both units must be open-minded and willing to look for the practical commonalities that unite them but also must acknowledge any differences that make them unique. How do students engage in learning and in creating new knowledge? What is our role in that? Library staff must be willing to work with trained student tutors who will question practices and need explanations in terms they can understand and convey to their peers. As collaborators, units will need to be able to answer questions such as the following in order to prepare librarians and writing staff to work in wider capacities: Is there a line between research and writing? What kind of resource is useful to a freshman writer? What is an authoritative source, and what confers authority? What constitutes successful research and writing within the various academic disciplines?

Above all, we will need participatory, shared training and activities that can help answer the questions that are posed above, and we need to teach a model of collaboration (i.e., no clear line between research and writing). This is very engaged, intellectual work that supports inquiry-based learning and is valuable to our campuses. Rolf Norgaard observed that we need to "spur and support the impulses for pedagogical reform already implicit in [our] initiatives."[44] We will need to pursue ongoing discussion among ourselves, but also with campus administrators and disciplinary faculty to solicit campuswide understanding, support, and resources for our efforts.

Notes

1. Craig Gibson. "Research Skills across the Curriculum: Connections with Writing-across-the-Curriculum," in *Writing-across-the-Curriculum and the Academic Library: A Guide for Librarians, Instructors, and Writing Program Directors*, ed. Jean Sheridan (Westport, Conn.: Greenwood Pr., 1995), 55.
2. Rolf Norgaard, "Writing Information Literacy in the Classroom: Pedagogical Enactments and Implications," *Reference and User Services Quarterly* 43, no. 3 (2004): 221.
3. Barbara Fister, "Teaching the Rhetorical Dimensions of Research," *Research Strategies* 11, no. 4 (1993): 211.
4. Allan Luke and Chushla Kapitzke, "Literacies and Libraries: Archives and Cybraries," *Curriculum Studies* 7, no. 3 (1999): 487.

5. Gideon O. Burton, "Silva Rhetoricae." Brigham Young University. Available online at http://humanities.byu.edu/rhetoric/Canons/Memory.htm [accessed 24 August 2004].

6. Quoted in Fister, "Teaching the Rhetorical Dimensions of Research," 215.

7. Thanks to Cleo Boyd for sharing her ideas on the Canons of Rhetoric and their significance to the organization, retrieval, and selection of information with her co-presenters: Cleo Boyd, Mary Ann Mavrinac, and Ian Whyte, "Scholarly Research or Information Literacy: What's in a Name?" Riding the Wave, Library Instruction from Coast to Coast, 33rd Workshop on Instruction in Library Use (WILU), Victoria, British Columbia, June 14–16, 2004.

8. See the work of Linda Flowers in *On Writing Research: The Braddock Essays, 1975–1998* or her textbook *Problem-solving Strategies for Writing in College and Community* (1985).

9. Carol Collier Kuhlthau, *Seeking Meaning: A Process Approach to Library and Information Services* (Norwood, N.J.: Ablex, 1993).

10. Ibid., xix.

11. Ibid., xxi.

12. Fister, "Teaching the Rhetorical Dimensions of Research," 216.

13. Ibid., 217.

14. Ibid., 216.

15. Gibson, "Research Skills across the Curriculum," 59.

16. Jennie Nelson, "The Library Revisited: Exploring Students' Research Processes," in *Hearing Ourselves Think*, ed. Ann M. Penrose and Barbara M. Sitko (New York: Oxford University Pr., 1993), 104.

17. Kuhlthau, *Seeking Meaning*, 7.

18. Norgaard, "Writing Information Literacy in the Classroom," 225.

19. J. Inman, "At First Site: Lessons from Furman University's Center for Collaborative Learning and Communication." *academic.writing*, 2001. Available online at http://wac.colostate.edu/aw/articles/inman2001/.

20. Fister, "Teaching the Rhetorical Dimensions of Research," 213.

21. Fister, "Connected Communities: Encouraging Dialogue between Composition and Bibliographic Instruction," in *Writing across the Curriculum and the Academic Library: Implications for Bibliographic Instruction*, ed. Jean Sheridan (Westport, Conn.: Greenwood Pr., 1995), 33–51.

22. Ibid., 36.

23. Luke and Kapitzke, "Literacies and Libraries," 480.

24. Ibid., 483.

25. Larry Hardesty, "Faculty Culture and Bibliographic Instruction: An Exploratory Analysis," *Library Trends* 44, no. 2 (1995): 356.

26. Fister, "Connected Communities," 36.

27. Hardesty, "Faculty Culture and Bibliographic Instruction," 152.

28. Fister, "Teaching the Rhetorical Dimensions of Research," 213.

29. Norman B. Hutcherson, "Library Jargon: Student Recognition of Terms and Concepts Commonly Used by Librarians in the Classroom," *College & Research Libraries* 65, no. 4 (July 2004): 350–51.

30. Wayne C. Booth, Gregory G. Colomb, and Joseph M. Williams, *The Craft of Research*, 2nd ed. (Chicago: University of Chicago Pr., 2003), chapters 8–10.

31. WPA, "Outcomes Statement for First-year Composition," *College English* 63, no. 3 (Jan. 2001): 321–25.

32. Nelson, "The Library Revisited," 116.

33. Paulo Freire, *Pedagogy of the Oppressed*, trans. M. Ramos (New York: Continuum, 2002), 72..

34. The Boyer Commission, "Reinventing Undergraduate Education: A Blueprint for America's Research Universities." Available online at http://naples.cc.sunysb.edu/Pres/boyer.nsf/ [accessed 2 August 2004].

35. Roberts-Miller, Patricia. *Deliberate Conflict: Argument, Political Theory, and Composition Classes*. Carbondale, IL: Southern Illinois U Press, 2004; Bruffee, Kenneth A. *Collaborative Learning: Higher Education, Interdependence, and the Authority of Knowledge*, 1st ed. 1993, 2nd ed. 1999. Baltimore, Md.: John Hopkins University Press, 1999.

36. Jonathan Mooney and David Cole, *Learning Outside the Lines* (New York: Simon & Shuster, 2000).

37. C. Severino, "Writing Centers as Linguistic Contact Zones and Borderlands," in *Professing in the Contact Zone: Bringing Theory and Practice Together*, ed. Janice M. Wolff (Urbana, Ill.: National Council of Teachers of English, 2002), 231.

38. See James K. Elmborg, "Teaching at the Desk: Toward a Reference Pedagogy." *portal* 2, no. 3 (July 2002): 455–64; Susan Deese-Roberts and K. Keating, *Library Instruction: A Peer Tutoring Model* (Englewood, N.J.: Libraries Unlimited, 2000).

39. J. Inman, "At First Site: Lessons from Furman University's Center for Collaborative Learning and Communication." *academic.writing* (2001). Available online at http://wac.colostate.edu/aw/articles/inman2001/ [accessed 19 August 2004].

40. Ibid.

41. Ibid

42. Ibid.

43. Ibid. See also Jill I. Tyler and Sheril J. Hook, "The Communication Center: A Full-service Academic Resource in the Heart of the Library," *Crossing the Divide*, 10th National Conference, Denver, Colo., Mar. 15–18, 2001, 70–74. Available online at http://www.ala.org/Content/NavigationMenu/ACRL/Events_and_Conferences/tyler.pdf.

44. Norgaard, "Writing Information Literacy in the Classroom," 225.

Chapter three

Roots Entwined: Growing a Sustainable Collaboration

Lea Currie and Michele Eodice

The occasion for writing this chapter came at a time when we, a writing center director and a research librarian, wanted go beyond simply describing our library–writing center collaboration as conducting joint workshops or space sharing.[1] Although many writing centers across the country are housed in libraries and many writing specialists and librarians form instructional alliances, we recognized the limitations to this relationship and are seeking ways to move our collaboration to the next level. At the same time that we were reflecting on our collaboration, we realized that our university was entering a period of change, one that would involve collaborations in number and scope that have never been tried before. The opportunity to explore an expanded notion of what this kind of partnership can become—for our future work and for this chapter—could not have been better timed.

When Michele Eodice was hired in 1998 to establish a writing center at the University of Kansas (KU), in order to accomplish the primary goal of the writing center mission—access to writing services for student writers—she began a search for additional satellite locations for the writing center. Students suggested the need for writing consultants at multiple and convenient locations on campus. The KU libraries were a natural choice. In 2000, a Writer's Roost (the name for our satellite writing centers) was established on the main lobby floor of Watson Library (one of seven libraries in the KU system) with a grant from the Student Senate. Limited resources kept the KU writing center from establishing another Writer's Roost in Anschutz Library, an even busier and more centralized location. However, while the KU writing center now has an established presence in Watson Library, the extent of the collaboration is based on physical space only. So far, our relationship has led to the construction of a recognized collaborative learning environment within the main undergraduate library, strengthened the academic image of the writing center while contributing to a more student-driven service atmosphere in the librar-

The authors would like to thank colleagues, students, and staff in the KU Libraries and the KU Writing Center. In addition, participants in the roundtable discussion were an invaluable resource. We appreciated the feedback from Moira Ozias, Emily Donnelli, Larry Hill, and Kami Day.

ies, and produced recognized scholarship.[2] However, as we begin to look for ways to strengthen our collaboration (by combining some of our instruction, for example), we find that several other collaborative initiatives are taking place simultaneously on our campus. Interestingly, the many persons and projects we describe below do affect our work, but we have found that as more participants enter an era of innovation at our university, the library–writing center collaboration is looked at as an exemplar, a model to follow.

The Current Context at KU

This is a time of change for the University of Kansas. The KU libraries have a new and innovative dean, and a new vice provost was recently brought here to lead a new unit called Student Success, which comprises more than twenty offices and programs that were formerly fragmented by traditional student affairs models of service delivery. It seems long overdue, but like other large decentralized public research universities, KU may finally be moving in the direction of more collaborative efforts, recognizing the interdisciplinarity of its programs and seeing the need for a more seamless delivery of student services. For example, the libraries may soon be moving toward an integrated help desk, combining reference, circulation, interlibrary loan, and so on in a single area, with cross-trained staff to ensure smoother transactions. At this same time, a number of task forces at the university, called HVC2 (High Velocity Change through High Volume Collaboration "squared"),[3] are looking at restructuring information services and increasing collaboration among the KU libraries, Academic Computing Services, Instructional Design Services, and other services including those under the Student Success umbrella, such as advising, enrollment, and orientation. As part of the HVC2 effort, several work groups across the campus are developing models for enhanced student services, looking at the possibilities for one-stop shopping models, collaborative learning spaces, and virtual help desks. Because these groups are initiating such fundamental change across the university, the HVC2 program drew the attention of the Educause Center for Applied Research (ECAR). ECAR, directed by Richard Katz, provides research and analysis on information technology issues to help higher-education administrators make informed decisions. A research fellow, appointed by ECAR, is following the progress of HVC2 and will write a "living case study" narrative of the work group process. Another timely initiative comes on the heels of a national report on student writing ability.[4] A new campus group, formed to explore ideas for infusing and supporting writing-across-the-curriculum, is led by the director of the KU writing center and involves faculty, student services staff, the Center for Teaching Excellence, and the libraries.

With so many collaborative exchanges taking place on campus, it seems natural that the continued collaboration of the KU libraries and the KU writing center should become a part of these discussions, especially because both instructional arenas share a commitment to student learning that ranges from supporting writing-across-the-curriculum to tending collaborative learning spaces to promoting information literacy.[5]

In his coauthored book, *The Social Life of Information*, John Seely Brown, chief scientist at Xerox, explained why so many predictions remain just that ... predictions. "The way forward," he stated, "is paradoxically to look not ahead, but to look around" if one wants to see a glimpse into the future.[6] KU libraries dean, Stella Bentley, recently called for a next wave of change for the libraries but admitted, "there is no grand plan." Like the dean, we are poised for change and will attempt to "look around" rather than simply going forward for the sake of going forward. The "looking around" reveals how many campus units and current initiatives affect our work, and this climate invites us to collaborate. As the dean of libraries stated, "The main idea is to start moving in what amounts to an open field, without a detailed plan, relying on signs along the way to update our sense of the destinations."

We wanted this case study of the collaboration between the writing center and the library to reflect our own efforts to "look around." Rather than focus on what we have done, we wanted to explore what the new environment on our campus makes possible. To accomplish this task, in February 2004, we invited members of the campus community to a roundtable discussion concerning the collaboration of libraries and writing centers. This group included

- Stella Bentley, Dean of Libraries
- Kent Miller, Assistant Dean of Public Services in the Libraries
- Frank Farmer, Associate Professor of English
- Deborah Ludwig, Director of Library Information Technology Services
- Richard Fyffe, Assistant Dean of Scholarly Communications
- Kathy Graves and John Stratton, Co-Coordinators of Reference Services
- Kathryn Nemeth Tuttle, Associate Vice Provost for Student Success
- Dan Bernstein, Director of the KU Center for Teaching Excellence
- Carl Strikwerda, Associate Dean of the College of Liberal Arts and Sciences

The participants were invited because of their histories of working on collaborative efforts, their participation in and support of programs affected by libraries and writing centers, and their views on how a collaborative effort of this type could move forward. The key people involved in this roundtable offered a new level of conversation about our collaboration; they offered ideas and challenges; and they offered support not only for moving our collaboration to the next level, but also for drawing on even more programs and people from across the campus to help deepen our collaboration.

We created a handout to suggest issues for discussion so participants could gather their thoughts ahead of time. Participants were asked to think about the barriers and the challenges of collaboration on the KU campus and how programs that simply share locations can better demonstrate true collaboration. They were also asked to think about costs of blending programs, staff training issues, and meeting information literacy competencies. We asked: Given an infinite pile of money and the most powerful and enlightened leadership, what could or should happen? Finally, participants were asked to think about predictions for what the future holds concerning technology, different institutional structures, service delivery models, impact on recruitment, retention, and graduation, and the impact on faculty.[7] Carol Ann Hughes (2001) in her conference talk, "The Changing Landscape of Scholarly Publishing: Print Collections E-Books and Beyond", stated that "the future will require librarians to think creatively and adopt a new entrepreneurial spirit to advance the core services they wish to maintain as the 'common good' for their constituencies."[8] We invited this group to think creatively and with an entrepreneurial spirit; admittedly, while planning the discussion, we predicted that the group might dwell on negative issues, particularly the putative institutional/financial barriers to collaboration, but we were pleasantly surprised by the direction the discussion took.

The resulting conversation provided the framework for this chapter. We organized the text around the themes of institutional support, space, and the power of peer—the themes that emerged in the roundtable discussion—and related them to the current context at KU. The following three sections represent the highlights and implications we identified as we reviewed the audiotapes of the roundtable conversation. We hope our interpretation suggests ways for other campus leaders to find and develop collaborations.

Institutional Support

Support for campus initiatives, although vital, can take many forms. In our discussion, we recognized that one type of institutional support is less tangible, but equally important to the success of any collaborative venture: the ethos of the campus culture needs to invite and recognize collaboration. Faculty, staff, and students must be confident of this ethos in order to proceed.

A key question that arose at our roundtable was, How do we know when we've arrived at a solid collaboration? We wondered how embedded in the institution a collaboration needed to be before it was established permanently and would continue whether or not the original planners were involved. We hoped to avoid a case of a people-based initiative; evidence of these attempts is rampant. As many academic programs can attest, relying on the same individuals to create projects is a risk to sustainability. In order to steward these projects into the future so that they will thrive even if the original players are no longer involved, an institutional support structure that includes values commitment, dedicated funding, and a plan for assessment will need to be in place.

The second type of support, one that most of us see as required, is fiscal support. Just two years ago, the university raised tuition for the first time in many years. With input from students and statewide constituents, a pool of funds earmarked for special projects and for supporting direct services to students was created. We believe the KU libraries and the KU writing center are deserving recipients of these funds and hope to develop the next level of collaboration (peer and tier model) with this financial support. With HVC2 and tuition enhancement funds, we see great potential for seed money; but whether programs can be sustained is a matter of the third type of support—academic mission.

Universities rely on curriculum and instruction to drive needs for faculty and program development. When information literacy competencies, for example, become embedded in the curriculum through changes to the general education goals (which is a distinct possibility at our institution due to a current revision of the goals) and thus reshape the goals of faculty, staff, and students, the responsive areas, such as libraries and writing centers, will need funding to provide high-quality resources. An academic mission is only as strong as its leaders acknowledge it to be, and initiatives not embedded within the mission cannot be sustained.

David Shulenburger, KU's provost, has been involved in supporting writing and the libraries in significant ways by convening the Writing Matters @KU task force, which explores the feasibility of a writing-across-the-curriculum component, and he has demonstrated a commitment to exploring information literacy across the curriculum as well. His work on issues involving scholarly communication is recognized at the national level.[9] When Marily Goodyear, vice provost of information services, proposed a new position, dean of scholarly communication, the provost gave his support. In addition, he recently issued new guidelines for our campus on intellectual property and copyright and supports the use of Turnitin.com, a plagiarism detection program administered by the KU writing center. Joint workshops offered by the KU writing center and the KU libraries continue to orient students and faculty to a range of issues impacted by contemporary research and writing challenges, such as online research methods, avoiding plagiarism, and digital scholarship. The work we already do collaboratively is congruent with the message we hear from our upper administration, and we sense this work is becoming a part of the institutional support structure.

Space

Kent Miller, now assistant dean of public services for the libraries, was managing facilities when the first library satellite for the writing center was set up. He has maintained a strong interest in furthering the collaboration. Currently, he is leading the collaborative learning spaces work group for HVC2. Proposals from this group seem to confirm the need to shift conceptions of learning spaces away from seeing and using them as purely instructional spaces; Kent has defined the areas they are looking at developing as learning spaces that bring together both the print and electronic resources with learning tools (which we see as including peer coaches) to assist in collaborative learning.

His review of other institutions' initiatives shows that many have fallen into the "space is space" trap, filling environments with equipment and furnishings without setting the spaces up to speak their mission, making the learning that takes place there less visible and less measurable. Certainly, for writing centers across the country that house satellites in libraries, this represents a departure. As many writing centers seek shared space, the initial motivation typically has had more to do with their perceived marginalized status and unstable funding sources. Teaming with libraries in more ways than simply becoming casual tenants is vital to making both the spaces and the values inherent there sustainable.

As writing centers seek spaces, libraries are trying to be less constrained by their traditional physical locations and to be seen as a service that can be used in many places. And because neither the KU libraries nor the KU writing center has the staff to reach all the KU students (more than 25,000, including graduate students), a shared space collaboration may be required for survival and the roundtable voices supported this notion. Yet, Kathryn Nemeth Tuttle, an associate vice provost for student success, stated that, for example, infusing student services in the residence halls has not always been successful. Students have a tendency to want to separate academics from their residence life. She believes that we need to create an environment in the residence halls that the students will want to be in—for both social and scholastic activity. Libraries are no different. The KU libraries have seen an increased gate count just by adding sleek Gateway computers, new furniture, and a coffee cart, so this method of attracting students has worked at KU to bring in the students. But even significant improvements to the environment and concerted efforts to address student desires for convenience are no guarantee: Katherine Furlong and Andrew Crawford, librarians at the University of Maine, found the adage "If you build it, they will come" was not entirely true. Following extensive and expensive renovations, the library was not attracting users. Campus misconceptions about the potential of their twenty-first-century library led them to reassess their user needs and create a marketing strategy that involved direct peer influence. The Information Literacy Program teamed with the campus writing center to develop a peer outreach and cross-trained tutoring strategy. From their perspective, the results included, among other things, enhanced skills for student tutors and student users and demonstrated that "student advocacy of library services and resources is effectively changing our campus curriculum."[10] This confirms for us that students are sophisticated users and expect more than simply a cutting-edge environment; they want effective help within that environment.

Naturally, we need to recognize that these types of interactions are neither automatic nor easy. And as one experienced librarian reminded us, we cannot take it for granted that all libraries would embrace our vision: "Some in the American Library Association see collaboration as trendy, or that it might erode what the library really does, and some don't want to share an agenda outside of the library. But others are progressive, even to the point of pushing on a trend just to keep things moving, changing, and that is often not such a bad thing." With competition for resources, many libraries may be protecting turf, just as departments also protect resources and limit collaboration. This competition for resources could be identified as the primary barrier to collaboration, often demonstrated from the faculty perspective by an institutional devaluing of coauthorship, for example, or when the message many faculty get from the moment they step on campus is to fulfill requirements for tenure by not venturing too far outside the box. In other words, some believe that collaboration takes time and energy better reserved for research and thereby miss opportunities that could benefit them in both scholarship and teaching.

We have tried as much as possible not to view our work together as either stemming from or dominated by the writing center side or the library side. Although eliminating this perspective, we do acknowledge that motivations for collaboration from both parties may be different at the start, but the pleasant surprise is how much of what each of us needs, does, and plans reveals our common vision.

- Writing centers may initially reach out to libraries as they are trying to break free of small, remote, unappealing location(s); to expand their number of locations; or to create satellites in diverse locations. Linking with libraries makes more visible the importance of writing to an interdisciplinary environment and helps a writing center demonstrate a commitment to the academic mission through closer affiliation with a library (which is traditionally associated with academics, more so, say, than student affairs or student services units).

 • From the library standpoint, collaborations can increase gate count (raw number of visitors), demonstrate the authentic connection between research and writing, and enhance staffing needs by developing peer and tier services. Integrated instructional models can send strong messages to faculty and administrators; constructing the library as a student-friendly, user-driven environment reinforces the mission of preserving the library as a "place" while developing alternative methods and locations of service delivery.

The Power of Peer

As any good reference librarian knows, students often approach the reference desk thinking they know what they want, but not really knowing what they need. A "reference interview" takes place so that the librarian can ascertain what will truly help the student with his or her research. Similarly, the consultants at the KU writing center find that students have difficulty articulating what they need. Writing consultants must ask a set of strategic questions to find out how they can help the student. According to Sheril Hook, Claudia Timmann, among others: "Both writing and research share common processes—brainstorming, drafting, and revising—that are not always obvious but easily understood when the connection between the two is described."[11] Information literacy competencies, the ability to evaluate information critically, and the ability to write and communicate are mutually dependent and certainly required for academic success. At East Carolina, the method for highlighting this goal came under an "umbrella of information literacy" initiative. Teams from across the campus, including faculty and student support partners such as residence hall staff, work together on all aspects of the program, including planning and evaluation.[12] Caroline L. Russom and Regina Clemens Fox even "attribute the improvement of student writing to the learning environment enhanced by [the] collaboration" between a library instruction module and a first year writing course.[13]

The KU writing center depends on a well-trained staff of KU students to provide peer-to-peer writing consultation services. This model has worked well, and abundant literature on peer tutoring in writing centers supports this, dating back to Theodore Newcomb's claim in 1966 that "the peer group is the single most powerful influence in undergraduate education."[14] Additional literature looking at a range of campus services also supports the blending of peer tutors into the overall service model for academic support. More than ten years ago, Ann Klavano and Eleanor Kulleseid reported in "Bibliographic Instruction: Renewal and Transformation in One Academic Library" on the ways they strengthened instructional partnerships through the development of a peer tutoring program for information literacy.[15]

In general, faculty and administrators at KU have expressed a "buy-in" to the idea that peers can and do represent a legitimate, highly accessible, and high-quality monitored delivery of services to students in areas ranging from academic tutoring to help desk services.[16] With the path cleared for a more innovative university-wide student services help desk model, involving students in direct services to other students supports the mission of strengthening retention and graduation rates because it provides more seamless services. According to Marlesa Roney, vice provost for student success, students need not know or fully understand the structure beneath that drives services, they simply need to see a consistent, highly visible, and accessible service model.

For example, when the KU libraries added productivity software (such as Word, Excel, PowerPoint, etc.) to the public workstations, reference librarians working at reference desks were fearful of being inundated with technical questions. Deborah Ludwig proposed training computer-savvy students to handle technology questions. Her colleague, Marianne Reed, hired and trained students to install software and answer technology questions at a help desk near the reference desks in the two largest libraries on campus. Elizabeth Malia described a shift to a tiered services model in the John F. Kennedy Memorial Library at Eastern Washington University: "We were given two words as the imperatives: tier and rove."[17] Training needs challenged the solution, creating multiple levels of service that included student assistants, paraprofessionals, and seasoned reference librarians, yet all levels benefited from an intensive retraining of the reference interview, a fundamental element of front-line library services. Another study showed that more than 80 percent of main information desk and reference desk questions could be answered by "trained, nonprofessional employees," leading to a trend in blending students and paraprofessionals (which the University of Illinois at Chicago calls LTAs or library technical assistants) from various areas into the service delivery model of library instruction.[18]

Case Study: KU Info

Beginning in the fall of 2003, KU libraries also began a peer-to-peer model of providing reference services. About the same time, KU Info, a rumor hotline housed in student affairs since the1970s and operated by students, had evolved to answer students' general questions about class timetables, campus- and citywide events, services for students, and other pertinent questions that can impact student retention and success. In the fall of 2003, KU Info became a part of the KU libraries. With a walk-up service located in the busiest library on campus, students staff an information desk and take questions over the phone. Coinciding with an effort to give librarians more time for collection development and liaison duties, and with a goal to provide extended hours of service to students, KU libraries began a program of training KU Info students to answer more in-depth library reference questions. Based on a peer and tier model of reference, the KU Info students are now trained to answer basic reference questions, but to refer more difficult questions to library subject specialists. The students have found the work experience to be extremely valuable to their own academic pursuits, and library staff members enjoy the input from the students concerning their own services.

Librarians Catherine Palmer and Collette Ford described integrating learner services with a new staffing model. In their report, they identified four instructional models and rated their effectiveness; the "student as instructor" model and the "student self-paced instruction" model were seen to be the most effective in reaching more students while stretching resources.[19] Two other librarians, Susan Deese-Roberts and Kathleen Keating, agreed that "peer assistance can effectively supplement the work of reference and instruction librarians."[20]

Could the traditional liaison model of outreach to faculty (with assigned bibliographers or subject specialists) through the academic librarian be limited in its effectiveness? Typically, a subject specialist does not reach every faculty member (and thus, not every student) in any one department or discipline. In fact, subject specialist instruction to faculty may have little impact on actual faculty instructional methods. One way to reach more students is to provide a peer-to-peer model of coaching for library research and writing skills, a model that exploits the powerful learning motivation at the point of need. In 1997, librarian Peggy Sieden predicted that "an emphasis on facilitating group work will be required on a broad scale as group projects and peer or faculty coaching become common instructional strategies."[21]

As a way to solve staff shortages and provide valuable opportunities for students, the peer-to-peer model is a win-win proposition. Pools of student hourly funds are much easier to replenish, especially with new criteria for use of tuition enhancement funds; hiring and training a large cohort of coaches, who can work across library and writing center boundaries, is an economical advantage as well. Currently, the director of our writing center offers, as many directors do across the country, a credit-bearing course on the methods of tutorial instruction. To expand on this idea, we are talking now about proposing a joint training session in peer-to-peer instruction in research, writing, and the use of technology. Admittedly, then, our wish list includes developing a larger cohort of peer support geared to the whole campus, an especially attractive prospect should an information literacy component become part of a general education portfolio.

Seeking Sustainability

Although the current climate at KU is one that seems to be fostering innovation, we believe that even the best collaborative efforts are at risk. As most of us in academia realize, change takes time and often within any change time frame leadership and agendas can shift dramatically. Even though we recognize that collaboration requires the elements our roundtable identified (institutional support, space, and harnessing the power of peer), without an effort to provide for sustainability, these initiatives could remain superficial, people based, and contingent efforts. We started at the grassroots level, yet we now find that multiple and broad efforts are springing up across our campus. And unlike less visible and informal collaborations, ours is receiving administrative support because, we believe, we have been mindful to demonstrate the many connections our work has with the "big picture." Without involvement in the larger arena (for example, we are both serving on different HVC2 work groups), we would lack the leverage—the networking connections to key players and funding—to "entwine" our projects with the larger initiatives. This "entwining" is a necessary component to fostering sustainability. According to writing teacher Derek Owens:

> Sustainability requires that we envision ourselves less as autonomous individuals than as collaborators who are not only dependent upon but also literally connected to our local environments in complex ways.[22]

At this writing, the KU writing center and the KU libraries are considering a cross-trained consultation model, with peer-coaching locations in the residence halls (Student Success Center) and in a new Multicultural Resource Center (expected to open in 2006). As we plan, we are inspired by a 2001 project at the University of Arizona that focused on the challenge of reaching minority and international students as a model; they found that providing incentives such as new technology and peer information counselors who were deskside peer coaches for writing and research methods helped turn the marginalized, underfunded student cultural center into a hub for learning.[23]

Conclusion

David W. Lewis reminds us that "libraries must become adept at boundary spanning," and it does not surprise us that many other institutions also are working on partnerships that will tie technology, writing, and research together in new ways and in new settings.[24] These collaborations can be characterized along a continuum, from sharing space to integration of curriculum goals to instructional partnerships. Yet, we believe the essential component of a more authentic, sustainable collaboration may be missing.

Space sharing is only space sharing, and it is often based on the goodwill or special interests of a small number of individuals. Understanding that many efforts to collaborate might seem counterintuitive to the historic, decentralized complexities of the institutional infrastructure, collaboration must be designed as sustainable, able to thrive beyond changing generations of leadership. The shared vision and future planning generated through a collaborative process should be made visible and open to a broad group, where opportunities and responsibilities can begin to take on the look and feel of distributed networks.

As we continue to "look around" to find local initiatives to tap into, we are mindful of the challenges. Initially, we worked simply to build and continue collaboration across two programs. Now we have seen how the range of programs at our institution—whether it be students grouped together in residence halls by academic interests, students in a precollege student orientation, students-of-color retention programs, or a universal help desk—offers new opportunities. We have learned much from our work so far and plan to continue building on our collaboration in order to make such partnerships a deeper, more rooted expression of the university's commitment to student learning.

Notes

1. An online review of writing centers housed in libraries indicates a trend in that direction, but in all the cases we saw on the Web, the connection did not seem to go beyond shared space (typically, with a library loaning space to a writing center). See Marquette, Texas A&M, Fort Hays State, and the University of Vermont, among many others.

2. An obvious example of this is this chapter. The authors thank Jim Elmborg for the opportunity to reflect on our current collaboration. Also, former KU librarian Cindy Pierard was instrumental in originally securing the space in the library for the satellite writing center; partnering often with the director in developing instructional materials and workshops, often about evaluating Web sources and digital plagiarism, led to a coauthored publication in the National Teaching and Learning Forum (http://www.ntlf.com/html/ti/archives/surfing.htm).

3. In 2003, Marilu Goodyear, vice provost for information services, brought together Donna Liss, associate vice provost, Stella Bentley, KU Libraries dean, and Marlessa Roney, vice provost for student success, to brainstorm an integrated service model for the University of Kansas. To read an overview, see http://www.ur.ku.edu/News/03N/DecNews/Dec3/hvc.html.

4. Provost David Shulenburger served on the National Commission on Writing in America's Schools and Colleges and attention to the report (http://www.writingcommission.org/) led to formation of an informal group to explore possibilities for KU related to supporting student writing. See http://www.writing.ku.edu/writingmatters/ for documents related to this effort.

5. "Information Literacy Competency Standards for Higher Education." *Association of College and Research Libraries* (2003). Available online at http://www.ala.org/acrl/ilcomstan.html [accessed 20 March 2004].

6. John Seely Brown and Paul Duguid, *The Social Life of Information* (Boston: Harvard Business School Pr., 2002).

7. Outline prepared for roundtable discussion: included in appendix A

8. Carol Ann Hughes, "The Changing Landscape of Scholarly Publishing: Print Collections E-Books and Beyond" (2001). Available online at http://www. lib.umich.edu/conferences/ebook/presentations/hughes.html [accessed 13 March 2004].

Excerpt: "Dick Rowe, CEO of Rowe.com, noted in his address at the Information Online 2001 in Sydney that there have been three revolutions in the latter half of the twentieth century: the first was that of the computer itself and the second was the communications revolution (hooking up all those computers with each other). The third revolution we are now facing is that of convenience. He states, 'We are experiencing a global transfer of value and power from knowledge providers to knowledge users that will cause many revered institutions to collapse and many upstarts to appear.' In other words, information will not be provided to users solely on the providers' terms. Users will have increasing power in the marketplace and their demands will make or break the success of products and services.

In this 'competitive space,' the role of the library as the primary aggregator and purveyor of content to its community is less and less unique. Local collections and staff are no longer the only source for information services to serious learners and support for faculty in their research and teaching. This statement may not be a radically new call to action for we have told ourselves this for the past decade. But Jerry Campbell at the same EDUCAUSE meeting said it a bit more directly than I had heard it before. He asked: 'Would the lack of librarians cause our system of higher education to crumble?' Librarians have to make sure that students, university administrators and faculty would all reply with a resounding yes."

9. David E. Shulenburger, "On Scholarly Evaluation and Scholarly Communication: Increasing the Volume of Quality Work," *C&RL News* 62, no. 8

(Sept. 2001). Available online at http://www.ala.org/ala/acrl/acrlpubs/crlnews/backissues2001/september3/scholarlyevaluation.htm.

10. Katherine Furlong and Andrew B. Crawford. "Marketing Your Services through Your Students," *Computers in Libraries* 19, no. 8 (1999): 22–24.

11. Sheril Hook and Claudia Timmann, "Academic Libraries and Writing Centers: Practical Approaches to Collaboration," poster session given at the Annual ALA Conference, June 2002, at Atlanta. Available online at http://www.library.arizona.edu/users/timmannc/online_presentations/collaboration_files/frame.htm.

12. William Joseph Thomas and Carolyn N. Willis, "An Information Literacy Umbrella for Instruction," *Academic Exchange Quarterly* 8, no. 1 (2004). Available online at http://www.rapidintellect.com/AEQweb/cho24653j.htm [accessed 3 March 2004].

13. Caroline L. Russom and Regina Clemens Fox, "First-year Research and Writing Convergences," *Academic Exchange Quarterly* 7, no. 3 (fall 2003): 194. In Expanded Academic ASAP [database online]. Available from University of Kansas Libraries [cited 22 February 2004].

14. Nancy Falchikov, *Learning Together: Peer Tutoring in Higher Education* (London: Routledge/Falmer, 2001), xi.

15. Ann M. Klavano and Eleanor R. Kulleseid, "Bibliographic Instruction: Renewal and Transformation in One Academic Library," *Reference Librarian* 51/52 (1995): 359–83.

16. Expanded annotated bibliography on program models:

1. Tyler, Jill I. and Sheril J. Hook. "The Communication Center: A Full-Service Academic Resource in the Heart of the Library." Proceedings of the ACRL Tenth National Conference: Crossing the Divide, Denver, Colorado, March 15–18, 2001 pp70-74. Online at www.ala.org/ala/acrl/acrlevents/tyler.pdf

The librarian in charge of research instruction and the coordinator of the basic course in speech communication collaborated to "integrate institutional initiatives in information literacy with the general education courses in Speech Communication, and to build on what Research Instruction staff was already doing in the basic course in English Composition." Naming it the Communication Center, the students have an on-call staff in the library to obtain assistance with oral communication, written communication, and research instruction. "Faculty from the Departments of English and Speech Communication were asked to be involved in the development of this new collaborative academic resource intended to build on the individualized instruction, information literacy initiatives, and oral and written communication across the curriculum movements." Faculty members in research instruction, English, and speech communication recruited, interviewed selected graduate teaching assistants and advanced undergraduate students from the two departments. Students give the service high evaluations, recognizing the benefit of consulting with experts in their fields. Faculty report that the work of the students has improved;

anecdotal evidence of increased enthusiasm and improved evaluation and use of supporting information is included.

2.   Ivan A. Shibley, Louis M Milakofsky, and Cynthia L. Nicotera, "Incorporating a Substantial Writing Assignment into Organic Chemistry: Library Research, Peer Review, and Assessment," *Journal of Chemical Education* 78, no. 1 (Jan. 2001): 50–53.

This study describes a successful collaboration between a librarian and a scientific writing instructor. Students report that the writing assignment helped them understand chemistry better.

3.   Christy Gavin, "Guiding Students along the Information Highway: Librarians Collaborating with Composition Instructors," *Journal of Teaching Writing* 13, no. 1–2 (1994): 229–335.

This study describes a library program designed for an English 101 course. Refutes that students innately know how to use the library or know how to use it the way faculty do. "The Lab saves the composition instructors preparation time." "The Lab relieves pressure on the instructor to become an expert on research methods." This model can be adapted to satisfy subject-specific needs of upperclassmen and graduate students. The lab requires students to engage in methods to locate and search sources and determine the credibility of the author's work.

3.   "Leadership by Design: Collaborations and Cornerstones." ACM SIGUCCS Fall 2003 Conference (Sept. 2003). Available online at http://www.valpo.edu/library/pd/sig03/conf/sld001.htm.

This presentation describes professional and contextual influences, for example, coming together over a larger project, such as help desk, information services model, etc.

4.   Sheril Hook and Claudia Timmann, "Academic Libraries and Writing Centers: Practical Approaches to Collaboration," presented by The University of Arizona Library

Poster Session, ALA, Atlanta, June 16, 2002.

Excerpt: "Technology has made it possible for academic libraries to work with writing centers in exciting ways. Many writing centers are now online, providing virtual help, but also providing one-on-one consultations while sitting with a student at a computer. Traditionally, writing consultants have been able to intervene at all stages of the writing process. Now consultants can connect to libraries' gateways, which provide them with an opportunity to help students with the research process. However, do the writing consultants have the research skills to do this successfully? There are many possibilities for collaboration between libraries and writing centers, which would provide the consultants with the necessary skills to be successful when assisting students with the research process. At the University of Arizona, librarians have been working with the writing center coordinators to train consultants in effective library research skills. At this poster session, you will learn strategies we developed for creating successful library collaborations with campus writing centers.

- Strengthens the library's role on campus
- Develops information literate students through partnerships
- Serves students through shared goals and missions

17. Elizabeth Malia, "Triage and Tiers," *Library Mosaics* (Nov. /Dec. 1996): 19.

18. Karen J. Graves, "Implementation and Evaluation of Information Desk Services Provided by Library Technical Assistants," *Bulletin of the Medical Library Association* 86, no. 4 (1998): 481.

19. Catherine Palmer and Collette Ford, "Integrating the Learning Library into the Undergraduate Curriculum: Extending Staff Resources for Library Instruction," *Research Strategies* 17 (2000): 167–75.

20. Susan Deese-Roberts and Kathleen Keating, "Integrating a Library Strategies Peer Tutoring Strategies, *Research Strategies* 17 (2000): 229.

21. Peggy Seiden, "Restructuring Liberal Arts College Libraries: Seven Organizational Strategies," in *Restructuring Academic Libraries: Organizational Development in the Wake of Technological Change*, ed. Charles A. Schwartz (Chicago: ACRL, 1997), 213–30. According to Seiden, "creating alternative learning structures and environments will require collaborations across existing administrative boundaries, which may prove especially difficult because physical space and pedagogical turf are at stake. Other spaces on campus will be designed to accommodate activities with a library component but will not be library based. In those cases, the library will always need to be involved, sometimes as a consultant and sometimes as a full partner. Interesting examples of this can be found in the new undergraduate library at George Mason University, which shares a building with the student center, and in the Media Union at the University of Michigan, located with computer classrooms and laboratories. The instructional approaches we can anticipate will require large-scale access to technology, through either the installation of many workstations or the creation of new space with network access for student laptops. In either case, an emphasis on facilitating group work will be required on a broad scale as group projects and peer or faculty coaching become common instructional strategies. The library, as the central space for scholarly activity on campus and as the facility that has traditionally offered the longest hours of operation, should be the primary locus of these new spaces."

22. Derek Owens, *Composition and Sustainability: Teaching for a Threatened Generation* (Urbana, Ill.: National Council of Teachers of English, 2001), 1.

23. Elaina Norlin, "University Goes Back to Basics to Reach Minority Students," *American Libraries* 32, no. 7 (2001): 60–62.

24. David W. Lewis, "Change and Transition in Public Services," in *Restructuring Academic Libraries: Organizational Development in the Wake of Technological*

Change, ed. Charles A. Schwartz (Chicago: ACRL, 1997), 31–53.

Excerpt: "Traditional library organizations generally lack the flexibility and adaptability to respond to rapid environmental change, especially when players from outside libraries become central to what we do. Team-based structures will be required if we are to maintain effective collaborations with computing organizations and other campus units. And in working with faculty, librarians must carve out a new professional role in the development and delivery of networked curricular resources.

A way out of this untenable situation is, at least in theory, not terribly difficult to ascertain, though it will be hard to implement. Robert B. Barr and John Tagg distinguish between two approaches to the mission of the university: instruction versus learning ["From Teaching to Learning—A New Paradigm for Undergraduate Education," *Change* 27 (Nov./Dec. 1995)]. The *instructional* approach generally involves only rudimentary, stimulus-response interactions limited in meaning to a particular course. The method and the product are the same—a class taught or a lecture given. The assumption is that to get more learning you must do more teaching. In contrast, the *learning* approach embraces "education for understanding—a sufficient grasp of concepts, principles, or skills so that one can bring them to bear on new problems and situations.

Additional Readings

Eodice, Michele, and Cindy Pierard. 2002. "Surfing for Scholarship: Promoting More Effective Student Research," *National Teaching and Learning Forum* 11, no. 3. Available online at http://www.ntlf.com/html/ti/archives/surfing.htm [accessed 25 March 2004].

Mileham, Trisha, and Joyce Hicks. 2003. "Leadership by Design: Collaborations and Cornerstones." Paper presented at the ACM SIGUCCS 31st Annual Fall Conference, September, at San Antonio, Texas.

National Commission on Writing in Schools and Colleges. 2003. *Report of the National Commission on Writing in Schools and College: The Neglected R: The Need for a Writing Revolution*. Available online at http://www.writingcommission.org/ [accessed 3 March 2004].

Tyler, Jill I., and Sheril J. Hook. 2001. "The Communication Center: A Full-service Academic Resource in the Heart of the Library," paper presented at the 10th ACRL National Conference, Marxh, at Denver.

The University of Kansas, Office of University Relations. 2003. "KU Announces 'Revolutionary' Project to Improve Info Tech Services, Resources." Available online at http://www.ur.ku.edu/News/03N/DecNews/Dec3/hvc.html [accessed 20 March 2004].

Writing Matters. 2003. *Writing Matters @ KU*. Available online at http://www.writing.ku.edu/writingmatters/ [accessed 23 March 2004].

Appendix A

For a chapter in a book edited by Jim Elmborg, Assistant Professor in the School of Library & Information Science a the University of Iowa, Lea and Michele are writing about the KU Libraries and KU Writing Center collaboration. We plan to describe the history of the partnership, as well as raise issues of sustainability and design for future directions. The book is slated to be published as part of the ALA series "Publications in Librarianship."

We'd like to hear what you see as barriers to collaboration at KU and how we can overcome these barriers. We are also interested in finding out, from your perspective, what you see as the benefits of this kind of collaboration. We do not expect anyone to spend a lot of time preparing for this discussion. We will be recording/transcribing the discussion and can provide you with a transcript in advance of submitting our chapter if you wish to review your comments.

We ask you to think about:
- how difficult it is to be truly collaborative—and to do really open collaboration
- how programs that simply share locations can better demonstrate a true collaboration

A question from Jim Elmborg to our discussion group:

Higher education institutions place a heavy emphasis on individual achievement for faculty, the reward structures on campus in money, promotion, and prestige, the prevailing culture of higher education with its turf battles, etc. How do you work against all that in order to do collaboration like yours?

Challenges associated with collaborations of this type:
- Disrupt institutional planning and organizational structures?
- Costs of blending programs?
- Staff training?
- Meeting information literacy competencies?

A utopian vision: (The Jim Carothers Method) given an infinite pile of money and the most powerful and enlightened leadership (or legislature!)…what could/should happen?

Future file: What might we predict is coming down the road related to:
- Technology
- Different institutional structures
- Service delivery models (big giant help desk model, for example)
- Impact on recruitment, retention, graduation
- Impact on faculty

Chapter four

Yours, Mine, and Ours: Collaboration among Faculty, Library, and Writing Center

Sarah Leadley and Becky Reed Rosenberg

At the University of Washington, Bothell (UWB), collaboration among librarians and writing center staff spans more than a decade, two writing center directors, and more than a dozen librarians. For all involved, it has been an enriching experience. Together, we have learned much about the teaching of writing and research methods from this blending of disciplines. Equally important, we have collaborated with scores of faculty at every point—from proposing a course to creating the syllabus and assignments to conducting classroom instruction and final assessment of student work. From the inception of the campus in 1990, faculty and staff have made heroic efforts to erase the "skills" and "content" split that is so much a fact of institutional life in the academy, just as they have rejected the disciplinary divisions of academic life in favor of interdisciplinarity. The integration of writing and information literacy into the curriculum has been a fundamental value of the campus culture. Developing instructional approaches that accomplish this goal has been a heady experience, and we have come a long way. But old habits die hard, and, as we illustrate, the learning curve has been steep for those of us on the "skills" side of the relationship.

We begin with a caution: One of the most important lessons we have learned from the library–writing center partnership comes less from our successes than from our failures. Although we have always maintained that faculty involvement is central to the successful integration of writing and research skills, we sometimes have neglected to invite faculty engagement in the planning of the writing and research portions of workshops. As we (library and writing specialists) have learned to collaborate, we have arrived at some of our conversations with faculty with a set of templates in our bag and offered them up as models, which sometimes provide easy answers to hard questions

This article reflects the many lessons learned from the authors' work with creative, thoughtful, and generous collaborators on the University of Washington, Bothell, Interdisciplinary Arts and Sciences faculty and in Academic Services. We especially wish to thank Bruce Burgett, JoLynn Edwards, Cynthia Fugate, and Linda S. Watts for reading and responding to an earlier draft.

and reduce the richness of our collaborations. The challenge, as we now understand it, is to bring to our conversations with faculty the benefit of what we have already done without limiting the possibilities to only that set of experiences.

We will use this chapter to examine how these collaborations have developed over a number of iterations of "interdisciplinary inquiry," a required multisection course for students beginning upper-division work in the UWB interdisciplinary arts and sciences program. The library and the writing center have contributed to many redesigns of the course, most recently, to a model that includes a series of workshops focusing on critical thinking, reading, writing, and research and team-taught by the instructor, the writing specialist, and the librarian with an emphasis on the processes of identifying and reformulating complex research questions, examining the rhetorical structure of texts, evaluating and marshalling evidence, and developing group work/learning through social interaction. We will explore our successes, but perhaps more important, we will examine some of the barriers to collaboration that we have experienced, barriers that in some cases were of our own design. We also will trace the evolution of this course from a content-driven interdisciplinary model to one that foregrounds a "transdisciplinary" method of inquiry.

Description of the Institution

Established in 1990, the University of Washington, Bothell (UWB), is located approximately eight miles north of Seattle. It serves upper-division and graduate programs in business, computing and software systems, education, interdisciplinary arts and sciences, and nursing. When the UWB campus was established to provide educational excellence to a time-bound, place-bound student population, the founders placed critical thinking and lifelong learning at the center of their vision. They recognized the crucial place of literacy in its many forms—for example, critical reading, writing, information, technology, and numeracy—and determined to integrate these into students' educational experience across the curriculum. Academic Services has evolved over the past decade to help meet that need.

Academic Services is the administrative department that houses the campus library and media center (resources now shared with Cascadia Community College), information systems, the Writing Center, the Quantitative Skills Center, educational technology, and the teaching and learning center. Working in close collaboration with faculty to support student success through the seamless integration of literacies in our interdisciplinary curriculum, each unit has achieved a high level of innovation, pedagogical sophistication, visibility, and accessibility to students and faculty. The joining of these services in a single organizational umbrella has provided a level of communication and collaboration among Academic Services staff members that stimulates both innovation and integration of instruction. Many of the practices that are now standard on our campus are a result of the close relationship among Academic Services units and between Academic Services and the academic programs' faculty and staff. With student success as the central goal, this structure and the relationships it nurtures have created an environment in which faculty and staff share responsibility for exploring, articulating and reconceiving their purposes, pedagogies, and instructional approaches. These joint undertakings and the sense of shared vision and responsibility have fostered ongoing assessment and reassessment of our activities.

Learning to Collaborate

Neither of us was prepared for the kind of collaboration made possible by the UWB experiment. Sarah had no formal training as a teacher and, as a new librarian, was learning by degrees the fundamentals of classroom teaching and instructional design. Just teaching the basic information literacy skills of finding and evaluating resources seemed a large enough task to occupy an army of instruction librarians. Furthermore, she had never taken a composition course or visited a writing center, and the processes of writing instruction were completely foreign. Fortunately, the library had a strong instruction program, fueled by the creativity and intelligence of its founding instruction librarian, Esther Daniels. Daniels created a program that stressed the teaching of critical thinking and faculty collaboration. She mentored new teaching librarians according to a model of instruction that was intellectually engaging, innovative, and very proactive. From the beginning, there were many successful partnerships among librarians, writing specialists, and those faculty members open to such collaborations.

Although Becky arrived at UWB with many years of experience teaching writing and modest forays into collaboration with faculty across the curriculum, she had only limited experience collaborating with librarians. Her training as a historian left her with enormous respect for the powers of archivists as partners in research. They were invaluable sources of insight because of their intimate knowledge of collections and how other scholars used them. As a composition instructor, she had encouraged students to see librarians as great resources for locating useful information but had never attributed to librarians the same range of insights that she attributed to archivists. The organization of the Writing Center in Academic Services put Becky into much closer contact with librarians, and she quickly learned that librarians did not only help "find stuff," but included in their purview selecting topics, developing research questions, evaluating sources, and integrating sources into research. If neither the librarian nor the writing specialist had exclusive dominion over these areas, they would have to work together to understand how each brought a perspective that enriched the process and they would have to learn how to share.

As a group, we instituted regular teaching meetings in 1996.[1] These standing meetings provided space for writing specialists and librarians to talk about a wide range of topics and questions about teaching and learning. We have used this dedicated time to talk about specific courses, research, and writing processes such as topic selection and source evaluation, and broader issues of assessment and student learning. One of the many advantages of this ongoing partnership and dialogue has been the development of a shared understanding of the interconnectedness of the writing and research processes, as well as the value of teaching these skills within the context of course content.

History of the Course and Our Work with It

We have selected interdisciplinary inquiry as an example of sustained collaboration among writing center staff and librarians. Our collaboration began as an opportunity to cover writing and research skills in order to prepare students for upper-division work in subsequent 300- and 400-level courses. Several models were designed and implemented by teaching teams of faculty, writing specialists, and librarians. We are going to focus on four iterations of interdisciplinary inquiry, over the course of which we have been able to experiment with a variety of assignments and workshops and assess their impact on student learning. With each iteration, we believe that progress has been made in more deeply engaging students as consumers and producers of research.

Round One: In the Beginning

Initially, the program required that entering students take two courses, one focused on writing and developing thesis-driven arguments, the other on research. These courses provided the opportunity to draw on the expertise of a wide variety of faculty members with different teaching styles and disciplinary training, often teaching in teams. This diversity opened up the planning dialogue in productive ways. Moreover, it was challenging to try to reconcile this diversity and integrate a consistent set of library, writing, and reading skills across the multisection course (even as participants debated precisely what those skills were and whether we needed consistency).

From the beginning, the writing specialists brought to our enterprise the tradition of Writing across the Curriculum (WAC), with its emphasis on process writing and collaborative learning strategies. This resonated with librarians frustrated by the limitations of tools-based workshops. Ironically, although WAC provided a partial model and inspiration, its advocates have not given much consideration to the value of collaborating with librarians, although they have anticipated the need to expand their collaborations to include technology, service learning, and a variety of other teaching initiatives.[2]

The initial collaborations among faculty, librarians, and the Writing Center resulted in a series of experiments in integrating a sequenced approach to teaching research, writing, reading, and critical thinking. These projects included annotated bibliographies, source evaluation assignments and workshops, and a research proposal assignment that brought them all together. These processes were all designed to take students more deeply into the "conversation" on their topic, based on their critical reading of a range of popular and scholarly sources. The final assignment asked students to formulate a question that could function as the basis for a longer research project. Many of these experiments were very successful, despite a continuing tension between "content coverage" and "skills" instruction, thanks to the extraordinary teaching skills and flexibility of the faculty involved and their willingness to embrace a collaborative instructional model.

Round Two: A New Approach

After several years, a committee was appointed to put forward a proposal for the course's revision. The charge to the committee included collapsing the two-course sequence into one course. The committee was composed of faculty, librarians, and the writing center director. Over several months, the committee crafted guidelines that called for "integrat[ing] fully the skills objectives of the course with the rest of the course content" in a synergy in which "these two parts of the course … create a dynamic and valuable learning experience for all involved." The document enumerated abilities that students would develop in library skills, writing, reading, technology, self-assessment, as well as faculty and staff development goals. (See appendix A.)

Although adopted in draft form by the faculty, the skills guidelines were created with limited faculty input. They were not framed in language that invited faculty to adapt them to their content objectives but, rather, in terms that spoke with expediency and efficiency to the contributing librarians and the writing specialists. This "shorthand" made sense to us; we understood that the various elements were flexible and, when joined to critical thinking, could be combined, modified, and adapted quite easily. We saw that these guidelines had the potential to be used and modified within a variety of disciplinary and interdisciplinary contexts, but our vision was implicit, not explicitly modeled for faculty—and not based on a faculty-driven example. To faculty, it looked like a laundry list of add-ons that provided students with "rote" skills at the expense of content. Because the design seemed overly prescriptive, permanent faculty started to disappear from the teaching roster for the course.

With the program's need to identify additional faculty to teach this core class, Becky was asked to teach a section, which we treated as a laboratory for our ideas about the course. We decided to continue to experiment with the idea of a term-long research proposal assignment, placing more emphasis on framing research questions and process writing. As with the previous models, we felt this would enable us to take students through the process relatively slowly (to the extent that anything can be accomplished slowly on a quarter system), under-scoring for them how recursive the process is by not allowing them to complete the project but only begin it. We hoped that asking for a proposal rather than a completed research paper would encourage students to really engage with their questions and the process. We also decided early on to introduce regular opportunities for reflection on their learning process—both because we feel that reflective self-assessment is fundamental to learning and because in the program's senior capstone course students assemble a portfolio of their work and a reflection on that work. We wanted that final requirement to be foreshadowed and practiced from the beginning of the program.

Taking the research proposal as the final product for the course, we developed a series of staged assignments, supported by in-class activities, that led students through identifying a topic of interest to them, framing a researchable question about the topic, examining their assumptions about the topic, identifying the disciplines that would be most relevant to addressing their questions, finding research work, understanding and evaluating the research work, and selecting a re-search method for their own original project. At each stage, we asked students to reflect on their experience, for example, on what terms were most useful when searching databases, how they expanded their search vocabulary, what kind of questions they found addressed in different databases (as a way of understanding what kinds of ques-tions/problems different disciplines address), what they had gained when they found themselves in dead ends, what criteria they used to evaluate their sources, and so on.

What we discovered through this experience was that these processes required extensive in-class workshops, time that even we did not allow for. With substantial parts of the process assigned as out-of-class projects, many students either never fully understood the difference between the research proposal and a more traditional research paper (leading to frustration and confusion) or they did not take enough time to develop the research question portion of the as-signment, arguably the most challenging part of the process. Despite our intention to avoid the pitfalls of a traditional research paper and the lure of the formulaic progression through the stages of research and writing, we proceeded in a rather tidy and linear way to accomplish something we kept insisting to ourselves and our students was messy and recursive, an all-too-familiar trap for both writing instructors and instruction librarians.

As we worked with other faculty teaching the course, we arrived with a set of assignment templates we had designed for Becky's section and invited them to tweak the templates to accommodate the content on which they were focusing. Some faculty saw that the assignments addressed the skills guidelines well and therefore accepted them. These instructors developed syllabi to suit the assignments rather than develop assignments to suit their own course goals. As a result, our contribution to the course lacked the seamless integration of skills and content that we aim for. We were enjoying our collaboration but were frustrated that we could not communicate our successes to our faculty.

We were not entirely successful with students, either. Evaluations from students on the library and writing components of the course were skewed between those who found them extremely helpful and those who found them inappropriate to an upper-division course outside composition. Although we saw ourselves addressing skills at point of need and within the content area of the course, many students felt that the library and writing components were (our worst fears) add-ons and remedial.

Largely absent from our approach was attention to the issue of interdisciplinarity, foundational to the program and the course. Interdisciplinarity assumes questions and problems "too broad or complex to be dealt with adequately by a single discipline or profession."[3] Although we were very attentive to guiding students to research problems and questions complex enough to require the tools we were providing, we were putting the process before the problem, which was a breech of our commitment to point of need instruction.

Round Three: New Blood

The course was reinvigorated by a new tenured faculty member who decided to teach it. This instructor developed a course focused on critical reading and writing based not on the traditional thesis-driven approach but, rather, on discovery, engaging students in dialogue with the texts they read using a variety of strategies. She traded the model some of us had worked with that sought coverage of a wide range of disciplinary approaches for a much deeper reading and interaction with fewer texts, texts selected not on the basis of the range of disciplines they represented but, rather, the approaches to constructing knowledge and text. Many of her assignments invited students to use the texts they read as models for creating their own texts (e.g., an excerpt from Susan Griffin's *A Chorus of Stones* in which she uses multiple voices on multiple topics entwined around a theme). She also enhanced the metacognitive element of the course by asking students to prepare portfolios with extensive reflections on the pieces they included, the process by which they created them, their revisions, and so on.

The library and the Writing Center had a place in this inquiry-based transdisciplinary iteration of the course, specifically in helping students develop their own "Griffin-like text." In her book, Griffin examines war through a variety of lenses, including the history of weaponry from spears and catapults to the atomic bomb and the impact of abuse and violence on personal development.[4] Students were asked to identify a concern they would explore through multiple lenses. Here we came into the classroom to help students frame a concern, explore the kinds of lenses they might use, and find sources that would give voice to the perspectives they wished to represent in their final synthesis. These workshops emphasized the function of sources as evidence to be read and understood on their own terms (not just as places to look for good quotes). The faculty member was an active participant in the discussions, in many instances taking the lead in mapping students' topics to possible types of sources and evidence. This kind of team teaching reinforced for students the ways in which prewriting activities and library research influence—and are influenced by—the intellectual content of the course, which in this case foregrounded problem posing and inquiry-based learned. Our contribution to this course was collaborative, but this time it was faculty driven. Students experienced our workshops as wholly necessary for their success because the support we offered was driven by the assignment their instructor conceived and we jointly developed.

Round Four: A Manifesto Is Born

This new approach inspired other faculty members who developed their own versions of the course along similar lines. The most recent iterations have been faculty driven, yet collaborative. Once again, the emphasis is on inquiry, and space is created for students to develop and revisit research questions throughout the term. In small groups or "research clusters," students explore their topic in a variety of types of texts and modes of inquiry, including scholarly journal articles and primary sources. The course readings complement this integration by providing a meta commentary on these various modes of inquiry (qualitative, quantitative, archival, etc.), and class discussions focus not only on understanding the content of the texts, but also on the research methods used. This emphasis on critical reading and inquiry positions students to think as researchers in order to become better readers and consumers of research. This synergistic approach also functions to dismantle the division between "skills" and "content" instruction.

This version of the course includes a series of team-taught workshops that focus on formulating questions, finding sources via the library's online databases, and then reading these sources critically. The workshop process is structured to provide multiple opportunities for all of the "instructors" to interact with each group, modeling the types of questions that experienced researchers pose to their sources as they come upon them, questions that many student researchers have not yet internalized. Students typically are prompted to revisit and revise their search strategy or to reexamine the source at hand based on a new set of questions. The emphases of each workshop and subsequent group and individual assignment are on posing, answering, and reposing complex questions, and on developing students' skills sets and confidence as researchers, writers, and speakers. The opportunities for collaboration create multiple learning opportunities through social interaction. Short "dialogue paper" writing assignments require students to place their sources in conversation with each other and selected course texts. Students have commented that they have had to reread their sources as they attempt to accurately represent the authors' voices in this new context. The culminating project is a research prospectus and the second installment of a learning portfolio.

Although these projects do not reproduce all of the elements of a more traditional research paper, the emphasis on critical thinking and problem posing, practiced and reinforced by a variety of writing prompts and research exercises, provide what we feel is an excellent foundation for the type of extended research project students will be assigned in other upper-division courses. In fact, many students struggle initially with the expectations of these assignments and workshops, in part because they are prevented from lapsing into what for some is a more comfortable and familiar model of "report writing" that focuses more on "finding the answer" or taking a position (usually in the form of a thesis) than on carefully analyzing and interpreting the evidence their research uncovers and then reformulating their research question. This approach gives students a sense of what is involved in generating complex interpretive research questions, arguably one of the most challenging aspects of the entire process.

What has changed? From the vantage point of the library and the Writing Center, most significantly inquiry, or the "research problem," has replaced the process as the focal point of the course. Many events converged to make these changes possible, some of which we have alluded to. One of the keys was the institutionalization on campus of teaching circles.[5] Although our 1998 guidelines called for regular meetings of faculty teaching the course, it was difficult to sustain. With the campuswide inception of teaching circles, supported with some funding (each participant receives $300 per year in credit toward professional travel or materials), the faculty teaching interdisciplinary inquiry coalesced, meeting regularly throughout the year. Among the many benefits of this model is that when those of us working with the course come to the table, writing and library staff do not outnumber faculty as we do when we meet with an individual faculty member planning the course. Faculty have a rare and rich opportunity to discuss the role of the course in the program, share what they are doing in the course, explore what is and is not working, and discover and assess new approaches. A tangible outcome of this process has been the creation of a new set of course guidelines. (See appendix B.) This "manifesto" describes the outcomes of the course more broadly, but perhaps more important, establishes guidelines for the ongoing collaboration among faculty and academic services staff.

Learning to Collaborate Revisited

Change is not easy—and we have weathered a good deal of it with this course. We both were deeply invested in the 1998 guidelines for the course, but Becky probably was more invested than Sarah because (1) the guidelines were developed in her first year at UWB and (2) she was instructor of record for the course twice in the early days of the guidelines and fashioned a course that she felt reflected a lot of her teaching goals. As different voices began to make themselves heard, she often felt protective and defensive about the work she had done, which was being rejected or surpassed by newcomers to the course. She chose to sit out the first year of the teaching circle to allow the newcomers to the course to develop their ideas without having to contend with her resistance.

Sarah was an active member of the teaching circle from the beginning. Her approach to collaboration, as it has evolved over the past decade of team teaching, places communication and ongoing dialogue above all other concerns. Although some of the initial conversations regarding the 1998 course guidelines were somewhat uncomfortable, it was heartening to see so many faculty engaged in talking about what had become a problematic course. Collaboration in this context is an incremental and evolutionary process and does not necessarily result in a formal program or standardized curriculum. It is a process that must provide space for faculty to experiment with new approaches to pedagogy and interdisciplinary studies, approaches that do not necessarily map well to existing research and writing models. A certain amount of uncertainty and discomfort seem to come with the territory. Talking about our classroom practice makes us vulnerable, and creating a climate in which ideas can be shared, risks taken, and frank talk about what is not working can occur are what ultimately lead to more cohesive partnerships.

That said, although this process can create an environment in which creativity and collaboration are rewarded, it also is very time and labor intensive. It has been crucial to have the support of our director (Cynthia Fugate is director of the campus library and UWB Academic Services). She appreciates the value of this collaboration and within the library has helped us to identify ways in which to streamline other activities so that we may dedicate more time to our teaching.

Next Steps

This latest version of the course is generating enormous excitement on the part of faculty and students. Although we are still looking for ways to improve our contribution, we are much clearer about how to collaborate constructively and about how important listening and watching are to successful collaboration.

After interdisciplinary inquiry, students fan out into many different courses as they proceed through the program. Their work culminates in a capstone course with a substantial research requirement. One of our goals now is to work with the faculty to look at the overall curriculum strategically. Clearly, we cannot be present in all classes, but when faculty ask students to work with multiple texts of different genres (e.g., scholarly, popular, literary), we want opportunities to support them, again at the point of need. We anticipate that some of this will be enabled by the recent creation of a teaching circle devoted to the senior (capstone) seminar. As we clarify the goals of that course, we will inevitably have to look back to what happens between the introduction to the program and the capstone.

Because we cannot always be in the classroom, it also is critical that faculty appreciate the importance of giving explicit attention to reading, writing, and information literacy and that they feel confident about their ability to address those issues in their classes. For this, we need to be sure we are offering faculty adequate individual consultations and faculty development opportunities.

Increasingly, program faculty are using course portfolios to facilitate students' ability to see the course as a whole and appreciate their journey as learners and researchers. These offer a variety of benefits for developing the writing and library components of the curriculum. First, portfolios provide a robust array of materials for assessing student learning, their process and their needs, particularly as they reflect change over a term. They are required to create a program portfolio when they enter the capstone course, which gives them an opportunity to assess their learning and to set some goals for their work in the course. As our experience with portfolios increases, we will understand better how to ask students for portfolio reflections that encourage them to relate their development as critical thinkers to specific tools they are learning to use.

We also are working within Academic Services to integrate into our collaboration with faculty more effective means of identifying their learning goals for students and clarifying the relationship between those goals and the literacy practices that will serve students in reaching those goals. This process has underscored for us the need to develop our own understanding and skill in assessment. Our initial forays in this area have been stimulating and frustrating; as with our experience in interdisciplinary inquiry, we realized that we were moving ahead collaborating with each other but forgetting to include faculty. As is always the case with collaboration, increased inclusiveness will require a lot more time and planning but will have a much richer result. We are now in the process of planning a series of structured conversations with faculty to articulate learning outcomes in writing and information literacy and to develop some rubrics to assess those outcomes.

As we have pursued the goal of seamless integration of literacy development in the curriculum, the work of the library and the Writing Center has met with the work of the relatively new Quantitative Skills Center (QSC). As the QSC director has joined the teaching circle's discussions of the course, faculty have come to a new understanding of quantitative reasoning as a fundamental and essential literacy and have begun to find ways to integrate it into their instruction. The circle of collaborators is growing.

Conclusion

The model of writing and information literacy/research instruction toward which we are working cannot succeed if it is not fully integrated with course content. In practical terms, the faculty must be able to address student questions at point of need, at least in terms of what Ann Grafstein refers to as discipline-based knowledge—evaluating the content of arguments, assessing the validity of evidence, and proposing original solutions.[6] The concepts and skills that the library and the Writing Center strive to communicate can wither in isolation if not practiced and assessed in terms of students' abilities to think critically.

What we in the library and the Writing Center have learned, in addition to developing a deeper mutual understanding of the theories and practices that drive our disciplines, is the value of "good talk about good teaching," to borrow from Parker Palmer, a long-standing advocate of creating opportunities for faculty engagement in dialogue about teaching and learning.[7] Our most successful experiments in the integration of reading, writing, research, and critical thinking have emerged out of partnerships with faculty in which there is shared intellectual ownership of the design and implementation of assignments and workshops that address writing and research, in which the faculty member's goals for critical thinking and content learning are served by exercises in reading, writing, and research that take students more deeply into processes of problem posing, synthesis, and knowledge construction. The lessons we have learned thus far position us to participate fully in a shared vision for learning with faculty and students.

Notes

1. Sarah Leadley, "Teaching Meetings: Providing a Forum for Learning How to Teach," *Reference Services Review* 26, no. 3–4 (1998): 103–8.

2. See, for example, Susan H. McLeod, Eric Miraglia, Margot Soven, and Christopher Thaiss, *WAC for the New Millennium: Strategies for Continuing Writing-across-the-Curriculum Programs* (Urbana, Ill.: National Council of Teachers of English, 2001).

3. Julie Thompson Klein and William H. Newell, "Advancing Interdisciplinary Studies," in *Handbook of the Undergraduate Curriculum: A Comprehensive Guide to Purposes, Structures, Practices, and Change*, ed. Jerry G. Gaff, James L. Ratcliff, and associates (Jossey Bass: San Francisco, 1997), 393.

4. Susan Griffin, "Our Secret," in *Ways of Reading: An Anthology for Writers*, ed. David Bartholomae and Anthony Petrosky (Boston: Bedford St. Martin's: 1996), 319–66.

5. Bruce Burgett and Diane Gillespie, "Circles Have Enriched Teaching, Research on Bothell Campus," *University Week*, 10 July 2003. Available online at http://admin.urel.washington.edu/uweek/archives/issue/uweek_story_small.asp?id=1251 [accessed 12 November 2003].

6. Ann Grafstein, "A Discipline-based Approach to Information Literacy," *Journal of Academic Librarianship* 28 (2002): 202.

7. Parker J. Palmer, "Good Talk about Good Teaching: Improving Teaching through Conversation and Community," *Change* 25, no.6 (1993): 8–13.

Appendix A
Interdisciplinary Arts & Sciences Program Core: Skills Guidelines

The program core (BLS 300 Introduction to Interdisciplinary Studies) was created to introduce students to advanced reading, writing, thinking, and technological skills needed to succeed in the Interdisciplinary Arts & Sciences Program while also providing them with an intellectually exciting and pedagogically coherent discussion course. Faculty teaching the program core are expected to work closely with the resource specialists in the Writing Center and the library in order to integrate fully the skills objectives of the course with the rest of the course content. The skills portion of the course should appear not as a separate activity, but as much a part of the learning process as discussions, lectures, etc. The synergy between these two parts of the course should help create a dynamic and valuable learning experience for all involved.

Course Goals
*   Topics or problem-oriented generalist course
*   Introduction to a range of interdisciplinary sources
*   Emphasis on excitement of intellectual inquiry and the skills necessary to engage in upper-division course work
*   Introduction to UWB academic standards and expectations

Library Skills Objectives
*   Introduce students to the UW libraries system and UWB library services and staff
*   Develop basic library skills
    a.   Conduct searches in UW library databases. In-class workshop(s) include basic searching (known item and keyword/subject searching) and interpretation/analysis of search results.
    b.   Retrieve materials held by the UW libraries. Includes document delivery and electronic reserves.
    c.   Use library research to assist in topic selection and/or generating a research question.
    d.   Analyze types of sources (for example, comparison of popular [mass media] and academic sources).

Writing Objectives
*   Introduce students to UWB Writing Center services and staff.
*   Write paper(s) with (hypo)thesis and support.
    a.   Use a variety of prewriting/invention strategies.
    b.   Summarize (annotations, abstracts, etc.).

Writing Objectives (cont.)
c. Generate topic and thesis.
d. Use evidence/support.
e. Rewrite/revise.
f. Citing sources using APA, MLA, etc.
g. Understanding plagiarism.

Reading Objectives
• Ability to read analytically
a. Identify authors' essential ideas.
b. Analyze quality of authors' ideas.

Technology Objectives
• Introduce students to media services and information systems services and staff.
• Obtain e-mail account, become familiar with PINE (for example, participate in class or small group e-mail discussion).

Assessment
• Provide students with in-depth, ongoing assessment of their progress in fulfilling the objectives of the course.
• Integrate assessment tools or mechanisms that will assist faculty in measuring students' progress in the Interdisciplinary Arts & Sciences Program. Assessment should also address evaluation of teaching goals and practices.

Instructional Development
• Foster collaboration between core faculty, writing center staff, and librarians.
• Create file of sample syllabi, assignments, exercises, etc.
• Beginning 1999, faculty, writing center staff, and librarians attend spring quarter planning session(s). (For 1998–1999, meet late summer.)

Appendix B
Interdisciplinary Arts & Sciences Program Core: Manifesto for 2002–2003

The purpose of Interdisciplinary Inquiry (BIS 300) is to introduce and orient students to upper-division work in the Interdisciplinary Arts and Sciences program (IAS). It encourages students to take intellectual risks with the goal of improving their abilities to read closely, write and think critically, communicate clearly and creatively, research effectively, and work collaboratively. Faculty teaching the core work closely with the staff in the library, the Writing Center, and/or the Quantitative Skills Center, thus acclimating the students to the rich variety of resources and support services available to them at UWB. Recent faculty teaching the course have attempted not to think of it as a "skills" or "methods" course, one that "prepares" students for "advanced" work in the various "fields" represented by the IAS program. We have preferred to understand it as a flexible course, one that responds to students with diverse levels of preparation by encouraging them to think about how various types of knowledge are socially produced, how they as students can become active, creative, and self-critical producers of knowledge (in either academic or nonacademic genres), and why the IAS program as a whole privileges interdisciplinary modes of inquiry. To these ends, we have devised various (experimental) means. But we have also discovered through ongoing conversations that we share several core values and objectives that guide what we want our students to get out of the course. We list some of them below, though we do so hesitantly because we do not want to be understood as prescribing a set agenda for future teachers of the course. We prefer that these values and objectives provide a sense of where we stand in 2002–2003 (and where we may or may not stand in the future). We want students in the program core:

1. To understand and become excited about the interdisciplinary production of knowledge and the ways in which it underwrites different aspects of the IAS program;

2. To gain a critical understanding of the IAS program's diverse and interrelated (inter)disciplinary fields and methods of inquiry;

3. To become better critical thinkers and writers, ones who are capable of posing, answering, and reposing a variety of complex questions;

4. To become better researchers, ones who are able to use the resources at UWB and elsewhere in order to identify existing and complementary scholarly work while producing original knowledge through data gathering and interpretation;

5. To become better speakers, ones who are able to communicate clearly and engagingly about complicated topics, arguments, and issues;

6. To learn to work well collaboratively, as both learners and teachers.

Proposals:

1. We want to ensure both that collaboration continues to take place among faculty teaching the core and the library, Writing Center and/or Quantitative Skills Center staffs and that the results of that collaboration are publicized to the faculty as a whole in ways that invite others to teach and/or contribute to the core. To this end, we propose that all faculty and staff teaching the core meet at least twice a year: once in the fall in order to exchange ideas, preliminary syllabi, assignments, etc.; once in the spring (along with the p-core faculty for the following year) in order to revise/update this document and to present it to the faculty as a whole in the regular IAS meeting. The IAS meeting will then provide an opportunity for faculty not directly involved in the teaching of the core to make constructive suggestions and suggest ways in which they might be interested in contributing. (We also strongly recommend that a p-core coordinator be appointed as responsible for calling these meetings and that the faculty dedicate one of the campus teaching circles to the core course.)

Comment: The purpose of this proposal is to push the core toward developing dynamic norms that provide consistency among the various sections being offered during (and across) any given academic year. It implements a procedure that will allow us to think collaboratively about those norms from a perspective informed by what is pedagogically possible in a single quarter (and in relation to a specific cohort of incoming students). It also challenges to think about the core's relation to the outcomes desired by the program as a whole. Further, it integrates support staff into the planning stages of course development.

2. Based on our contact with incoming students and their (often inaccurate) assumptions about the program, we propose that students "opt" for a concentration toward the end of their first quarter of courses. For practical reasons (because most students take the core in their first quarter), this would be best implemented by having the core faculty instruct their students to meet with an IAS advisor and declare an option around the 6th week (when they begin to register for their next set of courses).

Comments: This change should allow students to be more knowledgeable about the program, its resources, and its structure before making their decision. It also provides a great teaching opportunity in the core course. (But it does not suggest that p-core faculty can or will become formal advisors for/of the incoming students. Nor does it mean that the core could or needs to become a "buffet" upon which the various "goods" in the program are displayed.)

Chapter five

From Cross-referencing to Co-construction: Contemplating Collaborative Potentials for Reference and the Writing Center at Southwest Missouri State University

Casey Reid

As an undergraduate student at Southwest Missouri State University (SMSU), I worked for three years as a student assistant in the Reference Department at Meyer, the campus main library. Halfway through my tour of duty in reference, I was hired as a tutor in SMSU's Writing Center, where I spent four years as a tutor (two years as an under-graduate, two years as a graduate student), the final year of which included acting as co-assistant director.

As I compared my experiences working at these two SMSU insti-tutions, I recognized the collaborative potential for Meyer's Reference Lɛᴩartment and the Writing Center and attempted to pave the way for future collaboration. Both libraries and writing centers act as important campus resources with service missions, but in contemplating their collaborative potential, I had to recognize and analyze the different models they use to accomplish their service goals. Framed within my perspective as an experienced tutor and reference assistant, this chapter primarily explores two models for library–writing center collaboration, examining both the similarities and differences between both lines of work. Ideally, the ideas presented in this chapter will provide reasons and possibilities for moving the Reference Department–Writing Center relationship from cross-referencing to co-construction of an increas-ingly collaborative future.

Meyer and the Writing Center: Institutional Context

Located in Springfield, SMSU is Missouri's second largest university with more than 20,000 students enrolled in the fall 2003 semester.[1,2] As Missouri's third largest city with a metropolitan statistical area population of approximately 333,000, Springfield is the hub of SMSU's development.[3] During the 2002–2003 school year, the average ACT composite score of SMSU students was 23.3, and approximately one-third of SMSU's students ranked within the top 20 percent of their graduating class in high school.[4] (Student Information 2003). SMSU is a nonselective institution that accepts an average of 80 percent of the applicants who apply.[5]

Within Missouri's public university system, SMSU's role includes concentrating on "professional education, health, business and economic development, creative arts, and science and the environment."[6] To further differentiate itself from other Missouri public universities, SMSU has a statewide public affairs mission, meaning that the university concentrates on community building and molding its students into active, productive citizens. To obtain this goal, SMSU set out, among other things, to "Produce a broad literacy in the primary public issues."[7]

Campus services such as the Writing Center and Meyer Library have the potential to serve as models for broadening literacy and improving interaction and community building. Located on the Springfield campus, Meyer Library is the main library for the SMSU campus system and inherited a long institutional history of libraries at SMSU. In fall 2002, Meyer was renovated and substantial additions were made to accommodate collection growth, computer and office space, and other campus services. Within its Reference Department alone, Meyer employs six tenure-track librarians, one full-time staff member, and six part-time student assistants.

The SMSU Writing Center resides in a different portion of campus than the library and has a much shorter history within the university, having opened in a classroom in Pummill Hall in 1988. Despite its physical location within the same building as the English Department, the Writing Center has functioned independently since 1994, with the director reporting to the vice president for academic affairs. Though the writing center director and the dean of library science both report directly to Academic Affairs in SMSU's administration, the director is the Writing Center's sole faculty member, whereas the dean heads several departments and faculty members. Besides the director, the Writing Center employed fifteen undergraduate tutors; six graduate tutors, including two assistant directors; three staff tutors; and four receptionists during the 2003–2004 school years.

Despite sharing numerous responsibilities, Meyer (and especially its Reference Department) and the Writing Center have rarely collaborated in the past beyond referring students to one another's services, the Reference Department having gone so far as to keep Writing Center bookmarks on hand for students. More recently, the Reference Department and the Writing Center linked Web sites in an attempt to market reference's new individualized research consultation service. Currently, the two are considering options for further collaboration, including writing center research handouts and reference librarian– or reference student assistant–led tutor training.

Building Blocks: Similarities Recognized

Unlike many collaborators who move together out of a pressing need, I began considering collaboration only after recognizing the similarities between reference and writing center work. Like anyone immersed in his or her own culture, I did not recognize these similarities while working at both Meyer and the Writing Center. Recognition came only when I began learning more about the theoretical underpinnings of writing center work in graduate school. While making sense of my experience as a tutor, I also began to make sense of my experience as a reference student assistant, viewing my reference work within the theoretical framework of writing center tutor theory.

On a broad level, I recognized how intricately linked the research and writing processes are—both play off one another. The amount of research and types and sources of research affect the content of papers, and vice versa: as students write, they may have to continue or change their research direction as their writing leads to new insights and other research avenues. In fact, the relationship between research and writing can be described as a chicken-and-egg issue. Which comes first—research or writing? Papers can be both inductive and deductive in nature, which highlights the interrelatedness of writing and research.

Additionally, in terms of the way it works with students, the Reference Department uses strategies that very clearly resemble the strategies used in the Writing Center. For example, both Writing Center and Reference Department staff begin helping students in the same manner: they greet students, ask what students need help with, ask about the assignment, and specifically request to see the assignment sheet, if possible. On a theoretical level, this desire to begin working with students based on their self-expressed needs—not the staff's—parallels Stephen North's ideas in his 1984 article "The Idea of the Writing Center." In this article, North proposed that writing centers be "student-centered," meaning tutors work on students' agendas for their papers—not the tutors'. In both reference and writing center work, though, staff–student exchanges often waver from this ideal because of the nature of exchanging ideas; the staff's ideas about students' topics intermingle with the students' ideas and ultimately influence the direction of student papers and topic searches, bringing staff agenda into the writing and research process.

Throughout their attempts to communicate with the students and faculty they help, the Reference Department and the Writing Center also use similar listening and questioning techniques. In both fields, practitioners can be found paraphrasing what students tell them, interpreting students' remarks, making statements to clarify they are on the same page as the students (a technique I learned to call "perception checking" in my writing center class), and leading students in both direct and indirect ways with statements and questions related to the topic.

Another interesting balance that both reference and writing center practitioners attempt to make is that of actually researching or writing for students and trying to teach students to be better independent researchers/writers, a dichotomy in writing center work known as the "better products versus better writers" debate. In some situations (especially more complex research situations), reference staff might type keywords into databases for students and find the needed materials, whereas in others (notably in less complex research situations involving students for whom the library is more novel), reference staff might spend time with students teaching them how to use databases and search engines rather than pinpointing specific resources. Writing center staff has to deal with the issue of finding student errors for them versus helping students find their own errors every day, an issue that leads into another similarity between the fields.

Reference staff approach different types of student questions and student needs in ways similar to the way my writing tutor colleagues and I approach different types of student questions and needs. For instance, some students have quick, specific questions, such as where to find books under a certain call number or where to go for change; these are similar to specific questions in writing centers about how to cite specific types of resources and whether a comma is needed in a specific place. These questions can be answered quickly and directly.

Other questions and needs involving larger issues in the research process take much longer and require more thought as to how they should be approached. For example, like many students who approach the writing center for assistance, many students who approach reference staff for help know they need assistance but do not know what to ask to receive the assistance they envision needing, do not know what resources and options are available to them, and/or sometimes do not know exactly what they need help with—they know they need research (usually for a paper) but simply do not know where to start. By relying heavily on listening and questioning techniques and showing students how to use resources rather than using the resources themselves to find research, reference staff are often much more hands-off when dealing with these larger, more complex issues, a technique known in writing center work as "nondirective tutoring." In writing center work, rather than attempt to directly shape the students' writing process with specific suggestions and editorial-like revisions, tutors may use a nondirective or minimalist approach to try to involve students as much as possible in their own writing process, very much as reference staff attempt to spur students into thinking about the possibilities inherent to their research.

Besides their strategic similarities, the Meyer Reference Department and the Writing Center take similar approaches to hiring and training student help. Unlike many other campus services that hire any student with work study funds, the Reference Department and the Writing Center interview candidates for open positions and select only those who seem best qualified and most able to learn new responsibilities. They both also look for students with diverse backgrounds to add to their already-existing knowledge base and prefer students who can work at least one year because of the extensive training required for new student assistants and tutors. When I started working in the Reference Department, for example, I was told it takes at least a semester to learn the basics and was not allowed to work the desk unsupervised until I had worked more than a year. Although I was allowed to work unsupervised in the Writing Center my first semester, I was told much of my first year would involve becoming comfortable as a tutor, and I was required to write weekly journal entries to a more experienced tutor mentor and to attend monthly tutor meetings.

As I recognized similarities, I also recognized that SMSU students could benefit from a service that offered help with both research and writing. Partly because of the type of university SMSU is, many students enter with little or no experience researching and writing on the level expected of them in college. For writing, they at least are required to take two writing courses, but having experience teaching both levels of writing courses required of SMSU students, I can say that even those courses cannot completely transform the writing skills and habits of students in two semesters, especially if the students have little or no previous experience with the literacy practices required of college. Research is often part of these writing courses, as well as other writing-intensive courses, but it is only one of the many skills that must be covered in these courses; research rarely receives more than an hour of explanation in the one-hour course SMSU students must take to introduce them to the university. Consequently, the students I have encountered in the classes I taught, the Writing Center, and the Reference Department have an enormously difficult time grasping the complexities of research and the complexities of incorporating research into their writing.

Construction Considerations: Potential Models and Differences Surface

Interesting as these insights were, they only provided a glimpse into the relevance of these fields to one another, giving some rationale for why the Reference Department and the Writing Center could (and should) collaborate; they did not address the practical realities of such a collaboration. In contemplating possible models or steps in collaborating,

I envisioned two potentials: one based on training writing center tutors in research techniques, and another, more expansive model in which SMSU's separate research and writing assistance would be merged into some kind of joint research–writing assistance program. As I researched these collaborative potentials, though, differences within the fields of library science and composition/writing center work quickly surfaced, differences that would have to be navigated in any library–writing center collaboration.

Tutor Training Model

The first of these collaborative potentials—writing center tutor training—is obviously less intensive because it focuses primarily on expanding tutor training enough to make tutors more aware of the library and its services. This training would not necessarily be extensive or ongoing—it might involve meeting with tutors once a year or semester to bring their attention to pertinent aspects of research—and would not necessarily be intended to make tutors into miniature librarians. Additionally, library and writing center personnel would not have to navigate administrative channels to approve such training; giving presentations to various classes and groups about pertinent aspects of research is among the top priorities of SMSU's Reference Department and would only require a phone call the week before tutor training to set up a training/instruction session.

Librarian Katherine Furlong's 1999 article titled "Marketing Your Services through Your Students" discusses an interesting model for this kind of tutor training collaboration. In this article, Furlong described a program the University of Maine at Farmington (UMF) used to attract students back to their renovated library. The program entailed using students trained to assist librarians in an undergraduate teaching program to train UMF writing center tutors in library research skills. Conceived by a student in the undergraduate teaching program, the program has been largely successful in achieving its goal—that of increasing student library use—because after the training, tutors themselves better understand the library's role and actually take students to the library now.[8]

UMF's program strikes me as a particularly well-constructed model for library–writing center collaboration, especially when viewed within the perspective of writing center theory. Unlike library science, which places high value on the facultylike role of librarians as librarian-teachers, writing center research tends to emphasize the role of student peer tutors, a concept UMF's program incorporates by using students to train students. Recognizing the difference between librarian-teachers and peer tutors was somewhat murky initially for me because librarian-teachers are intended to share at least one common goal with peer tutors—in writing center–like terms, they attempt to make better researchers of students by teaching them to "find their own answers," instead of focusing on finding research for individual assignments.[9]

However, the librarian-teacher's status as a professionally trained instructor rather than a more informally trained practitioner markedly separates it from writing center peer tutors. Originally used as a way to make writing center–type services more human and to keep expenses low (students being "less expensive to employ than faculty"), composition theorists such as Kenneth Bruffee have formulated theoretical explanations justifying why peer tutors can actually work better than faculty in helping fellow students.[10] Using the work of Lev Vygotsky, Thomas Kuhn, and various collaborative learning researchers who argue for the socially constructed nature of knowledge, Bruffee argued that peer tutoring provides a discourse context more conducive to student learning than that offered in typical classrooms. As Bruffee saw it, many students having "difficulty adapting to the traditional or 'normal' conventions of the college classroom" do not use more mainstream avenues of assistance, such as faculty office hours, "because it seemed to them merely an extension of the work, the expectations, and above all the social structure of traditional classroom learning. And it was traditional classroom learning that seemed to have left these students unprepared in the first place."[11]

Consequently, writing centers turned to peer tutors to allow students to feel more comfortable working on their writing. Although numerous flaws in this concept have been—and continue to be—discussed (see Bruffee's "Peer Tutoring and the 'Conversation of Mankind'" and Nancy Grimm's *Good Intentions: Writing Center Work for Postmodern Times* for a few examples), the concepts reigns as the preferred method of working (or, as Bruffee put it, conversing) with students in writing centers. As Bruffee constructed it, the basic thinking behind the peer tutor concept is that students will feel more comfortable working on their writing if the people assisting them are fellow students experiencing college from a similar perspective.

Although UMF's program meets Bruffee's call for student–student interaction, it had to reconcile the status differences between the library and writing center's primary service providers—librarian-teachers and peer tutors. My suspicions about the difficulty of reconciling the differences between these roles was somewhat abated after reading Furlong's article. Furlong candidly wrote about the "initial qualms" of UMF's librarians regarding the program:

> Library staff had to give up a great deal of control and allow
> our student workers an unprecendented amount of freedom

to design and conduct instruction sessions. It was sometimes hard to let go. We knew we had succeeded when we allowed Andy to schedule the final workshop during a week that the professional librarians were attending a conference in Texas. We learned that if the students want to make something happen, it will happen, and our entire Information Literacy Program is the better for their efforts.[12]

In discussing collaborative potentials with a reference librarian at SMSU, the librarian acknowledged how difficult it would be to allow students to have as much free reign as writing center tutors have. She wondered how the writing center director maintains consistency among tutors and also brought up the possibility of tutors giving students incorrect information. I related that the director does as much training as she can but, ultimately, has to have a lot to faith regarding tutors and their interactions with students. She trusts tutors immensely, I noted, but also is prudent in addressing concerns raised by faculty members and others regarding tutors and tutor practices. "That is a lot of trust," the librarian replied.

The success of programs such as UMF's might help bridge the gap of trust librarians and writing center professionals grant student service providers. From my experience, my reference work helped me reach a group of students who might otherwise fall through the I-need-help-with-research cracks: students in the midst of papers, some of whom may or may not have gone to the library for research assistance. In reference, I generally helped students who were only beginning to research for their papers. They often only had a general topic they were researching, and whether they knew how they planned to approach the topic or not, they generally did not plan to start writing until they had some research.

Students entering the Writing Center for assistance or general conversation about a piece of writing come with different, usually unperceived, research needs from those of students I had helped in the library. For instance, one student I worked with came into the center wanting help making sure her paper met her professor's requirements. When I began asking questions about ideas in her paper, the student realized she was trying to cover too much information and would be unable to answer many of the questions I asked. She decided which section of the paper she wanted to focus on but did not know where she would obtain more information about the topic; she had difficulty finding information for that section when she initially researched and thought she had exhausted all research avenues. As I asked about the resources she used, I discovered she was unaware of the library's online indexes and databases. Ecstatic when I showed these to her, she admitted she had never stepped foot in the library because it intimidated her.

The above example demonstrates two facets of helping students research after they have written some or all of a paper: some students who enter the Writing Center discover resources they otherwise might not know existed, and some students realize they don't have the research (the amount, the kind, etc.) they need to make the points they want to make. In the latter case, most libraries generally are unable to provide this type of assistance; of the librarians I know, I doubt any would wish to include in their job description "reading student papers to assess the role of the sources used in the paper." Instead of adding to their growing list of responsibilities and taking on this role in the future, librarians can consider helping train writing center tutors to be more research savvy, thus allowing tutors to better help students in their quest to write more effective and/or personally meaningful papers.

Research–Writing Assistance Model

When I presented at the International Writing Centers Association–National Conference on Peer Tutoring (IWCA–NCPT) conference in Hershey, Pennsylvania, I came across a model for a more extensive type of library–writing center collaboration—that of actually combining research and writing assistance in a single service. I went to a session by the writing lab ("lab" being another term for "center") administrators and students of Bowling Green State University (BGSU). The session focused on their collaboration with BGSU's library in conducting Research and Writing Project Clinics (RWPCs), defined in their handout as:

> hour-long sessions for English 112 writers/researchers conducted by writing consultants at the campus library. During these sessions, students receive feedback on both their research and writing. Instead of bouncing back between librarians and writing consultants, students receive more integrated feedback.[13]

Although I envisioned helping a much larger clientele than freshman composition writers, I was quickly taken by BGSU's program, which so closely seemed to parallel my ideas for collaboration at SMSU. To learn more about the details of their program, I spent almost an hour after the presentation talking about BGSU's collaborative endeavors with one of the presenters and noted some interesting aspects of her commentary regarding the collaboration. Importantly, because she invited them to the Writing Lab to train tutors once a year, this presenter had an established relationship with the librarians, an element of library–writing center collaboration that I recognized as important early on. In addition, she reaffirmed my idea that collaborating would be a good way to build coalitions across campus, an idea I knew would appeal to SMSU administrators invested in the university's public affairs mission.

On a practical level, BGSU's program addresses one of the most difficult issues in contemplating library–writing center collaborations: staffing. If the librarians at SMSU are any indicator, I know librarians have enough responsibilities without having to consider the added weight of attempting to learn how to help students with writing and then having to devote further time to actually meeting with students to help them. These responsibilities alone would require several additional staff and/or faculty, people who would cost more than student tutors already trained in the writing end of the assistance.

Because of the more involved nature of a program such as BGSU's, joint research–writing programs have to contend with more of the practical and theoretical differences between libraries and writing centers. BGSU tended to use a more writing center–like model of assistance, using writing center tutors with little or no supervision stationed in the library. Although different institutional contexts require different solutions, I can see BGSU's model working at SMSU should Meyer and the Writing Center ever attempt to establish a closer relationship and collaborate: librarians could simply train more experienced tutors along with new student reference assistants, the center could set aside tutoring hours for the joint service, and the research–writing sessions could easily take place at the round tables in Meyer's commons area or at a table near its computer lab.

When considering such a program at SMSU, though, differences in the two fields and SMSU institutions under consideration emerged besides those I have already discussed. An exploration of these fieldwide and institutional differences is necessary to more fully understand the implications involved in a collaborative effort as extensive as a joint research and writing assistance program.

Differences in the Fields

After reading numerous sections of the Association of College and Research Libraries (ACRL) Web site, I began to see the librarian-teacher–peer tutor issue as one symptom of a larger issue—the different paths the fields have taken and continue to take toward gaining legitimacy as academic disciplines. In short, librarians have taken a fairly traditional route toward establishing legitimacy by using organizations such as the ACRL to regulate libraries. A quick glance at the ACRL's Standards & Guidelines page on its Web site includes imposing guidelines and standards for numerous facets of librarianship, including certifying librarians and libraries at various levels.[14] Rather than have staff positions, academic librarians now have faculty status at many institutions of higher education, partly because of the guidelines set forth by the ACRL.

Like the field of library science, the field of writing centers has gradually procured many of the traits of an academic field, including having peer-reviewed journals such as *The Writing Center Journal* specifically tailored for the field, having organizations such as the International Writing Centers Association (IWCA) that function like the ACRL, and having national and even international conferences specifically for discussing writing centers. However, writing centers tend to resist numerous other traditional routes of establishing broader academic legitimacy. Instead, they often prefer to use student help and to maintain a more marginalized status as a discipline so as to keep the espoused benefits of being marginalized, namely, the "capacity for providing an alternative to mass education," and to establish legitimacy within their specific institutions.[15] One of the best examples of many writing center advocates' belief in marginalization is Terrance Riley's article "The Unpromising Future of Writing Centers" in which he writes what has (paradoxically) become mantra for many writing center practitioners:

> Fall out of love with permanence; embrace transience. Stake your reputation on service rather than on publication. Acknowledge that directing a writing center does not involve the kind of difficulties for which advanced degree preparation is necessary. Stay impure: welcome mixed descent and cross purposes. Let last year's tutors handle the training. Allow that students may know what they need better than we do.[16]

Should any further collaboration be attempted at SMSU, the different places Meyer Library and the Writing Center hold in the university would have to be considered. For instance, if a BGSU model were used, one question immediately comes to mind: How could a collaboration taking place in the library, a place often considered as a focal point for the university, cultivate any of the sort of marginalized traits Riley describes as being integral to the work of writing center practitioners, the practitioners who (in such a model) would be primarily responsible for providing the joint service?

Differences at SMSU

Besides recognizing discipline-specific issues, I also began discerning differences and potential problems that might surface at SMSU, differences and problems that may or may not be indicative of larger discipline-specific issues. While talking about one potential for collaboration—having a satellite writing center in the library to offer research and writing assistance—a reference librarian related that she would have to involve the reference department head and the dean of library science. In the Writing Center, I was accustomed to discussing new ideas with the director and fairly immediately having the opportunity to try the ideas.

At this point, the most salient institutional difference I found was the different hierarchies within which Meyer Library and the Writing Center work at SMSU. Because the writing center director reports directly to Academic Affairs, it is relatively easy for me to discuss and attempt new projects with little or no administrative hassle. In Meyer, though, the chain of command is much longer, and any collaborative efforts would require substantial administrative maneuvering, the amount of which would also be affected by the department the Writing Center chose to approach, some department heads being more hands-on than others.

Additionally, while I worked there, the Writing Center experienced fewer budget cuts than Meyer, leaving the center in a better position to offer new or extended student services than the library. In fact, the Writing Center had attempted an extension service with SMSU's Multicultural Resource Center during my first year as a tutor, but the lack of interest ended the service within a semester of its start.

Thinking about my experience working in both the Reference Department and the Writing Center, more differences emerged. When I worked in the library, I sat in tall chairs behind a high desk while students and university personnel lined up to receive assistance. Behind the desk, the librarians and staff had their own space, separate from those they helped, for socializing and working among themselves and for keeping frequently used reference materials such as dictionaries and style manuals that tended to be stolen and/or misplaced. Although several other students also assisted at the desk, I, because of my student status, was rarely left to work the desk solely with other students. Librarians, most of whom were tenured faculty members, were almost always scheduled to supervise student workers and answer questions with which we needed help. (Incidentally, this belief in the need for student supervision may very well be a larger disciplinewide issue in library science. This belief comes across strongly in publications such as David Baldwin, Frances Wilkinson, and Daniel Barkley's 2000 book *Effective Management of Student Employment: Organizing for Student Employment in Academic Libraries* that attempt to inform academic librarians about recent trends in their field.) Being a curious person, I listened closely to the comings and goings of the librarians, all of whom I came to know fairly well, and became privy to the library's inner workings, including gossip and administrative-type information about how the library actually works.

In the Writing Center, I sit in normal-sized chairs around circular tables next to the students who make one-hour appointments to meet with me. There, appointments come first; walk-ins are helped only under specified conditions and I always seat myself based on where these students choose to sit. Until I became co-assistant director and was given a desk for completing administrative tasks, I never had space separating me from the students who came in for assistance. The Writing Center tutors' primary reference materials—all of which could be found behind the reference desk—are scattered among the tables and, though marked "Writing Center," could easily be taken because they are not tagged to set off alarms as books are in the library. Because I, as a tutor, deal with a much smaller space and am not segregated to a separate space from other students, though, I am better able to keep track of Writing Center reference materials than I could in the Reference department. In the center, I have only one supervising faculty member, the director, and even with the help of a twenty-hour-a-week assistant director, she, with her dual role as a tenured English Department faculty member, could never supervise all forty-eight hours a week that the center is open. Thus, I became accustomed to working without faculty supervision early in my tutoring experience, and because of the center's student orientation, I do not have to depend on others to learn about gossip or administrative workings; even as an undergraduate, I was and am an active creator of the center's gossip and policies.

My portrayal of these places' basic workings highlights some obvious differences. As discussed earlier, there are obvious differences between the status of student help, including differences in the amount of supervision they receive. In the library, students are rarely unsupervised, whereas writing center peer tutors are rarely supervised. Librarians in their library-teacher role serve as the primary figures in library culture, whereas student tutors are the main actors and influences on the Writing Center's culture.

Additionally, the physical trappings of the two places provide insight into the different perspective of the places regarding the separation of and difference in status between the people being helped and the people helping. In Meyer, the reference desk, as well as most other service desks in the building, are at what Elizabeth Thomsen calls "counter height," meaning they are "designed for staff to be standing or perhaps sitting on high stools."[17] Thomsen successfully detailed the arguments both for and against counter-height desks, one con of which is their intimidating look. Many students have specifically discussed this intimidating feeling when telling me about their reluctance to approach the desk for help. Having used the library extensively before I became a reference student assistant, I can relate. Like many students at SMSU who come from rural and/or smaller school districts with few resources, I had never experienced a library as large as Meyer and I remember quite vividly how intimidated I was the first time I tried to use it. I must have walked around the building for an hour, attempting to avoid those tall desks with the lights shining down just like the lights in the police confession rooms I had seen on television.

Besides being intimidating, the setup of a typical service desk in a library serves to segregate those helping from those being helped, giving the former proprietary claim over the materials kept behind service desks. To combat this separation in recent years, reference departments, including SMSU's, have instituted roving reference services in which librarians "walk around the library offering assistance to patrons."[18] Although this technique serves to connect librarians to patrons who might otherwise not seek assistance, Meyer's Reference Department, as well as many other reference services, continues to rely more heavily on more traditional desktype service, but this type of roving service could provide an option other than scheduling appointments or sitting behind a desk for any type of joint research–writing assistance program.

Co-Construction: Uncertainties Remain

The future of any collaboration between Meyer Library and the Writing Center is uncertain, mainly because of budget cuts and staff changes. How the two would collaborate is certainly questionable. Would it be effective to simply train writing center tutors in research strategies, should a more inclusive step such as a joint research and writing assistance service be considered, or should another possibility be considered? If a joint service were implemented, who would staff, fund, supervise, and otherwise make decisions about it? Possibly more important for a joint service, how could librarians and tutors justify maintaining separate services in any form if they truly can function more effectively together? Whether the two collaborate or not, though, successful, workable models for navigating differences between Meyer Library and the Writing Center definitely exist that could allow these SMSU institutions to move their relationship from mere cross-referencing of services to co-construction of their futures.

Notes
1. Southwest Missouri State University, "History of the University" (2003). Available online at http://www.smsu.edu/history.htm [accessed 14 November 2003].

2. ———, "Southwest Missouri State University Home Page" (2003). Available online at http://www.smsu.edu [accessed 14 November 2003].

3. Office of Institutional Research, Southwest Missouri State University, "General Information" (2003). Available online at http://www.smsu.edu/oir/factbook/generalinfo.pdf [accessed 18 December 2003].

4. ———, "Student Information" (2003). Available online at http://www.smsu.edu/oir/factbook/studentinfo.pdf [accessed 18 December 2003].

5. Ibid.

6. Southwest Missouri State University, "Countdown to the SMSU Centennial" (2001). Available online at http://www.smsu.edu/countdown/ [accessed 14 November 2003.

7. ———, "Definition" (2002). Available online at http://publicaffairs.smsu.edu/what/what.html [accessed 14 November 2003].

8. Katherine Furlong, "Marketing Your Services through Your Students," *Computers in Libraries* 19 (1999): 22–25.

9. Elizabeth Thompsen, *Rethinking Reference: The Reference Librarian's Practical Guide to Surviving Constant Change* (New York: Neal-Schuman, 1999).

10. Elizabeth Boquet, "Our Little Secret": A History of Writing Centers, Pre- to Post-open Admissions, *College Composition and Communication* 50, no. 3: 463–82. Also in *The Allyn and Bacon Guide to Writing Center Theory and Practice*, ed. Robert W. Barnett and Jacob S. Blumner (Boston: Allyn and Bacon, 1999).

11. Kenneth Bruffee, "Peer Tutoring and the 'Conversation of Mankind,'" *Writing Centers: Theory and Administration* (Urbana, Ill.: National Council of Teachers of English, 1984), 3–15. Also in *The Allyn and Bacon Guide to Writing Center Theory and Practice*, ed. Robert W. Barnett and Jacob S. Blumner (Boston: Allyn and Bacon, 1984).

12. Furlong, "Marketing Your Services through Your Students."

13. LaTwila Ainsworth, Ashley Ford, Barbara Toth, and Sue Twayer, "Out of the Center: Research and Writing Consultation at Our University Library," presentation at IWCA-NCPTW 2003 Joint Conference, October 23–25, 2003, Hershey, Pa.

14. Association of College and Research Libraries, "Standards and Guidelines" (2003). Available online at http://www.ala.org/Content/NavigationMenu/ACRL/Standards_and_Guidelines/Standards_and_Guidelines.htm [accessed 19 December 2003].

15. Terrance Riley, "The Unpromising Future of Writing Centers," *Writing Center Journal*, 15, no. 1 (1994): 20–34. Also in *The Allyn and Bacon Guide to Writing Center Theory and Practice*, ed. Robert W. Barnett and Jacob S. Blumner (Boston: Allyn and Bacon, 1994).

16. Ibid.

17. Thomsen, *Rethinking Reference*, 116.

18. ———, *Rethinking Reference*.

Chapter six

Library and Learning Center Collaborations: Within and outside the Walls

Judy Arzt

Sixteen years ago, Saint Joseph College, located in Connecticut, reconfigured its minimalist, basement-style writing center into a full-fledged tutorial operation covering all subject areas. With the benefit of hindsight, the decision to locate the new tutorial center in the library proved fortuitous. Partnerships between the departments readily formed. We collaborated on workshops, tutorials, strategic planning, and committee work. Joint ventures transpired routinely. People from different departments could easily collaborate given the logistics of our location. Campus climate and the college's mission also fostered alliances.

The college's reputation for preparing students for professional careers in such areas as nursing, education, and social work and its strong liberal arts program, including strengths in the natural sciences, has contributed to a healthy enrollment, which has steadily inclined in recent years as new programs have been added to the curriculum. Founded by the Sisters of Mercy during the Depression, the college prides itself in its original mission. The mission focuses on promoting leadership skills, a lifetime commitment to learning, and access to a high-quality liberal arts education. Integral to a liberal arts education, writing skills have always been emphasized. The college catalog has consistently spelled out that competency in written expression is a graduation requirement. A strong, functional writing center, in turn, is core to the college's mission.

Based on changing times, by the late 1980s, an across-the-curriculum writing center was seen as more appropriate than a stand-alone one housed in the English Department. Writing was largely dispersed throughout the curriculum and a writing-across-the-curriculum writing center better suited the times. Scholars such as Toby Fulwiler and Art Young were leading movements across the country promoting writing in the disciplines and spearheading faculty development to support writing-across-the-curriculum programs.[1] At the same time, the process movement approach to writing instruction was already more than a decade old and enjoying much popularity. Leaders in this field such as Peter Elbow and Donald Murray were widely read,[2] and other scholars promoting collaborative learning, for example, Kenneth Bruffee and Lester Faigley,[3] were welcome voices in the field of composition studies.

A decision to create a writing-across-the-curriculum tutorial center at Saint Joseph College followed current research theory. The decision to locate this center in the library, however, was not necessarily based on theory or research but, rather, on local matters. Space in the library already existed, and the library already enjoyed a healthy reputation on campus. More to the point, the library also was a place on campus that served an across-the-curriculum purpose. By aligning a writing-across-the-curriculum center with an academic stronghold, the college in retrospect created an ideal partnership, allowing a department in its infancy to profit from the wealth of a well-established entity on campus. As on most college campuses at the time, the library was an anchor and a place that students and faculty frequented.

The Evolution of the Early Partnership

In the late 1980s, the technology that drives a college campus today was virtually nascent. For the most part, library catalogs were not online and students could not plug into databases and similar services from remote sites. Understandably, in those days, it was not surprising to find a correlation between student use of the library and grade-point average. Motivated students were library savvy and could finesse their way through the multistaged process of completing term papers and similar library projects. Students who frequented the library also studied there, and for the high-achieving student, long hours in the library translated to superior grades on quizzes, tests, and other academic markers. In those days, the library was a quiet place to study, a sanctuary away from noisy residential lounges. The library also was a convenient place to meet. Students might make plans to rendezvous in the library midpoint through or following a study session. For numerous reasons, the library was a routine part of a student's daily ritual.

At Saint Joseph College, situating a tutoring center in a high-traffic, academically oriented site meant a body of potential users existed within the walls. For us, the location in a library as opposed to a tucked-away cubbyhole in a discipline-specific building was a milestone. Moving a 1980s-style writing center to a prominent building on campus and redefining its services as a writing-across-the curriculum center resulted in shedding an identity as a satellite of the English Department. Furthermore, a home in a building that served a research-oriented purpose well complemented the function of a writing center.

Moreover, library staff were instrumental in helping the center in its early days attract students. Front-desk staff and reference librarians routinely interacted with students and recommended tutorial assistance, explaining the array of services available. It was a natural step for a reference librarian working with a student to walk that student to the center for additional assistance. Already familiar with the student's needs, the librarian conveniently set the groundwork for the ensuing tutorial, often explaining the kind of help needed and sometimes joining in, smoothing the segue from library work to any stage in the writing process, whether it be brainstorming ideas, out-lining, or beginning a draft.

In these early days, the librarians were the center's best marketers and recruiters. Their word-of-mouth advertising drew students to the center in record numbers, far exceeding the outreach of flyers, faculty announcements, and campus newsletters. The in-person presence of the library staff was a strong variable in ensuring that students did indeed make their way to the center. This was particularly true of a reticent student reluctant to use a tutoring center. The librarian could cheerily walk such a student to the center and along the way give a pep talk, encouraging the student and explaining the benefits of working with friendly, knowledgeable tutors.

Another advantage of housing the tutoring center in the library was the ease with which jointly conducted workshops could be planned and delivered. In those days, it was customary to conduct partnered workshops on such topics as how to write research papers and man-age time. Like tutors, librarians discovered that students experienced difficulty in completing projects on time, waiting until the last minute or underestimating the amount of time required. Librarians were well prepared to offer tips at time management workshops. For example, they clarified time lines for interlibrary loan and explained strategies to ease navigation of microfiche or microfilm readers.

One of our most successful early workshops, "Stop Procrastina-tion, Now!," was conducted by a professional writer, a writing tutor, and a reference librarian. The professional writer talked of procrastina-tion that sabotaged her professional career and how she overcame her self-destructive behavior to publish several short stories. She motivated students to get beyond procrastination in order to succeed in their academic careers and accomplish academic tasks in a timely fashion. The writing tutor outlined how-to-do note cards, explaining that when this step was done correctly, it fostered critical thinking and facilitated organizing and synthesizing research findings. Her pitch focused on how time spent up front saved time later and reduced the cognitive overload associated with juggling multiple tasks when composing a draft. The reference librarian extolled strategies for making the library research process go as smoothly as possible and pinpointed where to find key sources in the library. In unison, the team covered three topics, modeling for students the benefits of working collaboratively with others to save time.

Most of our mutually conducted workshops promoted a process approach to completing a project. If we conducted a workshop purely on the research paper, we outlined requisite steps, including a preliminary library search, narrowing a topic based on that search, skimming sources, and effective note card preparation. We also let students know that sometimes this process did not occur linearly as their composition textbooks might have indicated. Rather, researchers and writers sometimes found that they needed to cycle back on an activity, perhaps doing more research after they appeared to complete note cards. The librarian oriented students to where specific reference volumes were located in the library and explained how excerpts found in such volumes foretold of full-text versions and could help with eliminating unnecessary sources and aid in finding the most relevant and useful ones. Writing tutors demonstrated the logistics of compiling a working bibliography and writing note cards and introduced the concept of the I-Search Paper developed by Ken Macrorie.[4] With Macrorie's concept in mind, students were encouraged to start with a topic of interest to them and to build a paper outward based on their own expertise and inclinations. We advocated for the writing-as-process approach popularized by theorists such as Peter Elbow. We showcased Elbow's early texts, *Writing with Power* and *Writing without Teachers*, to help students gain confidence in their skills and to focus on process, not product, thereby reducing their anxieties about producing a perfect final draft on an initial try.[5]

In sum, the presence of colleagues from aligned, but slightly disparate, fields worked well. We checked each other's tendency to use arcane jargon from our fields, with the goal of making our workshops as transparent as possible for students. By bouncing off each other's ideas, we reinforced concepts. This meant that students heard the same message from people with different areas of expertise, lending credence to our words. From that perspective, we modeled the principles of interdisciplinary teaching and learning.

We also found it fruitful to run joint tutorials. For example, a student researching an American author would be aided by a writing tutor and a reference librarian in finding sources, brainstorming ideas for a paper, and beginning to skim sources for relevant information. Amid a tutorial session, a tutor helping a student might find that the student needed additional sources. The reference librarian could easily be called on to help and might bring sources to the tutorial, joining the tutor and the student at the session. A librarian working one-on-one with a student might discover that a student needed to know more about a topic being covered in a course. If the librarian knew that writing tutors had already helped students with papers for the same course, such tutors might be called on to join the research interview with the librarian.

Jointly led group tutorials worked well when students had a common assignment and could profit from the give-and-take of this format. A librarian and a tutor could mutually keep the group focused, asking key questions and providing common information that all student participants needed to hear. Furthermore, as a group, students could well articulate an assignment's requirements, thereby making it easier for librarian and tutor to grasp what the instructor wanted. These group sessions created a bubbling synergy with participants focusing on a common goal. Although these sessions truly replicated an ideal learning environment, they were not necessarily events that were scheduled. Often they happened serendipitously, when, for instance, a small group of students congregated in the library and approached a librarian with a question. A tutor nearby might overhear the conversation or be called on by the librarian to provide additional assistance. The opportunity for these kinds of occurrences to happen was largely attributable to the fact that the tutoring center was housed in the library. Essentially, geography created the circumstances. In thinking back on these scenarios, we can see the benefits of people from different disciplines working routinely with small groups of students to focus on a common assignment. We can recognize the benefits of housing tutoring centers in libraries particularly when tutors assist students with writing research-based papers, where the aid of librarians and writing tutors is critical to the assignment's expectations.

We also found that writing tutors were inclined to share research from their field of knowledge with librarians, thereby allowing librarians to brush up on new theories about teaching writing and student learning. The Social Constructionist approach to instruction, growing out of John Dewey's earlier Progressive Movement, was gaining popularity. In part, some of the collaborative learning theories associated with such composition theorists as Kenneth Bruffee and Lester Faigley were built on a Social Constructionism, which purported that knowledge was socially constructed and students learned best through active participation and collaborative learning strategies. Professors who turned to this approach used one-on-one conferencing and small-group instruction as part of their teaching repertoire. They saw their role as less authoritarian and more like that of a coach. This approach echoed many of the strategies already used by writing tutors and librarians who routinely worked with students one-on-one and on equal footing in accomplishing a task. Writing tutors in keeping current of theory helped librarians acquire a new vocabulary to describe what they were doing. Knowledge of Social Constructionism also filtered into education classes, where alongside with teaching about the Progressive Movement, instructors were providing students with a model of teaching and learning. As we reflect on the kinds of work that we did mutually as writing tutors and librarians, we can now readily see how we were affected by emerging theories gaining popularity in aligned fields on campus. We also can recognize how Social Constructionism worked hand in hand with the prevailing climate on campus, one that nurtured students, led to small class sizes, invoked writing-intensive assignments across the curriculum, and evaluated student progress based largely on the progression of writing skills. In such a college climate, reliance on librarians and writing tutors as key players in the student learning process was natural. Both departments on campus enjoyed strong support, and the approaches we used in instruction for individual, group, and workshop formats sprang out of research and institutional climate.

At times, librarians and tutors naturally found themselves dialoguing about the anatomy of the work that they did with students. Of all departments on campus, perhaps we did the most one-on-one instruction. Thus, we found comfort in common partners who relied on the same instructional technique. We also were professionals who served the unusual role of teaching students who were not in our classes. After all, what other professionals on campus worked in the dual roles of instructing students who were not their own as well as constantly relying on one-on-one or small-group format? Unlike teaching, which occurred in class settings, we worked outside the classroom providing students with academic support. In that regard, there was much to be gained by collaborating on our instructional approaches and watching each other work.

New and experienced tutors alike found it helpful to shadow reference librarians. They joined library tours that acquainted students with services and observed reference librarians working with students at various stages of the research process. In witnessing librarians conduct reference interviews, tutors learned tactics for questioning students about assignment requirements and appropriate sources. The opportunity to watch reference librarians perform their daily craft was particularly helpful for new tutors. Veteran reference librarians knew from years of experience how important it was to look over assignment sheets and confirm professors' expectations before launching into a project, and they could share stories of other students doing the same or similar assignments. In essence, they put assignments into a context rather than let students plunge in, perhaps going off path from a professor's expectations.

The behind-the-scenes look into the daily life of a librarian helped novice tutors establish credibility in other ways as well. For instance, midway into a tutorial session, they could easily get up and help a student find just the right source in the stacks, reference area, or periodical room. They came to know the contents of the many reference volumes in the library and knew exactly where they were shelved. Daily encounters with librarians also allowed tutors ample opportunities to hear jargon from the field of library science. The language gap associated with professionals of different backgrounds slowly dissipated, which we found was advantageous when we worked together on common projects. In that regard, a story told by two compositionists who had a different experience is worth repeating. In an issue of *Writing Lab Newsletter*, writing specialists Jean-Paul Nadeau of Bryant College and Kristen Kennedy of Wake Forest University recall a misgiving in planning a joint workshop with librarians. Although the parties met to set an agenda, the written draft that the librarians presented looked different from what the compositionists had anticipated and used vocabulary that they found alien. Nadeau and Kennedy sadly assessed the situation: "Clearly, we hadn't communicated our intentions as well as we thought.... Perhaps we were ... guilty of not hearing the librarians' intentions...[and wondered if] we had a distinct role in the workshop."[6] As professionals, we can accept that it is not always easy for people of different disciplines to plan mutual projects. An understanding of each other's discipline-specific vocabulary, however, helps. At Saint Joseph College, we found that by understanding each other's vocabularies, encountering each other often in a common building, and coming to know each other's work through day-to-day contact, we overcame barriers that might otherwise have been difficult to hurdle. We also came to believe that this level of compatibility was important inasmuch as we shared the common goal of bolstering students' academic success. We found that through respect, trust, and a spirit of camaraderie, collaborations were orchestrated smoothly. The time taken to get to know one another culminated in healthy professional relationships and eased working on projects in unison.

In our experience at Saint Joseph College, the location of a writing center in the library where the staff of two departments commingled daily was a strong variable propelling collaborations. We had abundant time to talk and share ideas. When we sat down to plan workshops, we moved forward and were not compromised in the way Nadeau and Kennedy described. In planning a workshop, we worked collaboratively at each step, from setting the agenda to outlining the content to designing instructional materials. The divisional boundaries that might separate departments on a campus disappeared. We worked together daily and found that, over time, we developed mutually compatible goals and approaches. The chemistry of the people involved and the college's mission also were important considerations. A nurturing college environment for students, in tune with the college's mission, provided fertile ground for colleagues to join together. In the final analysis, the common building also was a vital catalyst in the early stages. The shared space made it easy for people of different departments to get to know one another on an informal basis. Thus, college climate, mission, and shared space all contributed to the development of a robust relationship that set the stage for collaborations.

Students sensed the energy of the symbiotic relationship, adding to their reasons to enter a building where academic support from well-qualified personnel in two departments was abundant. They were secure in knowing that professionals with diverse backgrounds were readily available to assist. The cliché "one-stop shopping" was apropos. The staff of both departments could work with students at any stage of a project, breaking complex tasks into manageable chunks. Personnel with two kinds of expertise were not only on-site, but also knowledgeable enough about each other's field that a student might well be served by one professional. For example, in the process of helping a student find additional sources for a paper in draft form, a reference librarian was apt to make suggestions for content revision. Librarians were well versed in answering students' questions about documenting sources and brushed up on grammar by consulting writing center handouts and handbooks. In observing librarians' and tutors' understandings of each other's trade, students learned a valuable lesson—cross-training enhances one's professional repertoire.

A formal means for collaboration also existed per the college's governance structure. The directors of the library and tutoring center sat on the Library Advisory Committee with faculty from various academic divisions. The committee met monthly to discuss library issues. These sessions helped the tutoring center's director keep abreast of library resources, including books and audiovisual materials. Writing-across-the-curriculum discussions transpired as faculty discussed specific assignments and requisite library resources. These discussions often segued into discussions about the tutoring center and its interconnectedness with the library. The center's director also had opportunities to hear about upcoming assignments, and, like the librarian, could plan accordingly. At times, this planning might involve joint projects, such as scheduling orientation sessions for incoming students that informed them about the services of both departments.

The Library Advisory Committee in these days was one of several venues for promoting writing across the curriculum and information literacy. The committee was fertile territory for negotiating common outcomes and fostering collaborations. Meetings were opportunities for all to keep current of one another's roles and for planning joint, interdisciplinary endeavors. We found that by having the directors of the writing center and library on the same committee, a means existed for entwining academic support services into curricular revision. As spokespeople for our respective fields, we emphasized writing across the curriculum and information literacy as critical components in curricular renewal and faculty development, and suggested speakers and topics for faculty development days and workshops.

Midcareer Growing Pains

By the mid-1990s, the college's enrollment had escalated considerably since the days the tutoring center housed in the library first opened. In addition, in the interim, students came to rely increasingly on tutorial services. By 1992, the center was clocking 2,000 hours of tutoring for the year for a population of 1,200 students and the college was fast approaching enrollment close to 1,600. By 1994, the annual tutorial report cited 3,000 hours of tutoring accompanied by thirty workshops. Increasing student enrollment also meant the library was strapped for space. For both departments, the same quality of services was now expected for a larger student population. Thus, the tutoring center's continued presence in the library was problematic.

Top-level administrators and the directors of the writing center and library did some soul-searching to find answers. Technology resources on campus were simultaneously becoming outdated, and more computer facilities were needed to address enrollment trends. Two small computer centers housed in the main academic building on campus were insufficient. In looking at the larger picture on campus, a temporary solution was found that addressed a two-year period of expanding growth. From 1992 to 1994, the tutoring center was offered another room in the library, one used as classroom space, not for library purposes per se. In this space, a computer facility was built and tutorials occurred there. This plan doubled the center's space without the library sacrificing additional space. In fact, the library gained space inasmuch as students using study carrels were now sent to the new facility to word-process papers. This multiprong approach helped three departments—the library, the tutoring center, and computing operations. The new computer facility fell under the jurisdiction of the tutoring center, saving some money. A crop of students to work in the computer center did not have to be hired. The same students who already worked in the tutoring center served in this role. The center's director assumed responsibility for supervising these students. Students, in general, profited from the new arrangement. They had access to word processors and other computer programs in a setting where computer-literate student workers and tutors were available to assist. For the time, all were content. Most of all, students enjoyed a technology-rich computer lab housed within a tutoring center, which, in turn, was situated in a library. Thus, all the advantages that existed previously for easing students' academic needs continued with new ones added. Librarians also found another reason to come to the tutoring center. They, too, stopped in to use computers, resulting in additional opportunities to interact with writing center staff in a bustling environment humming with students working on papers at computer terminals.

But as the student enrollment continued to climb, the temporary solution no longer sufficed. At a small college, an additional fifty to sixty students per year created the same problem that an additional 500 to 600 students would at a larger campus. Space became a sacred commodity. Soon the college was enrolling double the number of students that it did when the center started in 1988, coupled by the fact that more academically at-risk students were straining tutorial resources. Already the center was a well-established entity on campus enjoying a steady clientele, and faculty and administrators alike realized that the trend was not going to abate. The center tried sprawling into adjacent rooms in the library, but the creep effect was apparent. The library also needed more space to shelve books and periodicals. A permanent solution to an increasingly pressing problem was desperately sought.

Jointly, the librarians and tutoring staff worked with administrators to find an immediate solution to the situation facing both departments. The college's provost devised a solution that was well received by members of each department. He offered underutilized space in another building that could be renovated over the winter intersession as new quarters for the tutoring center. By the end of the winter recess, the move occurred. As the tutoring center staff boxed books, supplies, and paraphernalia and moved across campus to the other building, the librarians pitched in and helped. They graciously gave furniture, letting the center retain tables and chairs passed along when it first opened. Books purchased with library funding also were retained. Thus a valuable collection of resources for tutors' professional development and for tutorial needs was kept intact. Although both departments were happy to have much-needed space, we soon found that the easygoing camaraderie between the library and tutoring staff was sorely missed. We no longer ran into each other routinely, and during the cold, snowy months of the winter, it was no easy task to pick up during a tutorial and join forces with a librarian. Joint workshops also dwindled. Following the move, the staff of the center had to devote energy to reconfiguring space for tutorial needs and establishing new strategies for marketing a center that was now housed in a new home, slightly off the beaten path of students' daily treks. Furthermore, the new location was no longer in a building that primarily served an academic purpose, so students unfamiliar with the center's services were not readily inclined to use it. During the first spring semester of the move, joint tutorials, small-group sessions, and workshops dwindled in number while other activities took precedence.

By the following fall semester, librarians, however, did return to their habit of walking students to the center, even if this meant a short trip across campus. The librarians in a caring spirit saw the merits of bringing students to the center, and when time did not easily permit for this to happen, they telephoned the center to schedule appointments for students who sat by while the call was made. Librarians also continued to give students the tutoring center's brochure and to explain its services. Tutoring center handouts were kept in the library and were another means for librarians to familiarize students with services. When supplies ran low, librarians walked over for new copies and also checked out other handouts and resources available, bringing paper copies back to the library.

During this period, librarians also continued to play a role in helping students understand the college's across-the-curriculum writing portfolio program, established in 1989 and administered by the writing center. Working with students daily, the librarians knew of students who experienced difficulty in completing this degree requirement. Sometimes a student shared with a librarian the results of a preliminary evaluation, which fell at the end of sophomore year and foretold of results on the final evaluation, occurring a year later. Students who did not succeed at either stage were inclined to share results with librarians whom they came to know over the years. Not only did librarians play a mentoring role, they were key players in reminding struggling writers to make regular writing tutorial appointments. They also provided the expertise of someone outside the field of composition studies in counseling students about the criteria used to evaluate portfolio as defined in the college's *Writing Portfolio Booklet*. In particular, librarians could help students address the requirement that at least one paper in the portfolio demonstrate strong research writing skills. For many students, the omission of such evidence kept them from completing their portfolio. With that in mind, it was not surprising that students turned to librarians for assistance. Moreover, librarians were another voice in helping students understand why proficiency in research writing was required. Thus, in tandem, librarians and writing tutors helped students navigate their way through the portfolio program—the librarians providing counseling, and the tutors, tutorial support.

Interest in each department's workshops also began to resurface in the late 1990s. The staff of both departments made it a point to attend each other's workshops. Library staff regularly consulted the schedule of tutoring center workshops and attended those on research writing, documentation styles, and study skills. Invariably, tutors conducting the workshops introduced librarians in attendance. This strategy worked well for students writing research papers, particularly those in the early stages who soon would need to be meeting with librarians. The library staff also kept announcements about tutoring center workshops in prominent places in the library and encouraged students to attend these. Likewise, tutors noted when library orientation workshops occurred and, when possible, attended these, learning of new sources, journals, and online references added to the library's collection. We found that by promoting and attending each other's services, we were able to maintain a spirit of collegiality and camaraderie even though we did not mutually plan and conduct most events. Direct e-mails, as well as announcements posted on the college Web site and through all-client e-mails, also provided a way to communicate and keep informed of upcoming events.

With time, the workshops run by both departments grew highly technical and specific in focus. For this reason, it was vital for staff from each department to keep abreast of trends. For example, instead of simply conducting workshops on citing Internet sources in the APA style, the writing center offered in-class workshops for specific audiences such as social work classes writing research study proposals. At these in-class workshops, librarians could provide focused guidance on specific online databases to consult. When librarians could not attend such workshops, writing center presenters tried to consult with them in advance about which available resources to mention. By consulting with reference librarians, the writing center presenters also set the groundwork for the kind of work that students would soon be coming to the library to do.

Library tours and library orientations also began to include greater focus on information literacy. With new services and online databases added and remote access to library resources becoming increasingly possible, tutors found it critical to attend sessions or to arrange for one-on-one consultation to keep current. When Internet connections became available on tutoring center computers and access to more library services were available online, tutors had to learn about these services to help students during tutorials. With some online services still confined to the library building, tutors also had to know which terminals provided access to what kinds of services, which printers were hooked to what terminals, and what protocols were necessary for using different databases. Thus, although librarians and writing tutors no longer worked in the same building, it was critical that they crossed paths in a variety of ways to fine-tune their professional skills.

One way to look at our evolving relationship is to draw an analogy. Whereas we once functioned as members of an immediate family sharing a common house, we now were like distant cousins meeting on occasion, savoring the moments spent together. A trip to the tutoring center for a librarian meant time to become reacquainted with staff and to replenish handouts, much like a relative might bring photos home to share with extended members of a family. A visit to the library for tutors entailed checking on new developments there—learning of new databases, finding out about upcoming events, and reconnecting with staff. Opportunities to get together were much like family reunions—times to catch up on news and learn of new developments.

In terms of partnerships through college governance, by the late 1990s, the Library Advisory Committee dissolved, outgrowing its function; yet, it was resurrected in a new form as the Academic Resources Committee (ARC). Instead of faculty being appointed to serve on the committee, they now were elected. In that sense, the new committee wielded more power. The directors of the library, the tutoring center, and information technology served as ex-officio members. The committee's mission focused on the intersections between academic support services and the academic disciplines. Faculty representation by division fostered cross-pollination of ideas. The new committee, per the governance document, addressed issues of global concern. Meetings brought together players who devised plans for collaborative projects that intricately intertwined library and tutoring services. Furthermore, opportunities for writing-across-the-curriculum projects evolved that included more players. If writing-across-the-curriculum experts were invited to campus for a faculty development day, members of the library, information technology, and the tutoring center were invited to attend. When development of a new academic integrity policy on campus was brought to the attention of the college's policy committee, the committee consulted the ARC. Because the ARC existed in part to buttress three departments that lent academic support to the campus, the new structure in effect gave these departments a greater presence on campus for shaping policy, program development, and curricular changes. Increasingly, academic departments were concerned with the kinds and levels of support that these departments could provide to the college's community. The ARC served as a formal mechanism for fostering shared decision making and came to play a vital role in ushering in changes for the new millennium.

Setbacks and Rekindled Collaborations

By the year 2000, new forms of partnership between the writing center and the library surfaced as the two departments increased their reliance on technology. Both departments designed and maintained topnotch Web sites suitable to a small college campus. The sites were characterized by a user-friendly design and a plethora of helpful resources. We found that instead of meeting in person to collaborate, we turned to each other's online resources for guidance. When we needed to talk, we used the phone or e-mail. In-person visits tended to be reserved for special purposes and committee work.

Most of the meetings in virtual space revolved around acquiring a solid knowledge of each other's Web resources. Tutors became adept at navigating the library's Web site, and online databases were now accessible from remote sites. New tutors needed to spend time developing expertise and agility with these resources. They needed to be prepared amid a tutorial to go online and help a student access the library site, its online catalogs, and its online databases, as well as its hyperlinks to external resources. Tutors were expected to be adept at independently navigating the library's virtual space, and for some tutors this meant learning from other tutors or meeting one-on-one with librarians to become facile with resources. In turn, librarians were reliant on the writing center's Web site, particularly for information in citing online resources according to the popular documentations used at the college. The writing center's Web site also provided online access to an array of handouts dealing with different aspects of writing college papers, tips for academic success, and URL links to national Online Writing Labs (OWLs) such as the one at Purdue University. In effect, it was critical for members of each department to become quite familiar with each other's online resources.

Through electronic resources, we kept current regarding each other's fields of knowledge. Librarians could find information on teaching writing and the writing process by checking information on the writing center director's Web site in addition to the department's Web site. There the director provided information for teaching writing as a process, including descriptions of prewriting strategies, tips for conducting peer review sessions, and information about upcoming faculty development opportunities dealing with the teaching of writing. By consulting these materials, librarians could learn about peer review strategies and allay students' fears about writing, for in-class peer reviews would yield opportunities to ask questions and seek advice before proceeding further with an assignment. The site allowed librarians to keep current of developments in the field of teaching writing, just as informal conversations in the past, when the center was housed in the library, allowed exchanges about current pedagogy and emerging theories to ensue. The center's director's Web site also made available papers that she recently delivered at conferences, providing a means for the librarians to keep aware of the kinds of topics shaping literacy education in the field of composition studies. Thus, whereas in-person collaborations declined, instances for meeting conveniently in cyberspace increased. In looking back on the past three decades and thinking ahead, one of the pioneering librarians in our joint ventures commented, "In this day and age of the libraries without walls a collaborative venture with an academic resource center should be an easier goal for most institutions to reach than it was for us in the eighties."[7] Her comment speaks not only to where we have come, but how she envisions partnerships between libraries and learning resource centers evolving in the future. We also had opportunities to collaborate based on recent curricular revisions. In particular, the reinvention of first-year seminar in 2001 as a three-credit course as opposed to an earlier incarnation of the course as a one-credit module prompted a partnership. In May following commencement, for the past two years, the faculty teaching sections for the upcoming fall convened for a week-long series of workshops, including ones presented by librarians and writing tutors. One goal of the workshop series was to help faculty who had not yet taught first-year students understand what to expect. The shared belief of the tutoring center and library staff was that an assignment that required students to learn how to use the library in an integrative context would capture students' interest. To that end, we placed emphasis on hands-on learning and kinesthetic and visual skills. During the workshops, we suggested that when classes began in the fall, instructors should bring students to a computer lab where they could sit individually at terminals and access online databases and search for materials directly related to an assignment. We claimed that this approach served multiple purposes: it helped students start the assignment, taught them to use online sources, and developed important information literacy skills. We provided instructors with needed resources and encouraged them to include in curricular plans assignments that reflected current theory about multiple intelligences and learning styles, topics also covered in the workshops by other presenters. With that purpose in mind, we demonstrated how the development of information literacy capitalized on different learning styles, some kinetic, some visual, some interactive, and some highly textual. By fall 2003, we found that an increasing number of faculty included hands-on seminars on information literacy in their curriculum, often involving reference librarians in the presentations done in either computer labs or the library's electronic demonstration classroom. The writing center staff followed suit, conducting tutorials that checked students' development of information literacy skills, looking to see if students gained confidence with navigating online databases provided off the library's Web pages.

The thrust to include an information literacy component in the first-year seminar program rippled into general education curriculum renewal. All new curriculum models under consideration include scholarly research and information literacy as baseline skills. Emphases in these areas have ramifications for the writing center and the library, placing them at the forefront of curricular change as vital players supplementing classroom instruction. It is anticipated that students will need considerable support beyond the walls of the classroom to develop these skills and that it is the writing tutors and librarians whom students will turn to for help. In unison, we can collaborate to ensure that we are of like mind, teaching students a uniform set of skills that we each reinforce. For example, it falls within our areas of expertise to help students critique online resources, learn strategies for conducting effective online searches, discern how different search engines work, and cull search results for relevant and reliable sources.

In addition to the first-year seminar opportunity, other forms of collaborations between the departments have evolved. The Advisement Center asked reference librarians and writing tutors to conduct workshops for nontraditional students and incoming transfer students, who needed to be aware of academic resources available on campus. Jointly, we ran a workshop for nontraditional students focused on the research paper process and another one for transfer students familiarizing them with our services, including a tour of our facilities. These opportunities harkened back to our pioneering days, but now we added components dealing with online databases and used software such as PowerPoint. We saw that we could capture some of the glory of the past by working together and capitalizing on new technologies that engaged students. For nontraditional students, we found that orientation to our online services was critical to their early success at the college, preventing them from floundering or feeling alienated, or falling behind their peers already familiar with services.

At the initiative of the Advisement Center and Admissions, the library and tutoring center also joined forces to offer summer workshops for incoming students identified as academically at-risk. Although we had offered such joint workshops as early as 1990, we intensified the format of our new offerings. We brought students through the steps of writing a college-level paper, taking them through brainstorming, outlining, drafting, peer reviews, instructor conferencing, revision strategies, and editing tips. We accelerated the library component and were sure to introduce students to several members of the library staff. Students learned how to conduct online searches, use online catalogs, and access online consortia catalogs. The summer program once again gave librarians and tutoring staff an opportunity to confer and mutually plan an in-depth project tied to student success. Tenets instrumental to our early workshops, such as teaching writing and research as a recursive process with steps that cycled back on one another, resurfaced. Most important, we emphasized right from the start of the students' college careers that librarians and writing tutors were key academic support figures. Including upper-class students as mentors in the program lent credibility to this stance; these students bore witness to the fact that librarians and tutors helped students at the college meet with academic success.

When the Faculty Development Committee asked librarians and writing center staff to do an orientation for new faculty, we focused on assignment design, online resources, and criteria for evaluating student writing. We spoke of students' struggles with integrating source material into research papers and offered strategies for helping students, including using conferencing strategies and providing feedback to drafts. We pointed out that the tutoring center's Web site included links to OWLs and other resources helpful for writing a college paper. Librarians covered the basics of online databases and general library services. In essence, the orientation familiarized new faculty with both the on-site and online resources of the two departments. Workshop leaders emphasized how the departments worked in tandem to provide students with an array of academic support services.

Today, when we describe to new staff in our departments how the tutoring center was once housed in the library, they remind us that we still work well together. Although new staff never enjoyed the luxury of working together in the same building, they claim with a clear objectivity that old members of the department cannot assume based on historical memory that, indeed, collaborations are still rich and that teamed tutorials still do, in fact, occur. One reference librarian, who recently joined the college, remarked, "I have had tutors ... bring a student over for a kind of joint session where I addressed the research needs and the tutor addressed the writing issues. I found these to be productive, and ... feel I learned from the tutor as well." She added, "that kind of thing could be encouraged more often."[8] Her final comment spoke to a desire to continue collaborations, particularly joint tutorials. Tutors likewise acknowledged that joint sessions were occurring, claiming that they scheduled appointments in the library with librarians participating. Such tutorials tended to focus on students' needs to use library resources as a prewriting or drafting strategy in completing an assignment. In effect, new hires rediscovered lessons learned early on: librarians and tutors by nature of the work that they do with students benefit from working collaboratively on specific projects.

With time, The Academic Resources Center (ARC), which brought the directors of the library, writing center, and information technology departments together with faculty, evolved to a new stage. Similar to the Library Advisory Committee before it, the ARC outlived its purpose, and an Education Technology Committee (ETC) formed to reflect emerging trends. The new namesake spoke to the changes that technology reaped. Once again, the library, writing center, and information technology directors served as ex officio members. The ETC dealt with distance learning issues, building new computer centers, equipping classrooms with emerging technologies, and addressing curricular revisions based on appropriate, evolving technology structures. Distance learning, already a vital part of the college, redefined to some extent the operation of the library and tutoring center. No longer did students have to come in person to use resources. The need to provide services online twenty-four hours a day, seven days a week, was realized. The tutoring center moved to offer services through a statewide consortium, allowing student access to tutors from any one of the participating institutions of higher education. A statewide consortium provided an Ask-A-Librarian service around the clock. These kinds of services, we found, were used by all students, not just distance-education ones. It was through the ETC that we shared ideas with faculty and helped them learn of the new resources that we provided. Information disseminated at monthly meetings and through our committee's online blackboard discussion forums was, in turn, shared at the departmental and divisional levels.

In speaking at a library–technology international conference, library specialist Lizabeth Wilson noted that in the Information Age where information literacy leading to information fluency is a critical progression, we can best advance students' skills through collaboration. From Wilson's perspective, it is important for faculty, librarians, and, I would add, writing center personnel to join forces. In short, Wilson claims, "Best practices are collaborative efforts and involve the broadest range of educators."[9] At Saint Joseph College through departmental, committees and other structures, best practices have been implemented for developing students' information literacy skills. Efforts such as the ETC, the collaboration of librarians and writing center tutors with first-year seminar faculty, and the initiatives from the Academic Advisement Center and Admissions to introduce information literacy skills through jointly conducted writing center and library workshops have attested to best practices regarding infusion of information literacy skills on a broad scale. In creating a new curriculum that will make information literacy a vertical progression, Saint Joseph College will ensure that skills learned early in a student's education are reinforced in upper-division courses. Our model follows recommendations set forth by the Carnegie Foundation's report, *Reinventing Undergraduate Education: A Blueprint for American Research Universities*. As noted by Ilene Rockman, manager of the Information Competence Initiative for The California State University, the report encourages librarians to forge alliances across the institution. From Rockman's perspective,

"[I]deally, curricular restructuring helps students at various places in their academic studies by seamlessly weaving information competence horizontally and vertically throughout the curriculum, with ample reinforcement occurring in both lower- and upper-division courses."[10] Such an integrated approach requires that both writing and library specialists take active roles in the conversation based on their knowledge of how students advance in their literacy education.

Future Plans and Conclusions

As we move further into the first decade of the twenty-first century, librarians and writing center staff find themselves playing cutting-edge roles in information literacy skills and the development of students' scholarly research skills. Students must be well versed in critiquing online sources, adept at crafting research papers that integrate scholarly sources, and facile with citing sources, including those not easily classifiable according to style manuals such as those of the Modern Language Association (MLA) and the American Psychological Association (APA). As professionals, we continue to share the common goal of helping students succeed with academic endeavors. We also recognize that we live in a time where interdependency and interdisciplinary approaches are indispensable. As our institution fashions its new general education curriculum, we realize that skills taught in one discipline are reinforced in another and boundaries separating fields of knowledge are artificial.

Although we have learned much since our pioneering days and sometimes wax nostalgic for the past, we know the future awaits us. Where will we go from here? As librarians and writing tutors, we have come to appreciate the advantages of working mutually on projects. We have pledged ourselves to working on goals to facilitate collaborations between our departments.

These include:

• Setting aside times in our busy schedules to get together in person to plan common events such as workshops

• Continuing to designate places in our workplace and online spaces to display and disseminate information about each other's services

• Clarifying for students how our services intertwine and reinforce one another

• Working on common committees to foster faculty and staff development opportunities that engender an understanding of the role of information literacy in the future

• Requiring new hires and present members of our departments to participate in training that allows them to learn of each department's resources

- Encouraging ongoing professional development that will lead to mutually planned workshops and similar events

These are but a few of the ideas that we have proposed as we reflect on what worked in the past and where we would like to head in the future.

At present, plans call for librarians and writing center staff to move beyond first-year seminar classes as a venue for training faculty. We would like to design a series of collaborative workshops for the upcoming year that will attract large numbers of students and faculty. We believe that by working together on new projects, we can rekindle the synergic spirit characteristic of our past. We see popular campuswide workshops as one way to bring us to the forefront as key players in a period of vibrant curricular reform. We anticipate continuing to work with the curriculum committee to bring a new general education curriculum to fruition over the next several years, watching it unfold to encompass the work of our fields, particularly with the emphasis to be placed on core competencies in written expression, scholarly research, and collaborative learning.

When asked why our partnerships have worked and why the territorial divides that topple joint projects on other campuses have not surfaced, we would be remiss if we did not acknowledge the impact of our college's mission. The mission creates a culture that promotes collaborations. It engenders a climate for professionals to work together to foster student learning and achievement of academic success. A campus culture that makes student learning a top priority places a premium on the role of the writing center and campus library. In such a culture, it is easy for professionals to work cohesively to reach a common good. The philosophies of the two departments echo the college's mission. Saint Joseph College exists to provide access to education for students seeking strong leadership skills in a nurturing environment, where both a liberal arts education and professional programs are emphasized. The college seeks to create in students a desire for lifelong learning and a respect for academic excellence. An excerpt from the mission statement reads: "The College is a community which promotes the growth of the whole person in a caring environment that encourages strong ethical values, personal integrity and a sense of responsibility to the needs of society." The phrase "a community which promotes the whole person in a caring environment" resonates with the work that the library and the writing center have done together over the years. In working collaboratively, we have remained true to the college's mission. We believe that partnerships that reflect an institution's mission are sustained over time and become an integral part of that culture.

Notes

1. See Art Young and Toby Fulwiler's *Writing Across the Disciplines* for additional details.

2. Peter Elbow's two fundamental texts, *Writing with Power* and *Writing without Teachers*, and Donald Murray's *Writing to Learn* are useful resources on the early developments in the field of the process approach to instruction. Also, see Donald Murray's *Write to Learn* (Holt, Rinehart & Winston, 1984).

3. See Lester Faigley's *Fragments of Rationality: Postmodernity & the Subject of Composition* (University of Pittsburgh Pr., 1993) and *Assessing Writers' Knowledge and Composing Processes* (Ablex, 1985). See also Kenneth Bruffee's "Collaborative Learning and the 'Conversation of Mankind,'" *College English* 46 (Nov. 1984): 635–52.

4. Ken Macrorie's I-Searching concept of research writing is articulated in his early writing process book, *Searching Writing, A Context Book* (Rochelle Park, N.J.: Hayden Pr., 1980).

5. Peter Elbow's *Everyone Can Write* (New York: Oxford University Pr., 2000) outlines many of the principles found in his formative early works, *Writing with Power* and *Writing without Teachers*, and is a useful recap of many of his strategies for teaching and evaluating writing.

6. Jean-Paul Nadeau and Kristen Kennedy, "Re-configuring Writing Center Partnerships: Beyond In-center Tutoring," *Writing Lab Newsletter* 25, no. 4 (Dec. 2000): 4–6.

7. In reviewing a draft of this chapter, former Saint Joseph College reference librarian Catherine Posteraro, now of Saint Francis Hospital Library Center in Connecticut, made this comment via e-mail on March 29, 2004.

8. I am indebted to reference librarian Lynne Piacentini of Saint Joseph College for this quoted contribution.

9. See Lizabeth A. Wilson, "Information Literacy: Fluency across and beyond the Curriculum," in *Library User Education: Powerful Learning, Powerful Partnerships*, for a discussion of "best practice" characteristics of institutions succeeding with infusing information literacy across the curriculum.

10. Ilene Rockman, "Strengthening Connections between Information Literacy, General Education, and Assessment," *Library Trends* 51 (fall 2002): 195. The article provides an overview of interdisciplinary partnerships, curricular revision, and assessment outcomes with the goal of entwining information literacy into instructional processes.

Bibliography

Bruffee, Kenneth. 1984. "Collaborative Learning and the 'Conversation of Mankind.'" *College English* 46 (Nov.): 635–52.

Elbow, Peter. 2000. *Everyone Can Write: Essays toward a Hopeful Theory of Writing and Teaching Writing.* New York: Oxford.

———. 1981. *Writing with Power: Techniques for Mastering the Writing Process.* New York: Oxford University Pr.

———. 1973. *Writing without Teachers.* New York: Oxford University Pr.

Faigley, Lester. 1985. *Assessing Writers' Knowledge and Composing Processes.* Greenwich, Conn.: Ablex.

———. 1993. *Fragments of Rationality: Postmodernity & the Subject of Composition*. Pittsburgh, Pa.: Pittsburgh University Pr.

Macrorie, Ken. 1980. *Searching Writing*. Rochelle Park, N.Y.: Hayden.

Murray, Donald. 1984. *Write to Learn*. New York: Holt, Rinehart & Winston.

Nadeau, Jean Paul, and Kristen Kennedy. 2000. "Re-configuring Writing Center Partnerships: Beyond In-center Tutoring." *Writing Lab Newsletter* 25, no. 4 (Dec.): 4–6.

Rockman, Ilene. 2002. "Strengthening Connections between Information Literacy, General Education, and Assessment Efforts," *Library Trends* 51, no. 2 (fall): 185–98.

Wilson, Lizabeth A. 2001. "Information Literacy: Fluency across and beyond the Curriculum." In *Library User Education: Powerful Learning, Powerful Partnerships*, ed. Barbara I. Dewey. Lanham, Md.: Scarecrow Press, 2001.

Young, Art, and Toby Fulwiler, eds. 1986. *Writing across the Disciplines: Research into Practice*. Upper Montclair, N.J.: Boynton/Cook.

Acknowledgements

Linda Geffner, director of the Saint Joseph College Library, has been a valued partner in building a common community between her department and the Academic Resources Center, the all-campus tutoring center at Saint Joseph College. In the early days, she contributed books, supplies, camaraderie, and the sacred resource of a home for the center. Her congenial, sharing spirit throughout the years has been an inspiration and naturally helped with writing this chapter. Catherine Posteraro, former reference librarian at the college, during my first ten years, was another valuable player. She trained tutors in the use of the library's resources and promoted joint tutorials and workshops. Both Linda and Catherine, along with Ann Williams, another valued member of the library staff, regularly stopped at the ARC and were friendly, guiding voices in the days when the ARC first opened its doors. Front-desk staff member Maria Ciogli, who went on to marry Catherine's oldest son, changing her name to Maria Ciogli Posteraro, was another friendly voice in the partnership. As a student and worker at the college, she lent her expertise on dual fronts in a continued spirit of collegiality. Through her years at the college, she was a guiding light, often bringing students to the tutoring center. Finally, the new reference librarians who joined the staff in recent years have been valued colleagues. I thank Lynne Piacentini and Antoinette Collins for their continued support. The willingness of librarians at Saint Joseph College to work with writing center staff is demonstrated again and again, one case in point being the fast turnaround that all provided to the drafts-in-progress for this chapter. Despite busy schedules, all responded promptly and took the time to suggest collaborative projects for the future. Even Catherine, who has since left the college, responded via e-mail in less than twenty-four hours, making substantive comments and acknowledging that Maria who started her career at Saint Joseph is now a reference librarian at Providence College, Rhode Island. Responsiveness and goodwill have always been characteristic of the library staff of the college, making collaborative projects endearing, cherished endeavors.

Chapter seven

"It Might Come in Handy." Composing a Writing Archive at the University of New Hampshire: A Collaboration between the Dimond Library and the Writing-across-the-Curriculum/Connors Writing Center, 2001–2003

Cinthia Gannett, Elizabeth Slomba, Kate Tirabassi, Amy Zenger, and John C. Brereton

> "A functional archive is one of the most valuable legacies a writing program administrator can grant to the next person who takes on the responsibilities of the position."[1]

> "Memory provides the background to everything else, and without it, we are continually shackled to a narrow presentism …condemned to reinventing the wheel."[2]

In this reflective essay, our collaborative research team (library archivist and writing center/ WAC) documents and discusses the development of the Archive on the History of Writing and Writing Instruction at the University of New Hampshire. This project, admittedly challenging in many ways, has enhanced the Dimond Library's physical archival holdings and research/instructional activity while strengthening the intellectual and cultural identity of the writing programs at the University of New Hampshire. Together, we have created a collection that can be used within and across the institution and by scholars and researchers nationally.

The collaborative process of developing the archive was enormously valuable as well: the writing center/WAC staff learned a great deal about how archives are constructed and participated directly in the composition and collection of the archive itself, choosing the artifacts, labeling them, creating important connections and categories that will help create a functional and accessible archive for the future. The university archivist came to value a variety of artifacts related to writing pedagogy and writing program administration and the development of student writing across the curriculum that might not have been identified traditionally as making a significant contribution to a writing program archive. She found innovative ways to incorporate and connect the more informal and ephemeral materials related to curriculum and pedagogical changes and student writing-in-process with the more typical types of holdings, such as course catalogs, prize-winning essays, or published student literary journals. This broader view of writing and writing development has prompted her to shift her own research and instructional work accordingly. Finally, we consider the future of the archive and our collaboration, both in terms of its ongoing development and its possible uses, as we begin to understand more fully how very "handy" this kind of archival project can be.

Local and Institutional Contexts

The University of New Hampshire, Durham (UNH), the flagship campus of the state university system, is located on the southern seacoast of New Hampshire, an hour's drive north of Boston. Founded in 1866 as a land grant institution devoted the agricultural and mechanic arts, UNH has become a major research institution serving a student population of approximately 10,500 undergraduate and 2,000 graduate students. Two notable features of the culture at UNH set the backdrop for this interesting collaboration between the Connors Writing Center and the Dimond Library Archive. First, broadly speaking, UNH shares a consciousness of the past with the rest of New England, a region where history and heritage pervade daily life. In New Hampshire, the past is on intimate terms with the present. It speaks eloquently in the landscape itself, in the stone walls bordering fields where crops are no longer grown, in clapboard houses added onto again and again by successive generations, and in the tiny clusters of rural gravestones naming families who once lived there. Each of the scattered towns in the seacoast region celebrates a highly individual local identity and supports a vibrant, active historical association. Knowledge and curiosity about local history are commonly expressed by the questions you are likely to get from anyone you meet, as people speculate about the cultural significance of your surname or birthplace. The past also surfaces in the many artifacts that have been preserved (or merely survived) in barns and attics, in museums and archives. In New Hampshire, "most people have someplace at home where they tuck away things that might be useful at some future date," writes essayist Phillip Simmons, who identifies thrift as a local "household god." He reminds us, "the poet Donald Hall has suggested that instead of 'Live Free or Die,' New Hampshire license plates should read 'It Might Come in Handy.'"[3]

The second, and more specific, feature of the educational culture at UNH that acts as a prompt for the archive project has to do with the distinctive identity of its composition studies program. UNH has played an important role in the development of writing process theory and pedagogy since the mid-1960s, when scholar teachers Don Murray and Don Graves and later Jane Hansen and Tom Newkirk began their important and innovative work, exploring and explaining how writers at any age learn to write. In a composition program focused on writing process pedagogy, students' writing (drafting, revision, and finished works) are valued as the core of the curriculum, potential research sites that can give us insight into composing processes, constructions of identity, and constructions of disciplinary discourse. Over the past thirty years, UNH has continued to attract a strong faculty in composition, developed a well-known first-year composition program, created its own version of the National Writing Project, and developed two doctoral programs in literacy and composition. Its graduates have contributed in significant ways to the current generation of composition studies and writing program administration nationally.

In the mid-1980s, UNH began a set of faculty development projects in Writing across the Curriculum and in the early 1990s formally initiated a full Writing-across-the-Curriculum Program, composed of curricular components (writing-intensive courses), a University Writing Center, permanent faculty development support, and a writing fellows program, codirected by Dr. Robert Connors and Dr. Cinthia Gannett. By 2000, the Times/Princeton Review's *Best Colleges for You* listed UNH as one of the top WAC programs in the country.

The UNH Writing Center and WAC Program was brought under the office of the vice provost for academic affairs in 1998 but retained its primary intellectual affiliation with composition studies in the English Department. Both the WAC and writing center directorships were held by tenured compositionists, that is, senior faculty people invested in the programs and imbued with a strong historical consciousness of the field and UNH's place in its development. Our graduate students have regularly consulted in the program, and several have held assistant directorship positions over the past ten years. In addition, the Ph.D. program in rhetoric and composition promoted composition scholarship generally and historical scholarship specifically. Dr. Connors, the writing center director until his death in 2000, was a leading historian in composition/rhetoric. As an archivist, he had been a prime mover in the development of the Beale Collection, the national composition archive, consisting of the papers of many leading figures (located at the University of Rhode Island) and an extensive set of early composition texts, which he kept in his office in the Writing Center for many years and which now are housed at the Dimond Library.

Indeed, there has been a surge of scholarly interest in the history of composition, writing programs, and writing pedagogy in the past two decades, which has led to considerable interest in the deliberate preservation, identification, and uses of primary and secondary documents and artifacts in the field.[4] As John Brereton noted in "Archivists with an Attitude," a multivoiced essay on the current status of and possibilities for the composition and rhetoric archive:

> Those of us who work in the history of rhetoric and composition know that over the past few decades our archive, the repository of primary and secondary sources, has been expanding dramatically. Some parts of this archive, student papers, for example, were collected quite haphazardly and barely examined; other material . . . has been in front of us all along, but didn't come into focus until historians began to look at it in unfamiliar ways. And still other material . . . was barely collected at all or existed in hard-to-find places and awaited the vision of scholars to come to life."[5]

Brereton enjoined compositionists to take action to ensure that this archive continues to develop more deliberately and strategically in the future, no longer relying on whatever might have been preserved but, rather, taking shared responsibility for taking stock of current holdings and actively contributing to the development of current archives and the creation of new archival projects. "As scholarship in rhetoric and composition grows, we need to begin asking what is missing from the archive and how it can get there. And we can also ask some questions while there is still time to act: Are there things we should be working to preserve right now? And what can we do now to make sure current practices and materials will be accessible in the archives of the future?[6]

In "Preserving Our Histories of Institutional Change: Enabling Research in the Writing Program Archives," Shirley K. Rose also provided a compelling case for the creation of local writing program archives, drawing on her experience as writing program administrator at Purdue. Noting that WPAs often handle more than a hundred documents a day and "might rather see the paper work disappear rather than take the responsibility for retaining, organizing, and preserving it," she argued that the value of such an archive far outweighs the work involved in creating and maintaining one.[7] "Archives have value for writing program administrators' research because they provide evidence of the functions and activities of the program and its participants. Research in our program archives helps us understand the history of our own programs."[8]

Rose argued that an effective archive can give us information beyond the formal reports and documents to offer information on values and beliefs, cultures and communities, policies, and practices that inform the shape and development of a program at any given point in time.

In the course of its dynamic, day-to-day and year-by-year existence, a writing program generates thousands of records that eventually should earn a place in the program's archive. Agenda and minutes from meetings of committees with responsibilities for directing the writing program, reports (such as annual reports or enrollment reports) prepared by writing program administration, correspondence related to the operation or direction of the program, descriptions of curricula, records of staffing practices. In order to preserve these records in a usable form for eventual use by researchers—by future researchers for the program and by other historians of composition studies, practices of writing program administration and other educational institutions—WPAs should establish archives for their writing programs.[9]

She offers several possible uses for a writing program archive, ideas that informed our own developing conception and vision of a WAC/Writing Center/Writing Program archive at UNH.

Archives can:

• Inform planning and decision making for program, curriculum, faculty development, etc.

• Provide facts and figures to identify significant trends and changes that can help identify successes and gaps and can be used to create rationales for current or proposed practices; can be used recursively to inform work on an ongoing basis

• Provide material to get "the big picture"—to see the program within broader institutional contexts

• Make a significant contribution to writing program scholarship institution-wide (other disciplines) and national-field based research[10]

More recently, scholars in the areas of composition studies related to WAC and writing center programs have been researching and recovering the origins of their own specific historical trajectories, which added another level of interest for the archive project that we had conceived. A National Writing Center Archives project has been initiated at the University of Louisville, under the direction of Dr. Carol Mattingly, and a book on the recent history of Writing-across-the-Curriculum Programs will be published sometime later this year.[11]

Despite these extraordinarily strong local and national traditions of inquiry, no archive had been created specifically devoted to preserving, organizing, or celebrating the intellectual and pedagogical culture of writing at the university. Even though the general archive holdings at the library included items related to writing, such as student publications, newsletters, papers of alumni, materials from writing conferences, and photographic images, these materials were not organized or brought together as a collection devoted to the common inquiry of writing, that is, they were not yet a writing archive.

Overview: How Did We Come Together and Why? Becoming Handy to Each Other

Cinthia Gannett

This collaboration, like most collaborations, was one part deliberate, one part circumstance, and one part pure serendipity. Fueled by the long-term interest by many in preserving the history of writing study and pedagogy at the University of New Hampshire, it was precipitated by a specific series of events that created a powerful rationale for creating a writing center/ WAC archive in a short period of time. The specific prompt began in the summer of 2000 with the sudden and untimely death of Dr. Robert Connors, founding director of the University Writing Center at UNH and historian of composition. As his colleague and cofounding director of the Writing-across-the-Curriculum Program and as chair of the University Writing Committee, I wanted to find an appropriate way to memorialize his life and work. I proposed to use a portion of the Connors Memorial Funds to create a Writing Archive, a collection that would preserve the kinds of ephemeral documents and artifacts that he loved to ferret out as he reconstructed various fascinating aspects of composition's national history. This archive would capture and preserve whatever it could of the history of the writing/ WAC/Writing Center programs at UNH as one of the centers of modern composition history and create a collection that would continue to sponsor the important archival work so crucial to our field.

That desire was intensified over that year as the composition program changed radically in personnel. Another of the four tenured compositionists—the writing program administrator who wrote the original proposal for the Writing Center and WAC Program in 1993—left the department, and I, the current director of the Connors Writing Center and WAC Program, would be leaving as well—at least for a full year. With so much turnover, we knew we were losing a great deal of the human cultural capital on which the program had been founded and developed. With the prospect of a completely new, nontenured composition faculty administration, likely to inadvertently "clean out" or be unable to interpret much of the ample documentary and ephemeral record created over the first ten years of the project, it became critical to safeguard whatever we could.

We did not want the Writing/Writing Center/ Writing-across-the-Curriculum Program to be shackled to what Bob Connors so presciently coined "a narrow presentism." And we had come to believe with Shirley Rose that "A functional archive [would be] one of the most valuable legacies a writing program administrator can grant to the next person who takes on the responsibilities of the position."[12]

In the original draft of the proposal, developed throughout the spring of 2002, I included support for a professional consultant, a historian of composition with extensive archival experience (Dr. John C. Brereton) and support for the two doctoral students in composition who had worked with me as assistant directors in the WAC/Writing Center (Amy Zenger and Kate Tirabassi) for the previous two years. The proposal made no explicit mention of the role that the Dimond Library Archive (and archivist Elizabeth Slomba) might play because my understanding of that part of the project was—shall I say— underdeveloped. The Connors Writing Center and the library were already working partners in other respects. That is, I understood that the Dimond Library might well become the storage site of the archive, and I knew that Robert Connors had collaborated with the library on the housing of the Beale Collection. The Dimond Library also had been hosting a satellite writing center site for consulting, and we had collaborated on information literacy support for consultants and clients. I was soon to learn how critical the library–Connors Writing Center collaboration would be to the success of this new project.

In the spring of 2002, the proposal was approved by the University Writing Committee, and at our first team meeting in May, our historian-consultant made it clear that our *first* order of business was to contact the university archivist as that person's knowledge, expertise, and cooperation would be essential to any possible chance of success for the archive. Our collaboration was about to begin. Our sense that we would "Hand stuff over. And the stuff would simply transform into accessible information and data" was simply uninformed. What we learned is that archiving is as much a process as a product; that *archive* is a verb, not a noun!

Dimond Library Archivist's Perspective: Creating a Writing Center-ed Archive

Elizabeth A. Slomba
Shortly after starting as a librarian and archivist at UNH, I received what seemed at the time an unusual request. An English professor and the director of composition, Tom Newkirk, asked me if the archives had any examples of "bad" student writing. I did not have a ready

answer. We did have some collections of student writing in storage that had been collected when the university archives was set up in 1993, but they were mostly prize-winning essays or publications of student literary and journalistic writing. The university library once had a circulating collection of political science papers from the 1940s. These papers were now in the archives but were presumably examples of "good" student writing because they were honors papers. At the time, I did not have an answer for Tom. Nor did I have a clear sense of why anyone would be interested in studying the whole range of student writing or why a university would want to archive such kinds of materials.

In the summer of 2002, I was about to find out. I was approached by the staff of the Connors Writing Center and WAC Program. The CWC was undergoing a significant change in senior staff (the current director and both graduate assistant directors would be leaving) and the future administration of the whole WAC program was uncertain. They wanted to document the development of the creation of the whole program and its ongoing work with faculty, curriculum, students, and the community before vital information was lost or dissipated. They also wanted to use this moment to begin the creation of a comprehensive historical archive dedicated to writing and writing pedagogy across the university in honor of the previous director of the writing center, who had been one of the leading national historians of composition. After some discussion about what they envisioned and what they were hoping for, I offered the expertise of the archives. The university archives collects, preserves, and makes available to researchers university publications and documents. The office files and other related materials would easily fit in our collections as documentation of a specific interdisciplinary program. But what the writing center people also wanted to do was to develop a research collection that they could build on and use in the future to study how writing has been taught and how students learned to write in different academic settings.

The archives already collects the usual student publications—the student newspaper and student literary magazines. But Cinthia, John, Amy, and Kate were looking at a broader picture of what they wanted for research material—photographs, supporting materials such as course catalogs, university and other publications that might have articles on teaching and course curricula, syllabi, assignments, and any materials that would shed light on how students learned—and continue to learn—to write and the institutional forces (initiatives, policies, programs, assessment, etc.) that influence the culture of writing.

This conversation radically changed my perspective on what materials could be used to research writing and what should be collected.

Collections already in the archives would supplement the writing center department files. We have course catalogs, nearly complete collections of all major student publications and some of the smaller publications, presidents' papers and other administrative files, university publications on curriculum changes and policies, the administration's newspaper and the student paper, photograph collections, scrapbooks and other similar materials. These materials could be used to study changes in both the teaching and learning of composition throughout the years by drawing on both the administrative side (policy, curriculum, requirements, and distribution) and the student side (surveys, samples, formal and informal writing, memoirs and journals, etc.). Indeed, student writing can be found in many other types of collections; for example, student letters, notes, and papers can be found in faculty papers and department files and student letters and petitions, newsletters, and other forms of advocacy writing in the administration files, such as presidents' papers and student life office files.

But what about actual student papers? Collecting student papers can be difficult because students usually do not save their work, much less think of donating papers to the archives. Sometimes student papers come to university and college archives through faculty papers and department files. Indeed, student papers pose tricky questions for archivists. Usually, when I had been urged to collect student papers before, the argument was that papers represented honors work, which should be kept as evidence of excellent college work or that students might review similar projects to determine what and how they should write. In some archival literature, archivists are encouraged to collect student papers to document student life on campus.[13] But in practice, there is a tacit bias against collecting papers because they are difficult to collect, do not have inherent research value as secondary sources, and do not immediately reflect in themselves the student experience. But what Cinthia, John, Kate, and Amy were advocating was the collection of papers for documenting both the process of writing as well as the textual products and along with evidence of writing pedagogies. This triangulation of materials made a difference in my understanding of the desirability of collecting all levels and stages of student work along with other program materials. And it also emphasized the advantages of studying writing in a university or college archive because the whole process could be studied from course development, to the kinds of specific genres assigned, to the resulting papers and teacher's responses and evaluations.

In addition to the various collections of student papers I already had in the archives from previous library collections and department files, the new writing center files included several hundreds of student papers at all stages of development that had been collected by

the center through years of consultations. Although this is an exciting and important addition to the archives, these particular papers
(and some already in the archives) create significant access issues
because they are considered student records and thus are governed
by The Family Educational Rights and Privacy Act (FERPA) of 1974.
Without a signed release by the student, such papers cannot be used
by researchers. Fortunately, because the writing center was attentive
to these issues when it set up its documentation procedures, many
of the papers came with a signed release forms allowing them to be
used for research purposes. Papers that do not have a signed release
will be removed from the collection when processed and will remain
in storage. These papers may not be released for very long time, likely
seventy-five to a hundred years from the date of creation, so access
remains a critical issue.

Challenges to collecting continue. Recently, I have had requests
from faculty researchers to find handbooks with the answers filled
in or books with student notes in them. These types of pedagogical
materials-in-process are often thrown out by potential donors before
they can be thrown out by librarians! Nor are these materials usually sold by used book dealers as they are considered "used up." The
ephemeral nature of these texts highlights the general problem for
collecting such student materials—some items desired are fugitive and
can be nearly impossible to locate or find. Early draft papers or papers
not necessarily considered "excellent writing" (outside such collections
as the writing center files) also may be difficult to locate because such
items most likely will not ordinarily be preserved and would rarely be
offered voluntarily to the Dimond Library Archive.

The Writing Center Archives project also has clearly influenced
my library instruction. Traditionally, archivists are used to working
with history majors and researchers and suggesting primary sources
selected for history papers. In the future, composition students and
researchers will be using primary sources from our own (and possibly other) archives in their work and may be using these materials in
ways somewhat different from other types of historical inquiries we
have supported previously. These new information-seeking needs have
challenged me to review my collections and discover new materials.
During the second year of the project, graduate students taking a course
in the history of composition were encouraged to make immediate
use of the developing archive and were required by their professor,
Dr. Paul Matsuda, to approach the archives staff for ideas on topics
and materials they could use for their seminar papers. Because of the
collaboration with Cinthia, Amy, Kate, and John, I expanded on the
usual sources I would have gone over in the reference interview and
suggested to researchers many more sources on writing pedagogy and

student writing than I usually would have. The traditional launching spots would have been student publications and the student paper, or formal course catalogs. Now I can suggest that students look at course bulletins, syllabi, administrative papers, reports and memos, presidents' papers, student affairs papers, photographs, and many other, similar sources that touch on the student experience and reflect changes in curricula, programs, and practices. As part of this new approach, I drew up an in-house resource guide for staff to use when assisting patrons and included it in staff training and support.

I realized that I also needed to take into account the inexperience many composition students may have with using primary sources, compared to history majors. So as part of instruction, I now integrate more explanation on how to use primary sources and how to find and retrieve the various kinds of information or artifacts necessary for their work. Generally, all students find archives and special collections difficult to use because primary sources are not neatly packaged sources of information; students need to be full researchers, identifying and evaluating materials for their validity and utility for a specific project. Because composition students and researchers are looking for materials that are difficult to find to begin with, I have realized we have to work with students to determine what their research goals are, how to locate relevant materials, and how to interpret and use the primary sources found. This challenge requires greater sensitivity to students' information-seeking needs, but it has made the archive a lively and living source and site of important and original work.

In sum, collaboration with the WAC/CWC staff offered an unusual opportunity to share critical expertise and build an important and usable collection that neither of us could have created alone. Also, by learning about the types of materials needed by composition and other educational researchers, I am much more ready to identify the significance of those materials when they appear and make sure they are given a place in the archive, instead of disposing of them as I would have done before this collaboration began. Finally, our staff has reoriented our instructional activities to take into account this new kind of collaborative work and the new scholars it has brought into the archive.

The WAC/Connors Writing Center Writing Archive has gotten off to a good start, and there have already been requests to use materials from the developing archive, but there is much to do. Future potential projects include continuing to develop the archives through collecting previous and current writing center and other writing program administrators' papers, creating Web-based resource guide for locating materials in the various archives collections and finding other ways to make the collection visible and accessible. (See final section.) Whether these can be fully realized will depend on whether the collaboration can continue with the present researchers or whether other interested compositionists will be able to continue the work.

Putting the Writing Archive Together: The Graduate Students' Perspectives

Kate Tirabassi and Amy Zenger

Many graduate students in composition work with archival material at one institution or another, but very few get the chance to help create an archive. When this collaboration was initiated, Amy was working as the assistant director of Writing across the Curriculum (WAC) and Kate was one of the assistant directors of the R. J. Connors Writing Center. We felt fortunate to have the opportunity to develop our understanding of archival work while learning more about our own graduate program in rhetoric and composition and about the more general history of writing at UNH and how it relates to national trends in theory and practice.

Our previous graduate course work and informal apprenticeships had provided us with a framework for valuing and interpreting the artifacts we would be collecting. As doctoral students, we had studied the history, theory, and practice of rhetoric and its more modern incarnation, composition studies; taken a course in the history, theory, and practice of writing–across-the curriculum and writing center programs; and taken a first-year composition pedagogy course. Robert Connors and Cinthia Gannett had been mentors for us when they were codirecting the WAC/CWC program, and they had shown us how to see current as well as historical documents and texts as worthy of preservation and study. John Brereton, composition historian and archivist, also had been an important teacher as he had graciously taken over classes and acted as an advisor for graduate students for a period after Dr. Connor's death.

At our initial lunch meeting, we collaboratively established the value of creating a writing archive and articulated a vision for how it might look. Afterwards, back at the writing center, the compositionists brainstormed every facet of "writing at UNH" that we could think of, filling a wall-sized dry erase board with possibilities. From this loose, but generative, exercise, we culled many lists: key people who had been associated with UNH writing programs; the variety of UNH writing programs over time and across disciplines; and important documents and artifacts (some of which were readily accessible in the center and others we would need to actively seek). (For the lists, see appendix A.)

These brainstormed lists became templates for the hands-on work we would be doing intensively for the next two months.

The current director, Cinthia Gannett, had brought together enough funding to hire each of us for one hundred hours in May and June of 2001. And the writing center was scheduled to close for the summer term, affording us the space we needed to begin collecting and sorting. One task we could tackle immediately was to compose a letter inviting present and former professors, doctoral students, and instructors in the various writing programs at UNH to submit materials to the writing archive. (See appendix B.) We collected contact information for the intended recipients of the letter, and Elizabeth sent it out on official library letterhead with her signature. After the invitation was sent, we turned our attention to gathering and sorting through existing materials in the Robert J. Connors Writing Center and WAC offices. At this point, realizing that we needed to know more about archival practices before we could decide what to collect and how to organize it for the writing archive, we turned to Elizabeth for advice and instruction.

One way that Elizabeth helped us to understand her work was to give us a tour of the recently renovated Dimond Library Archive. Not only did we see the public spaces, such as the reading room and the museum, but we also were given a tour through the modern climate-controlled storage facility, viewing materials in various stages of processing prior to being stored in the archive. We learned that staples and metal paper clips rust and mar documents and that documents must be kept in acid-free folders. We saw where the processed materials get stored and how they are labeled and organized. This tour of the archive gave us a clearer sense of how to work with the materials we were collecting and an understanding of the future destination for these materials.

Over the next few weeks, while we were going through materials in the center, we regularly consulted with Elizabeth on a variety of questions that arose. For example, when we had multiple copies of a single document, Elizabeth helped us understand that that the copy with handwritten annotations would be the most revealing and interesting from a historical point of view because it provides insights into how the document was used in real-life contexts. When we found documents that had no trace of authorship, date, or explicit purpose, we learned to write a brief explanation (in pencil) on the back to provide future researchers with information that would help them read the document. We discovered that "original order," that is, preserving the order in which documents are filed, is one of the key principles of archival work because the way documents are ordered can reveal a great deal about how the creators and users envisioned their own work. This meant that it would be important for us not to arbitrarily disturb the order of the files we decided to send to the archives.

The long library table that dominates the Connors Writing Center space soon became crowded with stacks of paper and boxes of files as we gathered workshop handouts, memos, minutes and agendas from staff meetings, records of meetings with faculty members, flyers advertising writing center services, and syllabi and proposals for writing-intensive courses. We also discovered several electronic documents saved on old computers and needed to decide whether to print a hard copy or to transfer them to a disc for electronic storage.

Our first conceptual challenge at this stage was to create useable categories out of the stacks of documents. Working with Cindy, John, and Elizabeth, we learned to think carefully about how to taxonomize the materials so they could be related to other kinds of relevant materials and made accessible to researchers, both local and national. We found that in the course of our everyday work, we had generated more documents and artifacts than we had ready categories for in the filing cabinets. The writing center and WAC programs were relatively new, and their record-keeping systems were effective for allowing the programs to function efficiently, but we needed to expand the categories. As we sifted through the piles, we started with the most apparent of categories, such as "Writing Center" (referring to regular operational activity on-site: student files, drafts, and writing consultations; tutor staffing and training; course work; correspondence, memos, policies, and workshops) and WAC (University Writing Committee minutes, reports, and initiative, writing-intensive course guidelines and proposals, faculty consultations, workshops, meetings, research, assessment projects, etc.). We moved to more complex divisions as we noticed that the simple binary divisions did not really work; the programs were integrated organically, and publicity fliers, or minutes from committee meetings, for example, could be important for both the writing center and the WAC program. We also found stashes of printed material from workshops delivered by invited guests or articles that had been important for us and needed to decide if and how those papers would be pertinent to this particular collection. If published materials had a specific reference to our program, were authored by someone in our program, or possibly were annotated by someone who worked in the program, we might consider it connected to work that happened in our center. Otherwise, it would not be included.

As we worked on each box, we saw how time-consuming the process of creating categories and sorting materials was, especially when the archive was in its beginning stages. We began to see the need to weave our archiving into the fabric of the daily work of the writing center and WAC program by systematizing how we created new documents, reconstructing our filing system to incorporate our new categories, and creating a schedule for routinely sending old documents to the archives. Newly conscious of future readers and researchers, we made sure that all new documents included the writers' names as well as dates, title, and other information that would explain how the document was used. Archiving made us more aware than ever that although written documents could be open to different interpretations, unwritten policies and procedures (even long-term practices) are quite vulnerable to any changes in senior staffing and could be undone instantly, thus significantly shifting the philosophical stance of the center and its culture without seeming to change the formal structure or operation. In response, Kate wrote a writing center manual to articulate policies and procedures that had been tacit. In addition, she consulted with Elizabeth to create a records management system that listed all the filing categories, specified the length of time that certain documents (such as client files) should remain in the center, and provided instructions about whether these documents should be sent to the archives or destroyed (as in the case of personnel files).

By the end of the summer, we had sorted more than fifty boxes of materials and sent them to the archives. Yet, many boxes were still unsorted. After the fall semester started, we no longer had space and time to devote to archive work because our regular administrative work in the WAC/CWC demanded most of our energy. Because we had not finished the initial processing of old materials, it was hard to find a satisfying rhythm or pace for archiving current materials. Over the year, we worked at the collection process sporadically, but it was not until each semester's work was completed and the writing center had quieted down, that we could tackle some of the projects left over from the summer.

As the academic year was coming to a close, our concern for preserving a record of the program was heightened by the uncertainties of the future for the Writing Center and WAC program. Because the program was likely to be reorganized and put under the "management" of professional staff or nondisciplinary faculty, the act of archiving became a political act, a means of remaining visible, of preserving the program's written legacy, of marshalling evidence of its strength and vitality. Despite the obstacles to continuing archival tasks, we were determined that before our graduate assistantships ended, we would complete a record of the program as it had existed while we were there and as it had been conceived originally by composition scholars—its founding directors, Robert Connors and Cinthia Gannett.

Although we are unsure about the CWC's future participation in the archival project, it is gratifying to know that the writing archive contains, among its many holdings, a rich archival record of the writing center and WAC program from its inception in 1993 to spring semester 2003, including several hundred samples of student writing from hundreds of courses across the curriculum.

Our own participation taught us how valuable it was to work with an archive librarian who is an expert not only in preserving artifacts and documents, but also in teaching others how to build collections and to do research in archives. The process of collecting documents was important for our graduate work because each document we worked with taught us a bit more about the program's development as it was built from the ground up over the past ten years and gave us a clearer sense of our own place as graduate assistant directors in that history. To encourage other graduate students to participate in building and using the archive, we presented a workshop for the graduate seminar on history of composition, and some students used archive materials for writing their seminar papers. Elizabeth also helped us present a workshop for all of the tutors in the Connors Writing Center in which we examined a range of historical documents together—old course catalogs, memos, photographs—and discussed ways of thinking about how they could be read in terms of broader ideas about education and the teaching of writing. We hope to foster a culture of archiving at UNH by inviting teachers to contribute their curricula, their own writing, and student writing to the writing archive, as well as thinking of ways that they could work with archive librarians to create writing projects based on research in the UNH archives.

"It Will Come in Handy." Putting the Archive to Work: A Historian-Composition Archivist's Perspective

John C. Brereton

"It's a poor sort of memory that only works backwards."*Lewis Carroll*

In this final section, John Brereton invites us all to look more broadly at the ways in which such collaborative archival projects between libraries and writing centers can be made to "come in handy."

With a widely representative team, including writing program faculty, graduate and/or undergraduate tutors, and the professional archivist, you can begin the process of assembling an archive of a writing program's presence on campus. The content of this archive will vary, of course, depending on what is available now and on how wide your purview. Will the archive of writing on campus include the school newspaper? the literary magazine? the yearbook? letters home?

class notes? Clearly, these are all key components of the rich writing environment that characterizes most campuses, even though they have not traditionally been thought of as part of the writing "program." You'll need to decide how much to include under the rubric of writing, but at the very least the literary magazine and the newspaper and yearbook will have links to the writing program, especially when they are not collected under the program's heading. And no matter what gets in, the archive will doubtless include many samples of the writing itself and, of course, many images of writing taking place in campus settings, some familiar, some unexpected.

You might find, as we did, that it is useful not just to consider collecting and assembling artifacts in themselves, but from the very outset also to consider the ways the archival materials will be used, presented, displayed. Just what are the most effective ways to make this project visible? Not surprisingly, the answer depends on how you imagine the task, both at present and for the future: Who are the potential audiences? What are the occasions? How many purposes do you have? For instance, the library's audiences and purposes might well be different from the writing program's, which is fine. Researchers and public relations people will have different needs that must be accommodated. We tried to incorporate as many audiences and purposes as we could, keeping the archive in a state of construction, a living assemblage that allows for many different types of presentation.

Assembling and then presenting the archive can accomplish many different objectives, depending on your own understanding of the archive's purpose, including:

1. Stake a claim on writing's importance over time. The archive you have assembled can demonstrate that the act of writing has been central to the life of the institution. That simple fact of centrality over time is crucial. There is a tradition of writing, of attention to the written word. (This is true even if the writing was not valued in ways we currently honor; showing the evolution of writing can be a salutary exercise.)

2. Demonstrate the historical presence of writing in many different disciplines as a *natural* occurrence. The photograph of UNH students in soil sample class with their notebooks is a marvelous example of how writing has permeated the curriculum, appearing in places where it may be least expected, but where upon reflection it seems perfectly appropriate. (See appendix 3.) What could be more obvious than any students, including agriculture students, being required to take notes? Yet, it is important for everyone to understand that one accurate and *totally characteristic* representation of agriculture students involves them in the act of writing. That is one thing that ag students are: *writers*.

3.   Represent the writing program to itself. Most participants in a program, be they the students themselves, the tutors, the graduate student TAs, the adjunct faculty, and even the so-called permanent faculty, do not see themselves as participating in an endeavor with a history, unfolding over time, connected both to the institution itself and to developments elsewhere in higher education. People, even within the program, need to see their program's goals and how it fits in locally and nationally. Sometimes they are surprised and pleased to learn that they a part of a coherent program with a distinctive philosophy and history.

4.   Represent the writing program to colleagues within the university. Most faculty and administrators, however well intentioned, are always in danger of seeing a writing program in old-fashioned ways, concerned solely with surface features and "grammar," rather than in up-to-date terms, concerned as well with higher-order concepts of writing as an intellectual discipline. An adequate representation of the program as it has grown over time can show the evolution from a low-level "clinic" to a more modern, comprehensive, rhetorically sophisticated operation. (This representation also is useful for program members themselves, of course.)

5.   Represent the program to its outside constituencies. Alumni, employers, neighbors, potential students, taxpayers, all the various "stakeholders," benefit from a coherent presentation of a program's participation in the life of the university. A brief, engaging presentation with a clear story line and attractive illustrations can do a lot to demonstrate the way a program thinks of itself. It is a story well worth telling, one people are happy to be associated with.

6.   Employ the archival process as a learning tool and the assembled archive as a teaching tool. As we quickly discovered while assembling the UNH archive, the process itself can be instructional for all participants. The writing program members learn from the archivist; those students who enjoy delving into archives get the greatest benefit because they are engaged in a research project close to home, with strong faculty interest. But the archivist learns as well, in this case, gaining a much richer understanding of how writing permeates a particular campus. Additionally, the archive can now be shown to other campus programs as an example of how to go about creating their own archive, using this one as a model.

7.   Present the archive, whether in a library display, a brochure, or a Web site, in ways that connect to a college or a program's objectives. A place such as UNH with a graduate degree in composition and rhetoric can send a brochure about the archive to prospective graduate students. An undergraduate college that prides itself on good written communication can display its historical commitment through an

archive. Recent research is making everyone see that the single acquisition many students point to in a rigorous liberal education is learning how to become an effective writer. This is the story an archive can tell, and it aligns even the most modest program with national goals and the latest scholarly research.

A rich, well-planned archive of writing, assembled in a collaborative manner with the guidance of a professional, is a living thing, constantly subject to growth and change. It will continue to expand and, if done well, will continue its role of representing a central part of the college's work. At the same time, it will continue to instruct both its creators and the general public.

Notes

1. Shirley K. Rose, "Preserving Our Histories of Institutional Change: Enabling Research in the Writing Program Archives," in *The Writing Program Administrator as Researcher: Inquiry in Action and Reflection*, ed. Shirley K. Rose and Irwin Weiser (Portsmouth, NH: Heinemann, 1999), 109.

2. Robert J. Connors, *Composition/Rhetoric* (Pittsburgh, Pa.: University of Pittsburgh Pr., 1997), 235.

3. Philip Simmons, "Unfinished Houses," in *Learning to Fall: The Blessings of an Imperfect Life* (New York: Bantam, 2004).

4. For a brief sampling of archive-based histories of composition, see John C. Brereton, *The Origins of Composition Studies in the American College 1875–1925. A Documentary History* (Pittsburgh, Pa.: University of Pittsburgh Pr., 1995; Connors, *Composition/Rhetoric*; Sharon Crowley, *Composition in the University: Historical and Polemical Essays* (Pittsburgh, Pa.: University of Pittsburgh Pr., 1998; Albert R. Kitzahaber, *Rhetoric in American Colleges: 1850–1900* (Dallas: Southern Methodist University Pr., 1990).

5. Brereton, "Archivist with an Attitude: Rethinking Our Archive: A Beginning," *College English* 61, no. 5 (May 1999): 574.

6. Ibid., 574–75.

7. Rose, "Preserving Our Histories of Institutional Change," 107.

8. Ibid., 108.

9. Ibid.

10. Ibid., 108–9.

11. This developing area of work can be seen in essays such as Beth Boquet, "'Our Little Secret': A History of Writing Centers, Pre– to post–Open Admissions," *College Composition and Communication* 50, no. 3 (Feb. 1999): 363–82; Peter Carino, "Early Writing Centers: Toward a History," *Writing Center Journal* 15, no. 2 (spring 1995): 103–15; Neal Lerner, "Writing Laboratories Circa 1953," *Writing Lab Newsletter* 27, no. 6 (Feb. 2003): 1–5. For a new article on how to construct an archive, see Karen Bishop, "On the Road to (Documentary) Reality: Capturing the Intellectual and Political Process of Writing Program Administration," in *The Writing Program Administrator as Theorist: Making Knowledge Work*, ed. Shirley

K. Rose and Irwin Weiser (Portsmouth, NH: Heinemann–Boynton/Cook Publishers, 2002), 42–53.

12. Rose, "Preserving Our Histories of Institutional Change," 109.

13. William J. Maher, *The Management of College and University Archives* (Metuchen, N.J.: Scarecrow, 1992), 64–65; Helen Samuels, *Varsity Letter: Documenting Modern Colleges and Universities* (Metuchen, N.J.: Scarecrow, 1992), 68–69.

Appendix 1
ARCHIVES BRAINSTORMING LIST

Things we have ready access to in the Writing Center WAC Web site
- OWL
- Student files with copies of papers and consultant comments. 2001–2002 WAC Speaker Series materials
- Cindy's papers
- Annual reports/statistics
- Minutes of University Writing Committee meetings Planning documents (development of WAC/WC)
- Systems Grant
- Proposal for "new" Writing Center Cindy's 910 teaching materials
- ENG 914 Special Studies in WAC ENG 728 Consultant Training course Fitchburg
- Publicity Ephemera
- Library
- WI files with proposals, correspondence, and syllabi
- Kudos
- Photos/films and other memorabilia Roster of peer consultants
- Consultant files
- Evaluation and Assessment records Forms, written policies
- Staff meeting agendas and handouts Preparing Future Faculty College teaching course
- Endowment
- Writing Fellows records, training, correspondence
- High School outreach documentation

Archival materials from other Writing Program projects Personal papers of faculty
- School of Education
- English Literature, Composition, Linguistics. Part-time instructors
- Grad Students theses, dissertations Student papers from writing courses English 401 outside review materials Textbook adoptions
- Articles and editorials in student newspapers
- UNH Conference in Composition Nonfiction program
- Personnel (CVs, Dept files, official hiring documents)
- NH Summer Writing Program Writers Academy
- Oral Histories
- Student literary magazines
- Entrance Exams
- Catalogs
- General Education materials
- ENG 401/501 newsletters and handbooks Correspondence
- Video of Writing Center opening Video of Bob Connors memorial

Appendix 2

July 8, 2002

Dear   ,

Because you have been a significant member of the writing community at the University of New Hampshire, we would like to invite you to participate in the newly created UNH Writing Archives Project.

In consultation with John Brereton, and in collaboration with Cinthia Gannett and doctoral students in Rhetoric and Composition, the UNH Archives is documenting the history of writing and writing instruction at our institution. With generous support from the Robert J. Connors Memorial Fund and the UNIT Center for the Humanities, we are establishing this archive to preserve the unique history of writing practice and theory at UNIT, and to make this work available to researchers, administrators, faculty, and students inside and outside the university. We believe that developing this archive also extends and strengthens the everyday work of writing program administration.

We have begun by assembling documents related to Writing Across the Curriculum and the Writing Center, including the original legislation establishing WAC, annual reports to the faculty senate, minutes from University Writing Committee meetings, photos and videos representing our work, Writing-Intensive course syllabi, student writing (with or without consultant or instructor comments), and writing consultant and writing fellow training materials.

We hope the collection will eventually encompass all other writing programs and extend the record back to the late 1800's. We would be very interested in seeing any of the materials you may have, such as manuscripts from articles, books or dissertations; Summer Writing Program materials; conference presentations; syllabi from courses you taught at UNIT; papers written by students in your courses at UNH (or by you if you were a student at UNH); photographs and videos; personal memoirs or correspondence referring to writing at UNH; forms and handouts and handbooks; interviews; and newsletters or other ephemera.

Anything you can contribute to this project will be greatly appreciated. If you can provide us with original documents, that would be wonderful. If not, copies would be welcome. The University Archives can pick up materials from those who live in the area and will make arrangements for delivery for those who live elsewhere. Thank you for any materials you can provide.

Sincerely,
Elizabeth Slomba, University Archivist
Cinthia Gannett, Director, Writing Across the Curriculum John Brereton, Brandeis University
Kate Tirabassi
Amy Zenger

Appendix 3

"Soils Class" ca. 1900,
NHC Photo Collection, University Photograph Collection
University of New Hampshire Archives

Chapter eight

The Wesley College Library and Writing Center: A Case Study in Collaboration

Michele R. Giglio and Constance F. Strickland

When Connie Strickland assumed directorship of the Wesley College Writing Center, it had already been a self-contained unit within the library for five years. Peaceful coexistence rather than cooperation was the governing philosophy of the existing library–writing center arrangement. Strickland approached Michele Giglio, Wesley's systems librarian, for assistance with the technological aspects of running the center. Giglio and Strickland had a previously established working relationship as Giglio provided bibliographic instruction (BI) for Strickland's English classes. The pair seized on the opportunity to work together to promote information literacy and writing skills to a campuswide audience.

A significant element of the Giglio–Strickland collaboration is the voluntary nature of the partnership. Inherited, rather than planned, the collaboration was a joint venture, building on the strengths of each, to promote use of the library and the writing center within the campus community. By combining efforts, they sought to elevate the visibility and use of both service centers. Both Giglio and Strickland employ a personal approach to service that communicates a genuine interest in students, faculty, and staff. This type of rapport in a small campus environment is essential to the success of their respective and joint programs.

At the heart of the collaboration is a shared commitment to student learning. Translating the philosophy from classroom (English and BI) to the global service area (writing center and library) is the overarching principle that governs their partnership. The missions of the writing center and the library are quite similar. Wesley's tutors are trained as peer teachers, not editors. Following Jeff Brooks' minimalist tutoring philosophy, the center is not a fix-it shop where papers are dropped off for editing.[1] Instead, the tutee must take ownership of his or her own writing. Tutors use an inquiry–guidance method to illustrate problem areas rather than aggressively make changes to text. The goal is not to produce "better papers" but, rather, to develop better writers through the continuous improvement of writing skills.

This process mirrors the classic library reference-interview technique of inquiry to establish understanding. Rather than simply fetch and carry, Wesley's librarians teach various methods to access resources. Information literacy is embedded into all of the BI classes, building on previous student interactions to develop a hierarchical set of skills. The goal is to encourage students to engage in the learning process, enabling them to gain skills and confidence.

The Campus Environment

Located in Dover, Delaware, Wesley College was founded in 1873 as a college preparatory school in covenant with the United Methodist Church. The college has grown to offer thirty bachelor's degrees and four master's degrees. It provides traditional full-time day programs for approximately 1,300 students, 60 percent residential. In addition, evening programs are offered at nearby Dover Air Force Base and the Center for Adult Studies (CAS), a satellite campus in New Castle, Delaware.[2] The relatively small on-campus student population affords service providers, such as the library and the writing center, the opportunity to know students on a first-name basis and develop lasting relationships. In this intimate climate, student perception of the service agency is inexorably linked with their perception of the provider. The library and the writing center attempt to establish equilibrium between the personalized service that students expect and institutional standards for student learning.

The Writing Center

The diverse philosophies of college administrations in the seventeen-year history of the writing center caused fluctuations in funding levels and, at times, interruptions in the existence of the center. The writing center had an image problem. Students as well as faculty and administrators viewed the center as simply a supervised word-processing lab. It took years of lobbying and consistent efforts of the English Department to convey that although the technology assisted in the effort, the center was primarily a writing-skills learning center. Beyond image, the center faced many challenges. Inconsistent funding for the director's position and changes in financial aid requirements limited money for tutoring positions. Problems with technical support, lack of compatibility with computers in other campus labs, and old software plagued the center. When one of the former directors was promoted to humanities chair, a reliable funding source, structure and mission were developed that finally secured the center's fate.

With the Internet revolution, students began using campus computers not only for writing papers, but also for Web surfing and checking e-mail. Limited word-processing and Web-accessible computers in the library were inadequate to meet student demand. Incorporating the library and the writing center into one space seemed a logical fit. With its twenty additional computers, the writing center was a welcomed addition. The director of the writing center provided writing tutors, and the library director updated software and maintained computers to combat vandalism.[3]

Today, the writing center director is responsible for recruiting, training, and scheduling peer tutors. In addition, advertising, maintaining equipment, and keeping current on contemporary writing center philosophy are key to the position. The director serves as a fulcrum, providing two-way communication among the disparate academic communities on campus. The writing center emphasizes the importance of written expression, serving as a resource for both students and faculty.

The Library

In addition to the writing center, the library is home to many other campus agencies. Within its 30,000 square feet are located the offices of academic support services, college counseling, the Campus Community School (CCS) Library (grades 1–12), the college computer center, a media arts lab, as well as several faculty and staff offices. Two thirty-seat classrooms provide overflow meeting space during peak hours and serve as group-study areas evenings and weekends. In a small college environment, this type of facility sharing is essential to maximize all available resources.

As one of the first private college libraries to belong to a public library consortium, the library shares a common catalog, KentNET, and a patron database with the surrounding Kent County, Delaware, libraries. In addition, it holds membership in regional (TCLC) and international (OCLC) library cooperatives. The library's collection of approximately 100,000 volumes, 250 current print periodicals, and numerous electronic databases support the academic programs of the college and its numerous affiliated groups.

With a staff of three full-time professionals and twelve part-time paraprofessionals, the library is open eighty-five hours a week during the academic year and forty-eight hours a week during summers and holidays. The primary library clientele consists of the students, faculty, and staff of Wesley College. Circulation and reference assistance is extended to the CCS student population and all local public library cardholders. There are twenty-four reference computers dedicated for student use and three OPAC stations for public use. The writing center accommodates overflow demand for research, typing, and e-mail during the library's regular hours. Each successive addition or change to the facility configuration has increased gate counts and the use of library services: circulation, electronic databases, print journals, and reference.

The collaborative model is especially evident in the library's approach to bibliographic instruction. Individual, small group, or class instruction is available, depending on student needs and the resources available. "Connection development—going to where the customers are rather than waiting for them to come to the library—has been expected and required of the instruction librarian to generate faculty interest in including information concepts in their courses."[4] In the library, writing center lab, or classroom, the librarians work with faculty, tailoring presentations for each assignment requested.

Writing Center Role in Information Literacy Instruction

Future library renovation plans include space for a bibliographic instruction classroom. In the interim, Strickland offers the writing center as a substitute. Librarians may schedule the lab for library instruction in all disciplines. Although other departments have secured grant funds to renovate computer labs, these spaces are restricted to use by specific constituencies. What sets the writing center apart is the commitment to institutional and student objectives external to any one department's function.

Strickland was already an advocate for the role of libraries and librarians in student learning. "A writing center that has made information literacy its goal can forge strong links with the library and with librarians, so that all tutors become comfortable using available technology and other resources that their students might need to conduct research."[5] Giglio provides training for the writing center tutors in research methods that students are likely to need. Cross-training the tutors increases their competencies and establishes a firm link between the writing center and the library. Tutors refer students directly to librarians for research needs beyond their scope.

With technological restrictions to prevent vandalism, students are free to use computers during all of the library's hours. Ten peer tutors provide forty-eight hours of coverage in the writing center each week. Extending availability of the lab to the general student population during non-tutor-staffed hours provides additional computers in a separate "quiet" environment. The writing center has become synonymous with research instruction, as well as writing instruction.

Cooperation or Collaboration

The literature relating to collaboration in libraries suggests that in order for true collaboration to occur, there must be a formal framework of clearly delineated roles, tasks, expectations, and outcomes.[6] Anything short of this model is deemed merely networking or cooperation.

Hermeneutics aside, this commonly quoted definition differs from the experience at Wesley College where there is both inclusiveness and exclusivity to collaboration relative to the other terms. The authors posit that the "defining moment" when true collaboration occurs is independent of assigned roles or anticipated outcomes. Collaboration is best defined by the actions, or more specifically, the motivation behind the actions of the participants. It is letting go of territoriality and self-interest to share the load and make sacrifices, when necessary, for the common good.

This is not to say that all is perfect. Frequently, they disagree or are faced with challenges that have no immediately discernable answer. The writing center lab is less than a hundred feet from the reference area; therefore, changes to one necessarily impact the other. For example, changes in hours or staffing of the writing center have an impact on the library as students look to the library staff to fill the void when tutors are unavailable.

Their established relationship was crucial during the installation of a pay-to-print system. Printers were previously available in both the writing center and reference areas of the library with unlimited free printing. Giglio and Strickland discussed the possible impacts a deterrent mechanism would have in the "student-centered" atmosphere they worked so hard to create. Input from several other campus agencies was incorporated during the investigation and implementation phases of the project.

By working together from the start, the library and the writing center presented a unified front, confident that the system implemented was the least restrictive to those requiring printing, while serving as an effective deterrent to excessive waste of paper and toner. Administrative support, even in the face of student and faculty complaints, was key to the long-term success of the system.

Many faculty expressed concern that the fee-based system would have a negative impact on the writing center. The prevailing wisdom asserted that a pay-to-print system would fundamentally alter students' willingness to pay for second and third drafts or print research articles. The statistics show that use of the writing center was quadruple that of previous semesters. (See appendix A.) Likewise in the library, use of electronic and circulating resources was constant, but paper consumption decreased by more than 70 percent.

Setting aside politics to achieve mutual trust in an academic environment is not easy. In the service setting, they are frequently challenged to balance the interest of the students with competing interests of the institution. Strickland and Giglio believe this works best through open communication. They frequently meet to discuss changes or new ideas. Central to the communication is discussion of "unforeseen impacts" on the other's service area. The collaboration is clearly evident to those outside their sphere of operations as Giglio and Strickland get mail requesting their services as a "unit." They participate in joint projects such as new student orientations, freshman seminars, and research methods course preparation.

Shared Vision

Giglio and Strickland have found that with open communication come improved relations, opportunities, and service to the college community. They constantly share ideas and brainstorm to improve current conditions. An unresolved issue is the use of shared space. Although the writing center needs more space outside the lab, this would encroach on the space already occupied by study hall groups, academic tutors, and catalogers who use the adjacent stack space for books-in-process. They hope to improve the functionality and aesthetic of the area by creating a more efficient space design to accommodate all the groups.

Other plans for the writing center include activities, such as cooperative workshops and faculty training. As faculty use resources, they are more likely to encourage their students to use them. Faculty have requested workshops on citation formats, scientific writing, electronic databases, and plagiarism prevention. The director, faculty, librarians, and peer tutors have volunteered to lead these sessions.

Both Giglio and Strickland stay informed in their respective fields to ensure that Wesley students receive competitive services. With expanded course offerings at satellite and branch campuses, service agencies must respond to new demands. Students rightly expect institutional services regardless of location. Addressing these new service paradigms is a priority that must also take into consideration existing staff and space constraints.

Negative Aspects of the Arrangement

Although there are many advantages to the library–writing center collaboration, it would not be realistic to address this topic without acknowledging the constraints and challenges imposed by collaborating. From the librarians' perspective, the writing center and myriad other agencies take up valuable space. The library has thousands of books in the catalog–processing area, and each summer shifts the entire collection to live within the constrained space limit. Classrooms and offices also occupy space needed for the library. Librarians have found that as faculty schedule time in the writing center, there is some confusion as to what constitutes the center proper. On numerous occasions, faculty have simply coopted the entire reference space as a classroom. Another difficulty for the library is that decision making becomes a group effort. All of the service agencies in the library expect to be consulted, advised, or simply informed before implementing changes. There is a ripple effect to nearly all of the decisions that in a self-contained environment would not be so cumbersome.

The writing center lacks space to grow. To do so would mean encroaching on space shared with academic support services and the library. The center inhabits an older, unrenovated area of the library and lacks space for private consultation areas. At present, when classes use the center during posted tutoring hours, the tutors must conduct the session in the adjacent study hall area of academic support services. The center itself is not oriented as a classroom; old cabling prevents a more presentation-friendly configuration. In addition, the director's office is located on the floor above the writing center, making direct supervision of the center cumbersome.

Positive Aspects of the Arrangement

Even in light of the various stakeholder challenges, the writing center–library collocation has been overwhelmingly positive. Librarians have a much-needed BI classroom to accommodate workshops and classes with hands-on instruction. Writing center tutors receive reference training from librarians that extends the reach of the library. Tutors have taken on the task of teaching citation styles in one-on-one and classroom presentations, allowing librarians to refer students to them as local experts. The library has benefited from increased use from its resident agencies and their constituent groups.

The writing center benefits from the increased "customer" base already in the library to work on papers. In proximity to resources and technology, tutors provide a safety net for students who may otherwise be reluctant to "bother" a librarian or professor with questions. Tutors provide support to students in the writing process and frequently assist with word processing and online research. Tutors encourage use of the library and librarians, walking students to the reference desk for personal introductions, if necessary.

The Center for Campus Computing has benefited from the arrangement as the system's librarian serves as a technical contact for both centers. Unified lab profiles reduce work for the computer technicians and provide students with a unified view throughout the library, regardless of whether the student is in the reference area or the writing center. Although the focus of this paper centers primarily on the writing center–library collaboration, it is not an exclusive relationship and frequently requires assistance and technology support of the computer center. The nonconfrontational, nonterritorial approach they employ when working together is equally successful when working with other campus offices.

Faculty benefit from the writing center within the library as it provides access to a technology classroom. Librarians are available to assist with classes and/or orientations and instruction classes in the center. The center serves to consistently reinforce the elements of writing that students are exposed to in freshman English classes. Tutors encourage students to actively revise and proofread with a "trained set of eyes," looking for specific content, grammar, and punctuation errors.

Summary

Clearly, the advantages outweigh disadvantages as the library and the writing center provide an ever-expanding range of reciprocal services under one roof. Students benefit from the unified approach and cross-referential services. In the library, they are assisted in dissecting assignments, receiving reference assistance, and using computers to type papers. In the writing center, students receive editing and citation assistance and, after several revisions, walk out with a well-researched and executed product.

Recognizing the voluntary nature of the collaboration is essential to understanding its success. Although at times inconvenient, the overall effect is uniformly positive for all parties. In a small campus environment, it is especially crucial as no one person can fill all roles. Giglio and Strickland recognize that if the partnership were dissolved, the library and the writing center could return to the prior status as self-contained units. They equate the collaboration as a necessary and pivotal part of their job descriptions.

What creates successful collaboration? Michele Giglio and Connie Strickland have learned that good communication and a realistic acceptance of different styles, along with selfless consideration, sincere compassion, and excellent listening skills, are all necessary. Developing this case study has enhanced awareness of their respective roles and opened additional dialog, thus strengthening their collaboration. Working closely has highlighted the other's expertise and realistic expectations of the other's philosophy and job description. They are committed to continue to identify areas where they can collaborate in the future.

Notes

1. Jeff Brooks, "Minimalist Tutoring: Making the Student Do All the Work," in *The St. Martin's Sourcebook for Writing Tutors*, ed. Christina Murphy and Steve Sherwood (Boston: Bedford/St. Martin's, 1995), 83–87.
2. Richard France, interview by author, Dover, Delaware, 29 January 2004.
3. Robert Dugan, e-mail to author, 16 October 2003.
4. Carla Stoffle, "The Upside of Downsizing: Using the Economic Crisis to

Restructure and Revitalize Academic Libraries," in *The Upside of Downsizing: Using Library Instruction to Cope*, ed. Cheryl LaGuardia, Stella Bentley, and Janet Martorana (New York: Neal-Schuman, 1995), 10.

5. Irene L. Clark, "Information Literacy and the Writing Center," in *The Allyn and Bacon Guide to Writing Center Theory and Practice*, ed. Robert W. Barnett and Jacob S. Blumner (Boston: Allyn and Bacon, 2001), 568.

6. Doug Cook, "Creating Connections: A Review of the Literature," in *The Collaborative Imperative: Librarians and Faculty Working Together in the Information Universe*, ed. Dick Raspa and Dane Ward (Chicago: ACRL/ALA, 2000), 19–37.

Appendix A
Wesley College Writing Center Statistics

	Fall 2001	Spring 2002	Fall 2002	Spring 2003	Fall 2003
Tutoring Weeks	12 Weeks	12 Weeks	13 Weeks	13 Weeks	13 Weeks
Tutors	6	11 / 8	7	10	8
Sessions	100	105	232	183	403
Students tutored	62	56	81	78	182
Courses	23	15	22	20	28
Departments/ programs	13	10	12	11	10
Attendance at APA workshops	N/A	19	14	33	8

Better-connected Student Learning: Research and Writing Project Clinics at Bowling Green State University

Colleen Boff and Barbara Toth

We live in a society where students have access to cell phones, the Internet, instant messenger, fast food, and mega-malls. Students enter higher education with expectations of convenience and instant gratification despite the reality that universities do not always function that way. They also are dealing with a significant life transition of being on their own for the first time. When they are trying to make their way through their first college-level research essay and need help, are they going to be ambitious enough to seek out research assistance from a librarian and writing assistance from the writing center consultant if the two services are in separate locations? The reality is that sometimes finding the laundry facilities is a more pressing concern.

To respond to this disconnect, librarians and writing consultants at Bowling Green State University developed a collaborative pilot project, offering combination Research and Writing Project Clinics (RWPCs) to first-year students. Currently, these appointments are offered for a four-week period during the peak research and writing time of the semester. RWPCs are provided to students enrolled in the General Studies Writing (GSW) program, a two-semester composition sequence most students take in their first year. Along with wanting to provide students with a more convenient service, the combined clinics came to fruition because librarians and writing consultants felt strongly about treating research and writing as a unit, acknowledging the integral relationship

Our project is based on the assumption that the research and writing processes are better treated as consciously related, particularly when connected student learning is at stake. Our project also is based on the assumption that research and writing are complementary parts of a recursive process of inquiry. We also believe that deliberate collaboration and sharing of knowledge and know-how between our respective units more effectively fosters student learning and better prepares students for negotiating the complex worlds of information and communication through writing.

Several presentations at the 2003 International Writing Center Association Conference focused on the relationship between libraries and writing centers, one describing the relationship as "long-lost cousins."[1] Other scholarship has addressed the importance of collaboration among librarians and faculty,[2] but research focusing on the specific relationship between libraries and writing centers is lacking.

Fortunately, both our library and writing center had scaffolding already in place on which we could base our pilot. In the library, for example, Research Project Clinics (RPCs), which provide students with hour-long, individualized research sessions in content areas, were already well established. In the writing center, hour-long, one-to-one writing consultation sessions, which serve student writers in basic composition courses as well as across the curriculum also were part of business as usual. Very important to the success of our project, we also had the benefit of a cooperative spirit between librarians and writing consultants. Despite different reporting lines, staff at both units supported each other's student-centered goals. Perhaps the flame of cooperation was fanned because we seemed to understand that in an academic environment, research means writing and writing means research. This understanding necessitates cooperation.

Campus Climate

Bowling Green State University (BGSU) is located in the city of Bowling Green, in the northwestern part of Ohio. Of the 20,200 students enrolled at BGSU, 17,300 are undergraduate students and 2,900 are master's or doctoral students. The library and the writing center are open to serve these students, as well as faculty, staff, and members of the greater Bowling Green community.

Jerome Library and the writing center are approximately a five-minute walk from each other. Aside from our pilot RWPCs, the only other student-centered support service available in the library is a full-service computer lab maintained by the campus technology unit. Space in the library is tight, and opportunities for "outside" student services to occupy space in the library, though valued, are rarely feasible. Currently, the writing center is located on the third floor of Moseley Hall, one of the three oldest buildings on campus. Although Moseley Hall *per se* is a prominent building, its third floor is not easily handicap accessible or furnished with the up-to-date technologies.

Until recently, the library resided in Academic Affairs. In addition to Academic Affairs and Student Affairs, our university now includes a third unit in its organizational structure. As a result of this reorganization, the library is now administrative siblings with Continuing Education, Information Technology Services, Human Resources, and the Office of Equity, Diversity and Immigration Services. The writing center is embedded in a unit called Academic Enhancement, housing several other subunits, including the Math Lab, the Studies Skills Lab, and Premajor Advising. The head of the writing center reports to the director of Academic Enhancement, who in turn, reports to the vice provost of Academic Affairs. When compared to other institutions, these reporting lines for both of our areas are not ideal. Libraries typically reside in Academic Affairs and writing centers are more effectively aligned with the composition program, the WAC program, or operate as a stand-alone entity.[3] Because of the peculiar placement of the library and the writing center on our campus, both are in the position of having to prove that our teaching and individualized instruction contribute to student learning. Despite physical or administrative hurdles, RWPCs are an attempt to explore the merits of having research and writing instruction more logically structured.

Misconceptions about the work that we do also have strengthened our will to create RWPCs. Consider how often libraries and writing centers are narrowly viewed as "support service." Assumptions that librarians spend their days shelving books and that writing consultants fix grammar, particularly commas, still dangerously and destructively abound. Perhaps, our outsiderness brought us more easily together.

A relationship between the library and the writing center has existed for several years. In particular, the relationship between the director and the first-year experience (FYE) librarian has been solid. Librarians often refer students to the writing center for assistance, particularly when the students' questions veer more in the "writerly" direction. Writing consultants often refer students to the library, particularly when the students' questions call for more research expertise and warrant a library setting. Although writing consultants are very familiar with the curriculum of writing courses, they are not trained librarians. Unfortunately, based on our referrals, students often find themselves arranging several appointments, walking back and forth between the library and the writing center just to complete one writing project.

Project Profile

Gradually, both units began to realize that starting a combined service in one physical location made sense. The library and writing center's model and philosophy of collaboration are similar. Both models focus on helping students help themselves within hour-long increments. Both try to put the students in charge of the sessions. Both try to start with what students know and help them make connections. Literally and metaphorically, both put researching and writing tools in the students' hands. These common denominators make understanding and cooperation between respective parties easier.

We decided to build the RWPC pilot on the already existing RPCs. Although not unique to academic libraries, our RPC program is one of the more successful of its type.[4] It is strongly rooted in the university community and is valued by students who have participated. Although RPCs are available to all undergraduate students, we decided to offer RWPCs only to students enrolled in our GSW composition courses that are required of all students and typically taken by first-year students. Students are required to write at least two, eight-page researched essays. We targeted this program for two reasons: there are not enough librarians to do in-person class instruction for the large number of sections, and the librarians felt that the writing consultants could handle most of the research needs of students at this level.

One of the learning outcomes for RWPCs is for students to become aware of the out-of-class instructional support, resources, and teachers in order to feel less intimidated about college-level research and writing. The level of research in the GSW program often focuses on current events and cross-curricular topics. It is not our intention with RWPCs to expose students to everything there is to know about library research and writing within the disciplines. The focus of the combined consultations is nondirective and more about the process than the product. These consultations are designed to help students get started and/or to focus on a particular aspect of the research and writing process.

For our pilot, writing consultants, rather than librarians, have been selected to interact with the students. The writing consultants are typically graduate students, who have taught GSW. Being familiar with the GSW curriculum, they understood the type and level of required research. They also were familiar with how challenged these students can be as they negotiate both research and writing processes and then attempt to synthesize them into their texts. We chose this location because it provided the consultants with convenient access to librarian expertise. By offering our sessions at the library, RWPCs can be scheduled beyond the currently scheduled hours of the writing center. RWPC consultants have immediate access to the library resources and are able to consult with the librarian at the reference desk during the RWPC appointment, if needed. Additionally, writing consultants felt their involvement with RWPCs at the library would help increase the visibility of the writing center.

At the time of this writing, RWPCs have been under way for two semesters. We began our pilot spring semester 2003 with five RWPC consultants. We selected peak times of the week during the RPC season when students seemed to be desperate for appointments, Sunday and Monday evenings. We scheduled one RWPC consultant on Sunday night for three hour-long appointments from 5:00 p.m. to 8:00 p.m. and another from 6:00 p.m. to 9:00 p.m. One consultant was available on Monday nights from 6:00 p.m. to 9:00 p.m. In total, twenty RWPCs took place out of twenty-eight available appointments.

A week prior to RPC/RWPC season, an e-mail message is sent to all GSW instructors and fliers are distributed in the instructor departmental mailboxes as well. The master schedule of available appointments is available at the library reference/information desk a week prior to the RPC/RWPC intensive season. When students ask for an appointment, they are asked to provide the following pieces of information: name, phone number, course number, type of assignment (research paper, presentation, speech, etc.), research topic, and type of materials needed (books, articles, Web sites, etc.). Professional librarians and student assistants schedule appointments. To ensure that students are funneled into the appropriate type of consultation (i.e., RPCs or RWPCs), students are asked the following questions: (1) What class is this appointment for? and (2) Do you need assistance with the writing process as well?

The day before scheduled appointments, the coordinating librarian reviews and e-mails the appointment topics to the RWPC consultants. If the topic looks problematic, the coordinating librarian calls the consultant to talk about ways to approach the research. This way, the RWPC consultant has time to do some strategizing and searching beforehand.

Project Evaluation

Each student and each RWPC consultant was asked to fill out an evaluation of the service. The students could do so anonymously. When asked if the session provided the kind of assistance expected, fifteen responded, "Yes, just what I wanted," four responded, "Yes, with limitations," one person responded, "Only partly," and one person responded, "No." In matching up the consultant responses to the six students whose expectations were not met, additional insight is provided.

Of the four students whose expectations were mostly met, but with limitations, one of the students claimed, "We weren't able to find specific articles or sources relevant to my topic." But when asked about her overall satisfaction with the consultation, she said, "I found out how to search better for my material, and I found out how to limit my search." Another student in this category had a similar response to the latter question: "The information seemed relevant and the consultant seemed knowledgeable." The complaint of another student in this category was that she wanted "a little bit more help with actually helping me write down some of it."

Two students, one whose expectations were mostly met, but with limitations, and one whose expectations were "only partially" realized, were enrolled in a business course and signed up for this service by mistake. From a librarian's perspective, the RWPC consultants did remarkably well in getting as far as they did with these students. Both were still generally pleased, and one of the students had this to say when prompted for his overall satisfaction with the consultation: "It helped me get the process going for [finding] information and [I] got good help working with databases."

Of the many positive comments we received about the service, here are a few that stand out:

- "She gave me more resources to work with and new ideas to add to my paper."
- "She was very helpful finding articles and talking to me about my research topic."
- "I was unsure of how and where to start my research and was having difficulty with my thesis. She helped me with both."
- "I was able to see what was wrong with my paper and what I needed to fix. I also found better articles that applied to my argument."

Additionally, the writing center director received the following praise from a student in an e-mail message: "I think the research and writing help is one of the best things I have come across so far in college. It helped me so much. I had been stressing out about my paper a lot, and both of my sessions really calmed me down and showed me that writing a research paper isn't as difficult as I thought."

We received interesting responses from an open-ended question about how to improve RWPCs. Eight students suggested we advertise this service better, two suggested that we have more appointments available, and four students said that the service was fine as is.

Cross Training and Education

Training for RWPC consultants includes the mission and scope of RWPCs, instruction about select resources and key research strategies, and details of setting up materials to use during the consultation. Our research environment is enhanced by our affiliation with a statewide cooperative, OhioLINK. Students have access to collections from more than ninety libraries as well as approximately 150 different research databases. Leading a student to one or two research databases in this entry-level course is appropriate. We try not to overwhelm them.

The training session takes approximately one hour. This may seem short, but most of the RWPC consultants have been through a library orientation session earlier in the term as part of a writing center professional development meeting for staff or have experience in teaching the composition curriculum.

The focus of RWPC consultant training is on three specific research databases. They are taught keyword searching, Boolean operators, and truncation, along with the mechanics of the databases, such as retrieving full-text articles or determining availability of articles in the library's periodical collection. All of them are familiar with the library's floor plan. A resource manual for RWPC consultants has been assembled and includes documentation on these research concepts.

The other aspect of RWPC consultant training involves familiarizing RWPC consultants with the procedures for setting up the wireless laptops. When the pilot began, the library did not have a word-processing package on the computer terminals in the main research area, which was problematic. As a solution, the RWPC consultants used two fully equipped laptops from the library instruction office. The library has since added word processing to the computer terminals in the research area. RWPC consultants do not have a designated workstation but usually elect to sit at a computer terminal close to the reference/information desk in case they have questions.

Librarian Response

The library administration is very pleased that the librarians have partnered with the writing center to provide this student convenience. With increasing budgetary woes, this type of cross-germination and creative approach to student-centeredness, despite limited resources, is much valued.

This collaboration and pilot project occurred because of the strong ties between the library, the GSW program, and the writing center. There is a high level of respect among the three areas, along with a trust that boundaries will be honored. Although the librarians are more than willing to explore the possibilities with this pilot, we have been very clear from the beginning that the pilot in its current form would not evolve beyond the GSW program. The research skills needed for GSW students is typically predictable and, for the most part, contained. Beyond this level, the research skills are more complex and fall within the expertise of a professional librarian.

The staff at the reference desk, including both student employees and degreed librarians, expressed frustration with the sign-up procedures. In some respects, having the two services run simultaneously is confusing.

From the perspective of the librarian whose responsibility it was to train the consultants, the investment of time it took to organize everything, train everyone, and communicate details about procedures is questionable in relation to the number of students who have taken advantage of the program. Like many new programs, it may just take a while to really catch on.

Writing Consultant Response

The small number of students using the service is balanced by the importance of each individual student and the future vision of creating a research and writing center across curricula. From the director's point of view, the opportunity to work with librarians and be educated by them in order to be better prepared to help student learning was invaluable. Writing consultants educated in helping students with global concerns (audience awareness, organization, development, etc.) now better versed and more knowledgeable about search engines, search techniques, and information grammar equaled a powerfully connected session for student writer/researchers. The librarians' willingness to let writing consultants into their physical and administrative house and to share knowledge and know-how was the sine qua non of the venture. This willingness is indicative of the genuine and deep level of student-centeredness among BGSU librarians.

Writing consultants who served as the RWPC consultants have indicated that they have been "enthused about more connected learning for students before, during, and after the RWPC experience." One commented on being more "strategic in offering research guidance during the RWPC compared to a regular writing consultation session," something she said she "had unconsciously shied away from before." Another commented on the importance of "modeling good practice for the student writer/researchers by walking with the student to the librarian during a session when [they] both were stumped about how to proceed with researching."

Another consultant said she was more comfortable entering the world of ideas during an RWPC rather than focusing on whether the student had remembered three arguments, counterarguments, to use transitions, etc. Finally, another commented that, "RWPCs bring together two entities that should be treated as a piece instead of being bifurcated. Sometimes the place where writing leaves off and research begins—and vice versa—is an artificially constructed point. The RWPCs are making us think more about this." Because of the RWPCs and the training involved, writing consultants are more informed writer/researchers and can help students to become more so as well.

The RWPC experience and training has influenced writing center procedures as well. For example, we now ask student writers about their topics when students phone to schedule a writing center appointment.

Lessons Learned: Tighten Up Training

When several RWPC consultants are involved, it is extremely important to schedule a training session early in the semester. Because of busy schedules, a common time to meet with all of the consultants for a single training session can be difficult to establish and may be unrealistic to expect. There are dangers in training RWPC consultants individually because slightly different information may be conveyed and the synergy of a small group is lost.

Lessons Learned: Simplify procedures

Sign-up procedures to schedule appointments need to be clear, precise, and repeated often to staff. Doing so prevents students who are not part of the targeted population from being scheduled for RWPCs. Likewise, procedures for the RWPC consultants need to be streamlined so that the consultants are able to focus their energy on the RWPC sessions and not become flustered by complicated setup procedures.

Lessons Learned: Timing Is Everything

Although we prepared for and offered RWPCs in the fall semester of 2003, none of the appointments filled. This is because the majority of students are enrolled in part one of the GSW program during the fall semester, which does not require use of the library research databases. As a result, RWPCs will only be offered spring semesters when the majority of students cycle through the second part of the GSW program in which instructors expect students to incorporate sources from the library resources.

Another timing issue is related to when RWPC appointments are offered during the week. Our appointments have been clustered at the beginning of the week on Sunday and Monday evenings. It would be more convenient to students if RWPC appointments could be available each day of the week or at least every other day so that they would have more scheduling options.

Future Plans

At this time, it is not our intention to expand the RWPC program beyond the GSW program. Research beyond this level can become complicated, and training more RWPC consultants in additional disciplines would take much more time. Given the high turnover rate of consultants participating in the RWPC program, this does not seem feasible.

Another option we have considered is to offer research project clinics and writing consultations separately, but in the same location. We envision a designated area in the library (with obvious signage) where students can get individualized help from a librarian and individualized help from a writing consultant, both conveniently located in one location

The library recently received funding for building group study rooms on the first floor of the main library. Part of the plan, when completed, is to use one of the group study areas as an in-house satellite writing center during the peak research season for students to drop in for writing assistance several hours each day.

As with all start-up programs, we will continue to assess student learning and make changes to improve not only RWPCs, but also to creatively imagine new possibilities for student-centered, convenient, and collaborative services. The positive feedback we received from students about RWPCs is enough to keep us motivated to be flexible.

Notes

1. C. Reid, S. Henderson, and A. Burroughs Kelly, "Long-lost Cousins: The Unexplored Links between Writing Center Work and Reference Librarianship," paper presented at the joint conference of the International Writing Center Association and National Conference on Peer Tutoring in Writing, Hershey, Pa., 2003.

2. Dane Ward and Richard Raspa, *The Collaborative Imperative: Librarians and Faculty Working Together in the Information World* (Chicago: Association of College and Research Libraries, 2000).

3. For a lengthy description of different models of writing center positioning on campuses, read Carol Peterson Haviland, Carmen M. Fye, and Richard Colby, "The Politics of Administrative and Physical Location," in *The Politics of Writing Centers* (Portsmouth, N.H.: Boynton/Cook, 2001).

4. C. Cardwell, K. Furlong, and J. O'Keefe, "My Librarian: Personalized Research Clinics and the Academic Library," *Research Strategies* 18, no. 2 (2001): 97–111.

Chapter ten

Gaining a Scholarly Voice: Intervention, Invention, and Collaboration

Donna Fontanarose Rabuck, Pat Youngdahl, Kamolthip Phonlabutra, and Sheril Hook

Introduction: The Context for Intervention, Invention, and Collaboration

Donna Fontanarose Rabuck

In May 2003, a month before the Writing Skills Improvement Program's Graduate Writing Institute was about to begin, I received a call from a graduate advisor in the Department of Second Language Acquisition and Teaching. He highly recommended that a first-year international student in their program attend our summer seminar. The advisor felt that Kamolthip Phonlabutra's participation in the Graduate Writing Institute would provide her with the tools for academic success that she was direly in need of as a second-language student and scholar. After meeting with Kamolthip, I was certain that she was indeed an excellent candidate for the institute and felt that the intervention and information the institute would provide about academic writing and research might contribute positively to her success in the pursuit of her Ph.D. as well as to the development of her voice as a scholar.

The Writing Skills Improvement Program (WSIP) is a unique writing center at the University of Arizona that was created more than twenty years ago by Dr. Roseann Gonzalez to provide professional tutoring to underrepresented students. The staff is composed wholly of teachers and writers who have their master's degrees or Ph.D.'s in English, rhetoric and composition, or English as a second language, and extensive teaching and tutoring experience. The program's primary goal is to offer sustained individual tutorials and mentoring to minority and economically disadvantaged students and to fill in the gaps in students' writing instruction (or lack of it). For more than two decades, WSIP has consistently proven that sustained professional intervention makes a marked difference in the academic lives of students, building skills, self-confidence, and developing voice. (See my article, "Giving Birth to Voice: The Professional Writing Tutor as Midwife," for more information about the philosophy and practical results of the WSIP.[1])

158

Over the years, Roseann Gonzalez and I have expanded the program and designed a series of weekly writing workshops, satellite center tutorials, and summer writing institutes created for and open to the academic community at large. WSIP also has collaborated with a number of different departments to address their students' specific writing needs as a professionally staffed writing center can do. Because part of WSIP's expanded mission is to offer programs that individual departments and colleges cannot provide but might need for their students, eight years ago we worked with Maria Teresa Velez, associate dean of the Graduate College, to create the Graduate Writing Institute. From start to finish, the design and implementation of the program is collaborative in nature. Born of the Graduate College's funding and commitment to assist graduate students to successfully complete their theses and dissertations, the institute offers fifty scholars of diverse disciplines a three-week intensive summer writing program composed of large group lectures, small group sessions, and professional individual tutoring to address their most pressing writing needs. Kay Kavanagh, associate dean of the College of Law, offers a beautiful professional setting for the large group lectures and small group sessions in seminar rooms, and the tutoring occurs across the street at the WSIP offices.

Part of the collaborative curriculum design of the Graduate Writing Institute includes two optional workshops provided by the University of Arizona (UA) library. Ruth Dickstein has been instrumental in leading these workshops and working with other librarians, including Sheril Hook, to present them. The first workshop is a general overview of how to use the library and resources the library has available for graduate scholars; the second workshop hones in on discipline-specific research. Both two-hour workshops are well attended. In yearly evaluations, they are mentioned consistently as being among the most helpful large group offerings. (Sheril Hook discusses this component in more detail later in this article.)

The overall curriculum of the institute has a progressive weekly focus, moving from (1) Engaging in the Writing Process to (2) Key Elements of Formal Writing and Research to (3) Elements of Editing and Revising the Finished Product. Topics such as overcoming writer's block, the process of writing the master's thesis or dissertation, writing the literature review, critiquing a professional journal article, ruthless revision, and writing the academic vita are covered. The teachers collaborate in the presentation of lectures and provide handouts and resources for further future use. The population of the Graduate Writing Institute is composed of roughly 35 percent minority, 35 percent nonminority, and 30 percent international students of varied disciplines, and it is challenging to invent and present a core curriculum that best serves such diverse needs. Each one of the institute teachers leads a small group of ten students in similar disciplines who are provided with the tools for constructive peer response to their writing in progress. Then, twice a week in hour-long tutoring sessions, each graduate student meets with another institute teacher for individual professional attention to and assistance with his or her specific writing project. Here, the teacher assesses each student's strengths and weaknesses as a writer, answers questions about the piece the student is working on, and offers guidance and suggestions as these scholars develop and refine their academic voices. The institute staff also offer a series of optional writing workshops that review grammar, punctuation, and syntax and, more important, assist many second-language speakers to move from relative silence (because of their inexperience with academic English) to written proficiency, fluency, and confidence.

Many graduate students, and especially second-language speakers, experience extreme isolation as they attempt to understand the discourse of their fields and write cogent, well-argued papers, complete literature reviews, develop thesis proposals, or write the chapters of their dissertations. The Graduate Writing Institute staff also have discovered that a majority of students suffer from a lack of familiarity with the university services available to them. The UA library is one such pivotal resource. Again and again, the staff have found that graduate students are unaware of how to conduct efficient and effective library research, or what information subject specialists in their fields have to offer regarding discipline-specific journals and online resources. This is why the workshops the library offers at the institute are key elements of graduate student success. Thus, the WSIP's Graduate Writing Institute provides a model of intervention, invention, and collaboration unique to a professional writing center with ties to many different units, with the library foremost among them.

In this article, we intend to show how the collaboration of the Writing Skills Improvement Program and the UA library led to the development of a doctoral scholar's academic voice in the case of a student who previously was essentially voiceless. To further support Kamolthip's growth as a writer and scholar, the collaboration continued after the Graduate Writing Institute's close at WSIP's satellite location at the library (which Sheril Hook was instrumental in creating more than a year ago). Here, Kamolthip's institute teacher and tutor, Dr. Pat Youngdahl, met with her in weekly sessions over the course of the fall semester. The library provided tutoring space, computer access, and subject specialist services. We believe that this collaboration offers an example of how "marginal" units can indeed play a pivotal role in ensuring academic success.

Collaborative One-to-one Tutorials as a Resource for Gaining a Scholarly Voice

Pat Youngdahl

Kamolthip Phonlabutra and I first began to collaborate in June 2003 during the Graduate Writing Institute at the University of Arizona. Though we were both at the institute's opening plenary session, we met personally for the first time when Kamolthip arrived at my office for our initial one-to-one tutorial hour. We greeted each other and sat down, and I began to ask Kamolthip about her goals. In those moments, we, both scholars with an interest in writing pedagogy, embarked on a relationship as student and teacher.

Whenever I teach, I seek to make more possible the authentic freedom and well-being of all. In my view, such teaching requires a conscious intervention in what bell hooks calls the "interlocking systems of domination" that shape our existence in the prevailing global culture of racism, (hetero)sexism, and economic exploitation.[2] In the tradition of Paulo Freire, I see teaching as a way to participate in "the creation of a world in which it will be easier to love."[3] Elsewhere, I have elaborated what such a world might look like and explored how we can transform oppressive structures by entering into more profoundly cocreative ways of relating to each other.[4] In what follows, I hope to show how the teaching and learning relationship that Kamolthip Phonlabutra and I are co-inventing subverts the established hierarchy between student and teacher, and contributes to the development of both our scholarly voices. Our collaboration exemplifies the ways of learning together that I seek to make possible with every student.

As Kamolthip requested, we focused our tutorials during the institute on her revisions to an essay on second-language research design. From the start, we collaborated in complex ways as we each stretched across boundaries of race, culture, language, and personal experience to create common ground for our work. I speak and write only one of Kamolthip's three languages and am a nonexpert in her field, but she was incisive and patient in helping me to understand the central explorations of her study. In my memory of these first few meetings, Kamolthip and I are leaning together over the pages of her essay, tracing through her sentences and paragraphs, zooming in at first on matters of syntax and usage, then sitting back in our chairs, looking more at one another, to talk about her dilemmas of how to write her way in to the academic community, construct a scholarly voice, put forth claims, present evidence, propose explanations, and cue her readers as to the organizational strategies of her argument.

As part of her effort to gain a scholarly voice, one of Kamolthip's core goals has been to investigate the conventions of scholarly writing in English, her third language. In response, I have sought to open up a shared inquiry into both established and innovative practices of contemporary academic research and writing in the United States.[5] This inquiry became central to our work when we began to meet each week of fall semester 2003 at one of the Writing Skills Improvement Program's satellite locations, a conference room in the University of Arizona's main library. Kamolthip's intensive interest in examining academic conventions is a potent resource for her development. As I have learned in my twelve years of teaching scholarly writers, both ESL and native English-speaking students find it difficult, yet crucial, to discern commonalities and differences in what is recognized as persuasive writing across various academic fields and also among the scholarly journals within their own areas of specialization. In our reflections on conventions in Kamolthip's field, second language acquisition and teaching, we look closely at her drafts in relation to articles by established scholars, searching for clues about what readers in varying contexts expect in terms of such questions as whether to use "I," when to employ the active and passive voices, what counts as evidence, and how to incorporate the findings and viewpoints of other scholars without losing one's own voice. In this approach, we help each other to read with a writer's eye, focusing not so much on the *what* as on the *how* of a scholar's writing.

So far, the most formidable challenge Kamolthip mentions as she strives to write in her own voice is figuring out how to refer to the work of other scholars in ways that maximize accuracy and avoid plagiarism. This challenge is most difficult when she is called on to write summaries of empirical research studies in highly specialized subjects such as psycholinguistics, where the writers of articles often make numerous brief references to distinctive terms, previous findings, or theoretical traditions that are considered common knowledge among insiders in the field. Finding ways to make sense of the lore and language of one's scholarly discipline is daunting for any newcomer. Kamolthip's struggle to paraphrase the writing of other scholars is compounded because she is still extending her fluency in English as well as in the language of her field. Together, over time, Kamolthip and I have met this challenge by combining the resources each of us brings to the table: she brings her expanding foundation of expert knowledge and her questions, and I bring broad experience with synonyms, sentence structure repertoires, and scholarly writing in English. Moving back and forth between the research article and Kamolthip's draft, we engage in a mutually instructive, collaborative dialogue that helps us "piece together" the meanings of the research and generate options for Kamolthip's articulation of her summary.

Over the course of the fall semester, our collaborative relationship deepened. Kamolthip and I continued to give close attention to her drafts of essays for course work, discussing concision, elaboration, claim structure, and the persuasive power of clear subjects, precise verbs, and pertinent details. Questions related to academic audiences remained at the heart of our discussions. But now and then, we also began to talk more directly about how important other supportive scholars are to the development of one's own scholarly voice. We told each other stories about what kinds of teaching had inhibited—or liberated—us in our experiences as learners. We talked about our own imperfection as teachers and envisioned together what sort of teachers we now yearned to be. Along the way, we also explored and embraced the possibility of joining Sheril Hook and Donna Rabuck in the writing of this essay.

The work Kamolthip and I do as closely collaborating coauthors sparks my creativity and brings me great happiness. Her memo in response to my first draft helped me to express my ideas more clearly, especially in my descriptions of our inquiry into academic conventions and our dialogic approach to the challenges of summarizing what other scholars have said. In her memo, Kamolthip asked generative questions that guided my revisions and also encouraged my efforts to avoid the "unreadable writing" she has often encountered in academic articles. "Unclear writing," Kamolthip writes, "is beautiful and safe." This sentence is a powerful reminder to me of Patricia Limerick's "Dancing with Professors: The Trouble with Academic Prose," an article about writing (and teaching) that Kamolthip now looks forward to reading.[6] Limerick, a widely acclaimed professor of history, demonstrates the extensive personal and social costs of perpetuating traditions of academic training that make scholars so afraid to take risks that they hide their ideas in prose that at first glance may impress or even intimidate, but with a closer look, turns out to be impossible to decipher. Kamolthip's questions and comments on my first draft helped me remember to let readers see what I really believe and do.

Further, Kamolthip's own first draft prompted me to risk saying more about what has inspired my particular ways of being a liberatory teacher, writer, and scholar. Kamolthip's draft made clear that in our work together, what contributed most of all to the development of her scholarly voice was how I listened to her. This insight surprised me, for we had not talked about it in our meetings. But Kamolthip's experience also affirmed a belief I have sought to enact ever since I began to study liberation theologies more than twenty years ago. With Nelle Morton, I believe that one practice we can use to extricate ourselves from oppressive, violent social systems is "hearing [each other] to speech," that is, listening with such profound receptiveness and respect that we create a space where another can come to recognize and express emerging insights more fully.[7]

I rejoice that our mutual practice of "hearing to speech" has contributed so powerfully to calling forth Kamolthip's scholarly voice—and mine—to new levels of maturity and richness. Moreover, I am delighted that our focus on developing our scholarly writing has, in turn, strengthened our common commitment to liberatory teaching that resists a pedagogy in which, as Kamolthip's memo to me puts it, "teachers tell, students listen and obey, and there is no space to critique anything." I share in Kamolthip's sentiments as she writes, "I love this work very much. It is a very practical academic essay in the sense that we tell our readers a real story of our relationship between teacher and student, along with our belief and our philosophy of teaching and writing. Finally, we actually create a product of our shared values." For me, such co-creation of a liberatory relationship—and then, of a potentially liberating gift to others—is the essence of collaboration.

The Power of Intervention and Collaboration in the Life of a Doctoral Scholar

Kamolthip Phonlabutra

I chose to pursue my doctoral study in the interdisciplinary Ph.D. program in second language acquisition and teaching (SLAT) at the University of Arizona because I believe that this program can lead me to accomplish my goals. One of my goals as a foreign-language teacher is to know how to teach in a way that matches learners' language acquisition processes. Another goal for me as a foreign-language scholar is that, by doing doctoral study in SLAT in an English-speaking country, apart from gaining expert knowledge in the field, I will gain a scholarly voice in English in addition to Thai and Japanese, my first and second languages. My ultimate goal is to share and contribute my foreign-language teaching experiences and research findings to many audiences, locally, regionally, and internationally through my varieties of scholarly voices.

I completed my bachelor's degree in Japanese from Thammasat University, Thailand, and my master's degree in the same field, Japanese, from the University of Tsukuba, Japan. Now, I am in my second year in the SLAT program, and my major is pedagogy. My writing skill varies according to my level of fluency in each language: Thai, Japanese, and English, respectively. However, as I did not have much training in academic writing from my previous education, I have a huge challenge and tremendous struggle with my academic writing in graduate school in the United States. I have not only the challenge with my third language, but also the difficulty of knowing how to produce scholarly writing that meets the norms and conventions of the disciplinary community. My first formal training in academic writing in graduate school in the U.S. was in the Writing Skills Improvement Program's Graduate Writing Institute. Honestly, I am totally amazed at how ignorant and uninformed I was about academic writing whether in Thai, Japanese, or English. Fortunately, I had the opportunity to receive instruction on the concepts of writing conventions, voice, audience, and peer response from the Graduate Writing Institute in the summer of 2003.

I first heard of the institute when my academic advisor recommended that I attend it after I had been struggling with my academic writing and qualifying exam in the first year of the SLAT program. In fact, I always had an idea before I participated in the institute that if I had received training in academic writing beginning with my first semester, my first academic year in the U.S. would have been less stressful. However, it was not too late for me to obtain the instruction and I still have many years in my academic career to enjoy my writing. I participated in all sessions of the institute for the entire three weeks. Three weeks of training might not be a fast medicine to cure all my writing errors due to my nonnativeness, but it illuminated much for me about the process of writing. The instruction that I received helped reduce my fear of writing. I cannot emphasize enough that this kind of teaching is a sort of academic shelter for students, especially ESL students, who need to improve their writing skills. I am one of them. I am really happy to know that this kind of institute exists, and I believe that such instruction is invaluable for the success of graduate students.

In addition to the institute's workshops on writing, the sessions on library searching also contributed a lot to my study. The sessions provided rich information about how to search for materials in each specific field. I learned about tips for database searching in sources provided by several vendors, such as FirstSearch and EBSCOhost. These searching tips, especially for EBSCOhost, helped me search with ease for psycholinguistics articles for my course work in the fall of 2003. Because I gained the searching tips from these sessions, I now save a lot of time and can concentrate more on my reading and writing. The most fascinating thing was that the database searching also gave me a clue and led me to my first topic of interest for my future dissertation. I am interested in Thai graduate students' academic writing in English at universities in Thailand. However, according to my searching, most research concentrates on Thai students' academic writing at the undergraduate level. I am interested in Thai academic writing in English at the graduate school level because these students are going to be scholars and need to publish their papers in English for their professional advancement. The library sessions were especially useful for me because many of the resources I will need to examine in pursuing my research are not easy to find.

As part of the curriculum of the Graduate Writing Institute, I also received two hours per week of individual tutoring with Dr. Pat Youngdahl. I asked her to look at my paper, a final project for course work in the spring of 2003 (second-language research design). The title of my paper was "A Case Study of a Thai Doctoral Student's Disciplinary Academic Writing." My subject was a Thai health sciences doctoral student. I focused on the influences of this ESL writer's first language and cultural background, her academic training and her academic writing, and the process of her writing. Regarding the process of writing, I concentrated on a constructionist view of learning by investigating how my subject sought collaboration from her peers and disciplinary community for her writing. I submitted my final project to the professor who taught the course and asked him whether there was any possibility that I could present this project at any conference or publish it in a journal. My professor encouraged me to do so and recommended that I revise my writing. Thus, I worked on the revision with Pat. During our tutoring time together, we focused on various aspects such as language, conventions, and audience. This was the first time that I had a writing teacher sitting with me and elucidating for me every detail I should be aware of as an academic writer. It seems to me that having awareness of academic conventions and acquiring academic writing skills may work together, but the synthesis that results in mastery takes a long time. When the Graduate Writing Institute was over, although I had made great progress, I still needed further training.

Fortunately, in the fall of 2003, Dr. Donna Rabuck informed me that the Writing Skills Improvement Program (WSIP) would offer me once-per-week tutorial sessions for the semester at its satellite location at the library. I really appreciate that WSIP gave me this valuable training because it provides me with precious tools for my academic success, for both my writings for course work and my scholarly writings in the future. I would like to say that this kind of tutorial session is an ideal writing teaching program with an ideal writing teacher. As a language teacher myself, I am interested in not only *what* a teacher teaches, but also *how* a teacher teaches because these two factors greatly affect the learning outcome. Thus, for me to receive these writing tutorial sessions is a double fortune in the sense that I have a teacher helping me improve my writing quality and at the same time I have a very considerate teacher who truly cares to listen to my voice, that is, to what I want to say in my writing. This pedagogical philosophy is what I learned from Pat in addition to learning how to write. Listening to every student's voice is the pedagogy that I will carry with me along the journey of my teaching profession.

I will never forget the memorable first hour of tutoring with Pat in the fall of 2003. That first hour made me feel valued about my scholarly voice and my writing. Because it was the first tutorial hour of an early week of the fall semester, I did not have any writing assignment to revise with her. However, I had with me a rough draft about my topic of interest for my future dissertation that I had kept writing during the summer after I finished the Graduate Writing Institute. Pat was my first honored audience who carefully listened to my voice. That was the first time that I felt that my scholarly voice was heard after I had been struggling with my third language and academic writing for two semesters. Frankly, if it had not been for Pat, my respectful and amicable writing teacher, I never would have shared that rough draft because I would have been afraid of an outcome that might make me feel less confident about my writing.

There are two reasons why I decided to talk with Pat about my rough draft, which was still full of grammatical errors and nonnativeness. The first reason is that I had read one writing book recommended at the institute last summer. Peter Elbow, the writing theorist who is author of *Writing with Power*, suggests that writing is not just about writing, but is also about talking: "I think the process by which people actually learn to speak and write well is often [that] first they get an audience that listens and hears them (parents first, then supportive teachers, then a circle of friends or fellow writers, and finally a larger audience). Having an audience helps them find more to say and find better ways to say it."[8] This concept of talking to a reader, especially a supportive one, is a good strategy because it allows me to practice, in a friendly context, clarifying my thoughts and checking whether my audience hears what I really want to say.

The second reason why I risked showing such an early draft to Pat is because she is an ideal writing teacher whom any student with shaky confidence about his or her writing would feel comfortable to talk to. She listened to me. She assisted and trained me to transform my inner voice to the scholarly voice that would be heard by my academic audience. She helped me gain the tools to analyze audience expectations in various academic contexts. I am a beginning novice in my discipline and also my writing is still far from that of an English native writer. I never felt that my academic writings were anything more than challenging requirements for my course work. However, because of the first tutorial hour, I was overwhelmed by the greatest joy that my scholarly voice was heard by my respected audience. This has made me enjoy the process of writing more and more. I believe that if we do not enjoy or value the process of writing, it is difficult to create a good product.

As the semester progressed, I met Pat regularly once a week. Mostly, we worked on my course assignments for psycholinguistics such as article summaries and take-home examinations. Having had training in individual tutoring sessions for a semester, I now feel more comfortable with my academic writing. My progress, based on my self-assessment, is that I am better at voicing my thoughts in my writing and avoiding plagiarism. However, jumping from writing better for my course work to being able to participate in collaborative writing on this scholarly essay required a crucial support, a supportive scholar. I worked with Pat on several drafts of the present essay, and we reflected on each other's drafts to refine our scholarly voices. This collaborative writing is my first platform to share my experience as an English nonnative writer learning to produce academic writing for a broad audience and also the first platform for collaborating with other scholars. It would have been impossible for me to make this much progress in six months if I had not received the support of the Writing Skills Improvement Program and the University of Arizona Library.

Writing well, whether in a first, second, or third language, is not a given. One needs a lot of training. However, having an ideal writing tutorial session with an ideal writing teacher is a given that the University of Arizona offers for the academic progress and success of students. As a result of the academic intervention that WSIP provided, now I experience much joy in my academic writing in my third language, and I would like other students to have a chance to taste the same joy that I do.

Scholarly Voices in Collaboration

Sheril Hook

As a librarian, I celebrate the relationship that Pat and Kamolthip have. It is a relationship of extended intellectual discovery based on a mutual respect and trust in each other's work. Their scholarly voices emerge as they discuss both research and writing. Their work together exemplifies the collaborative, recursive, process-oriented approach to both writing and research that we seek to support at the University of Arizona Library.

The University of Arizona Library staff strive to create an environment that is not intimidating but, rather, inviting and collaborative. In 2002, an Information Commons (IC) was completed. It houses more than 250 computer workstations where students can work with a variety of software packages, use the Internet, or the library's gateway to resources. There also are a number of Internet connections for laptops and a wireless overlay. Additionally, the library collaborated with the Office of Student Computing Resources to offer a Multi-Media Zone for high-end software use and access to computing staff. The reference desk, staffed by librarians, staff, and students, is only feet away.[9] The space, as I mentioned, is intended to facilitate collaborative learning. Thus, there are group study rooms, faculty–student conference rooms, and a room and computer designated for writing tutelage, which is staffed several hours per week by tutors from both the writing center and WSIP. In creating a space where students can work with faculty, writing consultants, librarians, and computing staff, and collaborate with each other on group projects, the library has provided a much-needed location on campus that is open 24/5 with reduced hours on the weekends. It is usually packed, with students waiting for computers.

Important for me, though, is that the IC be a place that encourages students in a process-orientated approach to research and writing. That is, rather than sitting down in front of a computer (often preferred over paper resources) and gathering "everything" in one sitting that might be needed to write a paper or prepare a presentation, students work in a space that offers them a place to read, think, and confer with tutors, reference staff, computing staff, and faculty in order to develop their own ideas and contributions to scholarship. Providing a space that fosters this type of learning and collaboration should assist students in recognizing their work not as "communication of already discovered ideas but as a vehicle for inquiry and as a process of making and mediating meaning."[10] In other words, students, with assistance from someone like Pat, someone willing to sit down with them and discuss the information that they find and the inevitable discomfort they feel in doing research, could come to engage more meaningfully in their educations.[11]

The collaboration between the library and WSIP helps to facilitate Pat's work with students such as Kamolthip. Librarians and WSIP staff collaborate in four ways:

1. Librarians regularly offer two workshops as part of the WSIP Graduate Writing Institute's curriculum.

2. both the library staff and the WSIP staff attend training sessions provided by the other

3. They share space. Although WSIP is housed in another building on campus, it regularly holds hours in the library's Information Commons.

4. Both WSIP and the library refer students to each other.

Each of these forms of collaboration is discussed in more detail below.

WSIP Graduate Writing Institute's Curriculum

To make and mediate meaning, students need to feel comfortable using the library's disciplinary databases and other resources. They need to know how to access the discourse communities that represent the scholarly work to which they are contributing. To this end, librarians offer two workshops during the Graduate Writing Institute. The first workshop is intended for all graduate students. Librarians demonstrate resources and services that facilitate meeting graduate-level expectations for conducting research. These resources and services include databases such as WorldCat, Dissertation Abstracts, Citations Indexes, and services such as interlibrary loan, and subject pathfinders developed by librarians. The second workshop is geared toward resources in particular disciplines, so three sections are offered: science, social sciences, and humanities/fine arts. Graduate students enrolled in the Graduate Writing Institute attend the section most appropriate to their work. Each section workshop is led by a subject librarian.

Kamolthip notes in her essay that she found the library sessions "especially useful" and even got her first "clue" for her topic by exploring databases. These are databases that she learned about during the library sessions. Kamolthip learned how to find appropriate databases, to understand variations among interfaces (she mentions FirstSearch and EBSCOHost), and to locate articles on her topic. Although librarians have opened up a world of scholarship (i.e., a scholarly community conveniently and orderly indexed), Pat, in her role as writing tutor, has helped Kamolthip understand what to do with those myriad scholarly voices, guiding Kamolthip to find her own voice within what was becoming an identifiable (if not overwhelming) scholarly community within her subject area.

Shared Training Sessions

In 2002, the library and WSIP deepened their collaboration by providing workshops for each other. In the library sessions, the WSIP tutors become more familiar and confident in creating search strategies (e.g., Boolean logic, truncation, and proximity, understanding vendor versus database), selecting appropriate resources (e.g., particular databases, library gateway, print resources), and becoming aware of a shared role with librarians in reducing plagiarism and in understanding issues of copyright. When asked for feedback on the sessions, tutors indicated that they were very useful: "Enabled me to help students understand distinctions between the web and databases"; "I can coach students about how to experiment with the interface to find out how it works." In working with Kamolthip, Pat has used her knowledge of the subject pathfinders and database selection and searching to discuss with Kamolthip the process of creating and revising search strategies.

She also has encouraged Kamolthip to contact a subject librarian for in-depth research consultation. Pat can intervene at early stages of writing and revision to identify research needs and refer students, such as Kamolthip, to librarians and library staff when necessary.

In the session offered by the WSIP staff, librarians and reference staff learn about the services provided by the WSIP tutors. For example, tutors often help with all levels of the writing process, including brainstorming topics, development of claims, and citation style. This was a surprise to some librarians and staff who had not considered brainstorming or citation style to be within the role of the WSIP tutors and were pleased to know that they could refer students to writing tutors for help at all stages of the writing process.

Shared Space

In order to foster communication a shared space is important. Proximity to each other promotes continued awareness of services and encourages referrals. It also facilitates collaboration among units that have shared processes and goals for working with students. The library worked with WSIP to ensure that writing tutors have regularly scheduled reserved spaces in the library where they can meet with students to conference in either a private study room near the reference desk or at a nearby semiprivate computer station. Students can use drop-in hours or schedule an appointment in advance. The location of the room and the computer station remain the same every semester, but the hours are revised each semester depending on the schedule of the tutors. Signs are updated every semester to reflect the dates and times of writing tutor availability.

Referrals

Librarians include in their services one-on-one research consultations with students. WSIP staff highlight this service for the library by encouraging students to contact librarians for in-depth consultation, when needed. Similarly, the library staff keep fliers at the Information Commons help desk that detail the WSIP services and distribute them to students, when needed. In Donna's introductory essay, she notes that "again and again, we have found that graduate students are unaware of how to conduct efficient and effective library research, or what information subject specialists in their fields have to offer" and she notes that this is why the library's workshops are an important part of the Graduate Writing Institute. The WSIP tutors' understanding of this need and their willingness to attend library sessions in which they learn about library resources enables them to assist students in research and refer students to an appropriate subject librarian, when necessary.

Most important, though, what the tutors bring to research (or information literacy) is the evaluation of information. In her essay, Pat provided details of what evaluating sources entails: "to discern commonalities and differences in what is recognized as persuasive writing across various academic fields and also among the scholarly journals within their own areas of specialization." Together, Pat and Kamolthip reflected on writing conventions in Kamolthip's field, on avoiding plagiarism, and on finding one's own scholarly voice.

In conclusion, the library is pleased to participate in this collaboration because it reflects our mission to serve our customers by providing space and resources that support and encourage learning. The following conclusion was a collaborative effort among the cowriters of this piece. It represents our collective thoughts on future goals for our collaboration and demonstrates our co-commitment to teaching and learning.

Forward Thoughts

The collaboration between the library and WSIP was born in our openness to teaching and learning from each other as a way to improve our mentoring of students, and our visions for the future of our work together embody this collegial spirit. Our shared training workshops have helped us to sharpen our awareness of the potential for productive interplay between the recursive processes at the heart of both writing and research. Our goals for the future focus on making it easier for students to benefit from this interplay as, through research and writing, they seek to construct arguments that reflect critical analysis, well-integrated evidence, scholarly ethics, and creative insight.

At present, WSIP and the library share three specific goals. First, we want to continue to increase the number of referrals we make to each other. We have found that knowing each other personally makes us more likely to refer students to each other, more effective in explaining how to access each other's services, and better equipped to describe what kind of help students will receive. To build on this success, we plan to expand the network of connections between writing tutors and librarians, including through future shared workshops.

Second, both the library and WSIP would like tutors to be available to students in the library's Information Commons for more hours each week. An expansion in hours would require support in the university's budget, a goal that we plan to pursue jointly as part of the growth in our collaboration.

Third, we envision working together to establish a research/writing desk in the library's Information Commons, where students could confer simultaneously with writing tutors and research librarians as they formulate and develop their arguments. In such a setting, not only would students benefit from receiving both kinds of expertise at once, but librarians and writing tutors would have an ongoing practice by which to learn about one another's work and thus enhance their own.

These are our current dreams. Because we are engaged in an open and evolving collaboration, we trust that new goals will emerge as we continue to work together. We cannot anticipate these goals from here, which is part of what makes collaboration, for us, such an enlivening adventure. Yet, we trust that whatever shape our shared projects take in the future, we will be seeking to create the most vibrant, fertile context possible for our students to gain their scholarly voices.

Notes

1. Byron Stay, Christina Murphy, and Eric Hobson, eds., *Writing Center Perspectives* (Emmitsburg, Md.: NWCA Pr., 1995).

2. bell hooks, *Talking Back: Thinking Feminist, Thinking Black* (Boston: South End Pr., 1989), 175. For a critical and creative reflection on liberatory pedagogy, see also hooks's *Teaching to Transgress: Education as the Practice of Freedom* (New York: Routledge, 1994).

3. Paulo Freire, *Pedagogy of the Oppressed*, new rev. ed. (New York: Continuum, 1993), 22.

4. For more about how I link love, learning, and social transformation, please see my book, *Subversive Devotions: A Journey into Divine Pleasure and Power* (Tucson: Bean Pole Books, 2003); my essay, "Sacred Erotics in Louise Erdrich's *The Last Report on the Miracles at Little No Horse*," in *RED INK Magazine* 11, no. 1 (spring 2003); and my article, "Identification," coauthored with Tilly Warnock, in the *Encyclopedia of Rhetoric and Composition: Communication from Ancient Times to the Information Age*, ed. Theresa Enos (New York: Garland, 1996).

5. In my weekly lecture and discussion with graduate students from diverse fields at the University of Arizona, we critically analyze the politics of writing conventions, investigate trends in what practices are considered authoritative and credible among various scholarly audiences, and strategize about how to negotiate the disparate and evolving expectations of academic readers and publishers. For illuminating examinations of how scholarly writers construe, employ, and reshape the conventions in a wide variety of fields, see *Advances in Writing Research, Volume Two: Writing in Academic Disciplines*, ed. David A. Jolliffe (Norwood, N.J.: Ablex, 1988); *Writing in Multicultural Settings*, ed. Carol Severino, Juan C. Guerra, and Johnnella E. Butler (New York: Modern Language Association, 1997); Paul A. Prior, *Writing/Disciplinarity: A Sociohistoric Account of Literate Activity in the Academy* (Mahwah, N.J.: Lawrence Erlbaum Associates, 1998); and *Writing and Revising the Disciplines*, ed. Jonathan Monroe (Ithaca, N.Y.: Cornell University Pr., 2002).

6. Patricia Limerick, "Dancing with Professors: The Trouble with Academic Prose," *New York Times Book Review*, 31 October 1993.

7. Nelle Morton, *The Journey Is Home* (Boston: Beacon Pr., 1985), 127.

8. Peter Elbow, *Writing with Power: Techniques for Mastering the Writing Process*, 2d. ed. (New York: Oxford University Pr., 1998), 179.

9. For more information about the University of Arizona Library Information Commons see their website at http://www.library.arizona.edu/library/teams/pic/pic.htm.

10. Rolf Norgaard, "Writing Information Literacy: Contributions to a Concept," *Reference and User Services Quarterly* 43, no. 2 (winter 2003): 127. Available online at Academic Search Premier.

11. See Carol Kuhlthau, "Stages of the Information Process," in *Seeking Meaning: A Process Approach to Library and Information Services* (Norwood, N.J.: Ablex, 1993), 45–51.

Bibliography

Elbow, Peter. 1998. *Writing with Power: Techniques for Mastering the Writing Process*, 2nd ed. New York: Oxford University Pr.

Freire, Paulo. 1993. *Pedagogy of the Oppressed*, new rev. ed. New York: Continuum.

hooks, bell. 1989. *Talking Back: Thinking Feminist, Thinking Black*. Boston: South End Pr.

Joliffe, David A., ed. 1988. *Advances in Writing Research, Volume Two: Writing in Academic Disciplines*. Norwood, N.J.: Ablex.

Kuhlthau, Carol. 1993. *Seeking Meaning: A Process Approach to Library and Information Services*. Norwood, N.J.: Ablex.

L .rick, Patricia. 1993. "Dancing with Professors: The Trouble with Academic Prose," *New York Times Book Review*, October 31.

Monroe, Jonathan, ed. 2002. *Writing and Revising the Disciplines*. Ithaca, N.Y.: Cornell University Pr.

Morton, Nelle. 1985. *The Journey Is Home*. Boston: Beacon Pr.

Norgaard, Rolf. 2003. "Writing Information Literacy: Contributions to a Concept." *Reference and User Services Quarterly* 43, no. 2 (winter): 124–30. Available online at Academic Search Premier.

Prior, Paul A. 1998. *Writing/Disciplinarity: A Sociohistoric Account of Literate Activity in the Academy*. Rhetoric, Knowledge, and Society. Mahwah, N.J.: Lawrence Erlbaum Associates.

Rabuck, Donna Fontanarose. "Giving Birth to Voice: The Professional Writing Tutor as Midwife," in Byron Stay, Christina Murphy, and Eric Hobson, eds., Writing Center Perspectives (Emmitsburg, MD: NWCA Press, 1995). Severino, Carol, Juan C. Guerra, and Johnnella E. Butler, eds. 1997. *Writing in Multicultural Settings*. New York: Modern Language Association.

Youngdahl, Pat. 2003. "Sacred Erotics in Louise Erdrich's *The Last Report on the Miracles at Little No Horse*, " *RED INK Magazine* 11, no. 1 (spring).

———. 2003. *Subversive Devotions: A Journey into Divine Pleasure and Power*. Tucson: Bean Pole Books.

Youngdahl, Pat, and Tilly Warnock. 1996. "Identification." In *Encyclopedia of Rhetoric and Composition: Communication from Ancient Times to the Information Age*, ed. Theresa Enos. New York: Garland.

Chapter eleven

A Library, Learning Center, and Classroom Collaboration: A Case Study

Carolyn White and Margaret Pobywajlo

Many freshman English classes, and a few developmental English classes, require students to do research and to write about their findings. Writing about research is a challenge for most freshmen because they have had little experience with it prior to entering college. Part of their difficulty stems from a lack of experience with the library resources, so freshman English instructors often call on the librarian to provide library instruction to their students. However, the traditional method of library instruction is rife with problems. Too often, such instruction is delivered in one session, thus overloading the students with information. Furthermore, it is delivered out of context, that is, it is not situated in a particular research/writing assignment. Library instruction sessions necessarily involve a great deal of technological explanation, and the lecture/demonstration format precludes any opportunity for active learning or significant student interaction with the material being presented. Little opportunity exists for students to actively and critically engage with the information they find. Other factors that complicate the delivery of library instruction are the range of students in their level of preparedness for college, the range of students' ages (17 to 60+), and the diversity of native cultures and languages. To be effective, library instruction requires a developmental approach with opportunities for hands–on learning and individual tutorials.

At the University of New Hampshire at Manchester (UNHM), the librarians' ongoing efforts to improve on library instruction by incorporating critical thinking skills and information literacy theory into their information literacy program led to a collaboration among the library, the learning center, and two English instructors. In our pilot project, peer tutors trained and employed by the learning center were later trained by a librarian to deliver basic library instruction in the English classroom and to provide ongoing tutorial support to students in the research and writing process.

In this chapter, we describe the factors that enabled collaboration among the library, the learning center, and English instructors at UNHM and the process by which we implemented the collaboration.

Following our report of the outcomes for our pilot project, we evaluate the success of the collaboration.

Factors That Enabled Collaboration

The size of UNHM was key to developing the three-way collaboration. UNHM, the sixth college of the University of New Hampshire, is a small commuter college with 802 undergraduate-degree students enrolled in ten bachelor- and two associate-degree programs; another 800 students are continuing education students. UNHM's urban mission is to provide access to students in southern New Hampshire who might not otherwise have the opportunity to attend the university. The college attracts a wide range of students: 31 percent are nontraditional students over age 25; about 10 percent are English speakers of other languages; another 10 percent have documented disabilities. In order to provide greater access, the college offers a College Transition Program (CTP) through which students who do not satisfy the usual admission requirements for UNH can be admitted to an associate-degree program, providing there is evidence of the student's ability to succeed in college. Thus, there also is a range in students' levels of preparedness for college.

Because of the small size, faculty and staff get to know each other well and become aware of each other's goals, needs, and resources. For instance, librarians work closely with freshman English instructors and developmental English instructors to plan and deliver library instruction. Likewise, the learning center has worked with faculty to provide tutorial support for students in composition classes. One way that support has been provided is through the class-link tutoring program whereby writing tutors choose to be linked with writing courses they have already taken; this means they attend the classes and work with the students both in and out of class.

Writing tutors are trained to work with students on all stages of the writing process in a manner that Barbara Rogoff described as "guided participation" whereby learners "appropriate an incrementally advanced understanding of and skill in managing intellectual problems of their community" by working with experienced members of that community.[1] The amount of guidance and the level of structure or directiveness the tutor uses depend on the student's prior knowledge and skill level. For example, a student in a developmental English class is likely to require more direction than a freshman English student with better skills. An adaptable writing tutor learns to determine the student's need in relation to the requirements of the task and adapt his or her response accordingly.[2] The challenge for the tutor when the student needs more direction and structure in the beginning is to recognize when it is appropriate to become less directive and to provide less structure. Learning to adapt to individual students is not easy. Most tutors take considerable time learning to be flexible; however, working in a class-linked situation allows tutors more opportunities to assess students' needs and strengths.

The class-linked program is successful in meeting teachers' and students' needs because the tutor becomes very familiar with the assignments and the teacher's expectations for them. Students become familiar with the tutor and are more willing to seek assistance than they would if they were just sent to the learning/writing center. Class-link tutors tend to be more available to students than instructors are, and because tutors are still undergraduates, some students are more likely to work with the tutor than with the instructor.

The UNHM library director's familiarity with the English composition program and the learning center's peer-tutoring program, coupled with her knowledge of the problems of delivering effective library instruction, were the major factors that enabled our collaboration. While attending the national Association of College and Research Libraries conference in April 2003, the library director attended a poster session that described library initiatives in which peers were being trained to deliver library instruction. As a former UNHM class-link tutor, she immediately recognized the potential to utilize class-link tutors for the purpose of improving library instruction, and she brought the idea to the director of the learning center. Drawing on their close working relationships with faculty, the library director and the LC director recruited two instructors to participate in the pilot project, and the collaboration began.

Beginning the Collaborative Work

Responsibility for developing the collaborative project was delegated to the public services librarian who oversees the UNHM library instruction program. She met with the LC director and two English instructors, one developmental English instructor and one freshman English instructor. The group met three times to identify what issues might arise and to discuss articles about other institutions that utilized library peer mentors. The articles enabled us to formulate some questions, provided models for the assessments,[3] and confirmed several assumptions we had made about first-year students engaged in the research process. For example, we assumed that first-year college students would have little or no experience with library research and that students confronted with a significant research project would experience anxiety about using the college library and its resources.[4] Based on the experiences of the librarians and the instructors, we further assumed that some incoming college students who were computer savvy might be inclined to limit their research to materials found on the World Wide Web and accessed through major search engines such as Google. However, we also assumed that other students would be afraid of the technology, an assumption supported by our research.[5] Based on the articles, we also made some assumptions about the potential effects of using peer library mentors. For example, we assumed that students would be more comfortable approaching a peer tutor than a reference librarian for assistance,[6] that students' library anxiety and apprehension about using the technology could be reduced as a result of their work with the peer tutor,[7] and that peer mentors could provide students with more in-depth research assistance than could busy librarians at the reference desk.[8] We further assumed that, as a result of the peer-tutoring program, students familiar with the computer would be more willing to use a variety of sources instead of depending on the Web.

The articles helped us to foresee some possible problems (such as tutor underutilization[9]), but because none of the programs described were collaborative, they did not address some issues we faced. The first issue, not surprisingly in this time of reduced budgets, was money. Although the library fully expected to pay the tutors for the hours of training, it was unclear who should pay the class-link tutors for the time they assisted students with research. We decided that during the pilot project, the learning center would pay the tutors for the hours they spent with students, and we would monitor how many hours were actually spent on assisting with library research. However, monitoring turned out to be more difficult than we anticipated.

A second issue was agreeing on the theoretical bases for the program. We agreed that the theories of collaborative learning,[10] guided participation,[11] situated learning,[12] and information literacy[13] could provide the conceptual framework for our pilot project. Although these theories might appear to be in conflict with one another, we reconciled them by emphasizing or de-emphasizing some aspects of the theories. The learning/writing center is founded on the belief that one-to-one instruction enhances learning, a belief supported by the research on peer tutoring.[14] Peer tutoring is a form of collaborative learning in which the tutor and tutee work together to share their knowledge and create new knowledge.[15] Kenneth Bruffee emphasized the "peer-ship," that is, the equality of the tutor and tutee, and argued that the peer tutor's effectiveness is "a function of the degree of peership that tutors maintain between themselves and the tutees."[16] In a truly collaborative setting, the tutor works toward helping the student develop as a writer, reader, and researcher without compromising the tutor's peership. At UNHM, peership is regarded more as an attitude of shared authority that the tutor brings to the tutorial than as a prescribed way of facilitating a tutorial, although our emphasis continues to be on the role of guide rather than peer teacher. Bruffee also emphasized the idea of shared power. We de-emphasized this idea in order to stress the need for tutors to adapt to students' needs and to the new role as library mentors because the new role required tutors to occasionally take on an instructional role.

Several studies have shown that peer tutors need to be trained if they are to effectively meet the needs of students. Trained tutors are more knowledgeable, efficient, student centered, and strategic in their tutoring than are untrained tutors.[17] Another advantage of peer tutoring is that it can "help college and university teachers reach, indirectly, students who for a variety of reasons have not responded to direct instruction under traditional classroom conditions."[18] The librarians and the instructors agreed that training peer class-linked tutors to deliver basic library instruction would help the students make the adjustment to the college library and the research process; furthermore, they agreed that training the tutors in library skills would prepare the tutors to "guide and support" students while they used the research to write their papers.[19]

Guiding and supporting students through their "library anxiety" and helping them to become information-literate individuals are two goals of the instruction program at the UNHM Library. In its 1989 Final Report, the ALA Presidential Committee on Information Literacy stated that "[t]o be information literate, a person must be able to recognize when information is needed and have the ability to locate, evaluate, and use effectively the needed information."[20] Information literacy "enables learners to master content and extend their investigations, become more self-directed, and assume greater control over their own learning."[21] Inspired by the information literacy movement, the UNHM librarians seek to use library instruction as a mechanism to teach students not only how to access information so as to complete specific assignments, but also to appraise that information, to become critical thinkers and lifelong learners rather than passive consumers of received knowledge. Incorporating information literacy into a library instruction curriculum requires a shift in focus from a "tool-based" lecture/demonstration format to a curriculum that stresses fundamental research concepts, intellectual inquiry, and evaluation.[22] An information literacy curriculum calls for "a new model of learning—learning that is based on the information resources of the real world and learning that is active and integrated, not passive and fragmented."[23]

This focus on active, real-life application of new knowledge is also a principle of the situated learning environment. In the situated learning method, learning activities take place in an environment that reflects how the knowledge will actually be used. Students learn from demonstrations presented by "masters" or more knowledgeable peers and then practice applying the knowledge themselves so as to build new knowledge. Situated learning is essentially a collaborative activity; learning takes place when students interact with others in the educational community.[24] Whereas the learning center de-emphasized the peership of tutors and emphasized the tutors' need to adapt to the student's needs, the librarians de-emphasized the notion of tutors as "masters" and stressed the collaborative nature of the activity. Both aimed to improve students' skills, promote independent learning, and provide opportunities for students to negotiate their way into the academic community. This socialization into the community of learners is essential for the acquisition of real understanding because "it is the authentic social context in which learning occurs that offers the benefit of increased knowledge and offers the learner the potential for applying that knowledge in new ways and in new situations."[25]

The UNHM librarians saw the library skills peer-tutoring program as an opportunity to further incorporate information literacy and situated learning principles into their library instruction. Peer tutors could assist students with basic research skills through classroom demonstrations and one-on-one consultations, and librarians could focus on higher-level research concepts and evaluation. Both tutors and librarians could utilize active learning techniques to encourage students to engage intellectually with the process of research and inquiry. Students would become participants in the educational community, actively learning to apply knowledge through their interactions with the peer tutors. We believed we had reconciled our theories and practice to a degree where the goals of the library, the learning center, and the instructors could all be reasonably met. However, the reconciliation of theories worked better in theory than in practice.

A third issue was aligning our goals. To the learning center's usual four "T's"—tutee, tutor, teacher, and task—a fifth perspective was added: the librarians' perspective. Although the librarians' major goal was to improve information literacy, they had several secondary goals:

• To reduce students' "library anxiety" by giving them the opportunity to interact with the knowledgeable peer

• To encourage parallel problem solving between tutors and students

• To use active learning and inquiry learning techniques and exercises with students

• To have the freedom during instruction sessions to focus on critical thinking skills

• To allow librarians time to focus on analysis and evaluation during reference interactions

• To provide tutors with an opportunity to discover librarianship as a possible career choice

The learning center's goals, in addition to improving student learning, were focused on the tutors' professional development:
- To expand the class-linked tutors' roles and enhance their research skills
- To increase their opportunities to facilitate groups
- To enhance their critical thinking and problem-solving skills
- To transfer communication skills, particularly asking questions, from tutor training to the library setting

The two instructors' goals differed because of the nature of the two courses. The developmental English course focuses on improving the students' reading and writing skills and preparing them for the types of writing they will do in freshman composition. Library research is only one component of that class, whereas library research and writing about research is the major focus of the freshman English instructor who participated in the pilot project. The developmental English instructor's goals for the program focused on students' learning basic library concepts and resources as well as learning to employ critical thinking skills in the research process. She wanted students

- To learn "that research is a process" that "takes time"
- To comprehend the "search process" and the "vocabulary of research"
- To "learn to focus a topic" and to "ask intellectually curious questions about a topic"
- To "learn to distinguish between magazines and scholarly journals"
- To learn about the library's online catalog and electronic databases
- To "ask questions about sources to assess quality, credibility, [and] currency"[26]

Library research is a critical component of the freshman composition course, and the instructor who took part in the pilot semester already had incorporated research and critical thinking exercises into her syllabus. She hoped that the peer-tutoring program would help her achieve the following goals:

- "To expand the resources students have for receiving guidance in the research process"
- "To provide students with experiences which allow them to situate themselves in the world of critical thinking"
- To allow students to see "that a variety of people—not just the classroom instructor—are important to their learning"[27]

We found that the goals of the library, the learning center, and instructors were not only compatible; they often overlapped, and where they did not overlap, they complemented each other.

A fourth issue was how to incorporate library instruction into the course curriculum. The librarians saw in the peer-tutoring program a unique opportunity to integrate information literacy into the very fabric of the writing courses. Such integration is a core principle of information literacy: according to the ACRL's *Information Literacy Competency Standards for Higher Education*, "[a]chieving competency in information literacy requires an understanding that this cluster of abilities is not extraneous to the curriculum but is woven into the curriculum's content, structure, and sequence."[28] This level of integration requires flexibility and willingness to change on the part of an instructor because incorporating information literacy into a course's curriculum often involves significant changes to the syllabus. Integration is further complicated by various time constraints. Participating faculty need to cover course content while leaving adequate time for library instruction and exercises. In addition, instruction ideally should be offered at the point when students will immediately apply the skills, specifically at the moment in the term when they will begin research for a paper or project. As Kathleen Bergen and Barbara MacAdam pointed out, "students prosper most from any form of library instruction when it comes at a time of greatest need and relevance to their academic work."[29]

To get the maximum benefit from information literacy, classroom instructors need to be willing to adapt their syllabi so as to work the library instruction into a course at the ideal time. The two instructors involved in our peer-tutoring program were willing to work with the UNHM librarians to incorporate information literacy into the curriculum. The public services librarian and two instructors worked with the existing course syllabi to design an appropriate plan that addressed both the librarian's goal of incorporating information literacy into the classroom and the instructors' need to cover course content. Fortunately, both instructors had worked with librarians in the past to structure appropriate and effective library instruction sessions, and both agreed on the need to ensure that instruction be presented at the time when the students would need to use the knowledge and skills presented in the instruction session.

Although both instructors agreed in principle that library instruction should be integrated into the curriculum, the different focuses of the two courses meant that the two instructors differed in their willingness and ability to restructure their course plans to accommodate the proposed changes. The developmental English instructor had worked closely in the past with the library director to present focused, assignment-specific library instruction at two key points in the course of the class. On the other hand, the focus of the freshman English course is writing about research, and the freshman English instructor had always allowed ample time during class for library exercises and the development of critical thinking skills. As a result of this course goal, the freshman English instructor was willing to restructure her syllabus in order to add even more time for library instruction and research exercises and to use the class-link tutors as library skills instructors.

A fifth issue was selecting tutors for the pilot project. We decided to use only experienced tutors who already had received a year of tutor training so that the library training could focus on library skills, not on basic tutoring skills or the interpersonal or communication skills covered in tutor training. All three tutors selected for the pilot were females over age 25 who were first-semester seniors and previously had had class-link experiences; one tutor, however, had been a mathematics tutor the previous year, and she was new to the writing tutor experience.

Training the Tutors

Having worked with the LC director to select tutors, the library director and the public services librarian turned their attention to training the tutors in research skills, reference techniques, and the provision of basic library instruction. Together, the librarians decided that the tutor training would consist of one initial three-hour session followed by approximately five one-hour-long sessions conducted on an as-needed basis throughout the semester. The training sessions would be planned and conducted by the public services librarian. Finally, the tutors and the public services librarian would meet for a two-hour session at the end of the semester to discuss the tutors' overall experiences with library skills tutoring and ways in which the program might be improved from the tutors' perspectives.

The librarians' primary concern was to ensure that the peer tutors were well versed in all aspects of basic academic library research. The librarians decided that the initial training session would take the tutors through the various steps of the research process, from brainstorming topics and framing an appropriate research question to finding and evaluating resources, citing sources, and avoiding plagiarism. Of course, it was essential for the tutors not only to be able to execute an effective search strategy themselves, but also to model good research techniques to the students they would be tutoring. Thus, training included a description of techniques (e.g., the "reference interview," in which the librarian/tutor poses questions to the student in order to establish an information need) and exercises (e.g., brainstorming methods such as mapping) that could be applicable in a tutoring situation. The skills of negotiating a goal for the tutorial, negotiating authority, and posing questions were transferable from tutor training to library training. Indeed, such negotiation is similar to the questioning techniques of the reference interview, in which the librarian establishes the precise information need of a library patron/student by asking questions and establishing the prior knowledge and research skill level of the patron. However, the tutors assumed an additional role when they became peer library tutors—an instructional role. Because the library tutors would be conducting "mini" instruction sessions themselves, the training session itself served as a model of a library instruction class. Furthermore, the training included a discussion of when tutors should refer students to the reference librarians for assistance.

The public services librarian decided to use the initial three-hour training session to introduce the tutors to the ideas of information literacy and to provide them with a review of library resources. She and the tutors discussed library/reference ethics (such as privacy issues), explored reference techniques (brainstorming/mapping, the reference interview), and practiced using basic library resources (print reference materials, the online catalog, electronic databases) that would be most useful to freshman English students. Because one of the goals of the mentoring program was to include critical thinking as a fundamental part of the research process, the training session stressed the evaluation of resources and materials based on currency, accuracy, authority, and bias. The librarian used a combination of lecture/demonstration and hands-on exercises during the training.

The follow-up training sessions were used to reinforce the tutors' library skills, prepare them for their library instruction presentations, and serve as a discussion group where tutors could talk about their tutoring experiences and concerns with the librarian and the other tutors and receive advice and feedback. The freshman English instructor attended the initial three-hour session and offered her insights into student research habits; the instructors did not attend any of the follow-up training meetings.

Implementing the Program

As stated earlier, the role of library skills and research in the developmental English and the freshman English classes differs in fundamental ways. Consequently, the instructors used class-link tutors in different ways, and the changes made in library instruction in the classes differed in scale and scope. Furthermore, the experiences of the peer tutors in their one-on-one tutoring sessions diverged depending on the research needs of the students. It is necessary to consider the implementation and the outcomes of the program in the two classes separately.

Developmental English

The developmental English instructor and the library director had worked together in the past to develop what the instructor describes as "a two-tiered structure that is assignment specific and works very well."[30] The students are assigned two library skills projects during the semester; the librarian visits the class twice to discuss the specific library resources that are most useful for the completion of the two assignments. Although the librarians hoped to use the peer tutor in addition to the librarian to present several library instruction sessions, the instructor felt that the existing library instruction met the needs of the class. She and the library director compromised and continued to work together on their plan, while the peer tutor was used once in class during the semester to model student inquiry and to engage students in a discussion about research questions and strategies. The tutor presented students with a real-life problem that she was having with research in one of her own classes, and the students brainstormed possible solutions and practiced using the library resources that would help the tutor solve her research puzzle.

The developmental English peer tutor's main purpose in the class was to conference with students and, in the instructor's words, act "as a research mentor."[31] The instructor and the tutor met regularly to discuss student progress, and the students met frequently with both instructor and tutor to review assignments. When working on the library assignments, the tutor worked with students in the library to help them use the resources that had been presented to them in class by the librarian and to introduce them to additional materials that would help them complete the specific task at hand. After one-on-one sessions, the tutor completed the Session Evaluation Form, which asked her to describe and comment upon the session. (See appendix 3.) Students in the developmental English class wrote reflective pieces on their library experience describing what they had learned about the research process and about themselves as learners and student researchers.

Freshman English

The freshman English instructor has always made library research and critical thinking skills a fundamental part of her course plan. Students in freshman English are introduced to the library very early in the semester and immediately required to find and evaluate resources using various library tools. The librarians envisioned an instruction model in which the "traditional" fifty-minute library instruction session would be replaced entirely by smaller modules of fifteen to twenty minutes, led by either the librarian or the peer tutors. However, because library skills are stressed throughout the course, the instructor was reluctant to eliminate the initial library instruction in favor of "minisessions" presented at intervals throughout the term. Her experience with student researchers led her to conclude that students would benefit from the repetition and reinforcement of library skills. As a compromise, the public services librarian agreed to follow the instruction model recommended by the instructor, using the tutor and librarian-led minisessions as follow-ups to the typical library instruction lecture/ demonstration given toward the beginning of the semester.

Both instructor and librarian hoped that having the peer tutors lead library instruction sessions would allow students to see knowledgeable peers modeling good research strategies. The instructor and the librarian also sought to increase the visibility of the tutor as library skills resources, thereby making students more comfortable in approaching the tutor for assistance with research needs. The tutor would serve as a medium between the students on the one hand and the librarian and instructor on the other, helping students to negotiate research assignments. The tutors spent the first part of the semester preparing for the minisessions, and the latter part of the term (when students worked in earnest on their major research projects) saw an increase in their role as one-on-one tutors. Students scheduled time with the tutors through the learning center; one-on-one library skills tutoring sessions were conducted on computers available in the learning center or in the library itself. Tutors usually met with students for thirty minutes, although occasionally longer sessions were scheduled if needed. Like the developmental English tutor, the freshman composition tutors completed the Session Evaluation Form after tutorials.

Evaluating the Program

During the initial meetings, the librarians and the instructors discussed what evaluation tools should be used to assess the effectiveness of the peer tutors and the library instruction sessions. Students in the participating classes were given a questionnaire (designed by the director of the learning center and the librarian) at the end of the semester in which they were asked to answer specific questions about the instruction provided by both the librarian instructor and the peer tutor, their sessions with the tutor, and their interactions with the librarian. (See appendix 1.) The writing instructors also were asked to assess the peer tutors, the library instruction, and the tutoring program and its outcomes in a separate questionnaire. (See appendix 2.)

The peer tutors' library skills were informally assessed during training sessions through enhancement exercises. They also engaged in lengthy self-assessments after every tutoring session by completing an evaluation form that they created in collaboration with the librarian. The questions on the form prompted them to describe the goals of the session, what was accomplished, and what they would do differently in the future. At the end of the semester, the tutors were asked to complete a questionnaire and to participate in a discussion group to evaluate their experiences as library tutors and to suggest ways to improve the program. (See appendix 4.)

Outcomes

At the end of our pilot semester, we asked the instructors, tutors, and students to assess the program's effectiveness and to reflect on their experiences. For the librarian, learning center director, and instructors, the main question was whether we had met the goals we had for the program at the beginning of the term. Based on instructor, student, and tutor evaluations, we found that the outcomes of the program varied significantly between the two courses. As a result, it is necessary to analyze the impact of the project on the developmental English and the freshman composition classes separately.

Outcomes for Developmental English

According to instructor and student comments, the peer-tutoring program as implemented in the developmental English class was a success. The instructor was positive and enthusiastic about the impact of the tutor on her students' research skills, indicating that the research conferences with the students "worked superbly."[32] According to the instructor, more students completed research projects and more students got high grades on the research projects than in past years. She also stated that those students who met regularly with the peer tutor and who were prepared for their tutor conferences received high grades in the course as a whole.[33]

Student comments on their experiences with the peer tutor corroborate the instructor's conclusions. In journals, reflective essays, and the final questionnaire, the developmental English students gave "high marks" to both the tutor and the library director who taught the library instruction sessions. They were positive about the role that the conferences with the peer tutor played in their acquisition of library research skills. One student's comment that the peer-tutoring project is "a great idea" that "helped … tremendously" was representative of the student response.

Some student comments confirmed several of the assumptions that underlay the entire project. For example, we had assumed that the peer tutors would be able to spend more time with students than could a busy reference librarian; one student agreed, stating that the peer tutor was "helpful if the library is busy and a lot of people need help." This comment indicates that one of the goals set by the librarians was met: library staff had hoped that peer tutors would alleviate some of the traffic at the reference desk while providing students with focused, individual research assistance. We also had assumed that students would be more comfortable approaching a knowledgeable peer for assistance than going to the instructor or the reference librarian for guidance. One student agreed, stating that "sometimes it is easier to ask for help [from] somebody that is around your age." However, another student suggested that the librarians "would be more helpful because they know more." Such divergent views indicate that approaching a peer tutor for help rather than a librarian is a matter of personal choice and individual perception. The tutor is another resource available for those students who learn best in an intensive, one-on-one setting with a peer; as one student said about the project, "I think it is very helpful and gives the student more opportunities to get help."

Ironically, the peer tutor assigned to the developmental English course had a very different view of her role in the class and of the success of the project overall. Because research is not the main focus of development English and students in the class are only "getting their feet wet" [34] with library use, her assistance to students was at a very basic level. The tutor felt that she did not make a significant difference to student success with the research projects. In contrast to the instructor and the students who believed that the tutor made a significant impact on student library skills, the tutor herself felt that something was missing in her own experience as a research mentor. Further discussion with the tutor revealed that making the shift from her collaborative tutoring style to an instructional role created a state of disequilibrium. This tutor's experience is an example of an instance in which the blend of theories and roles broke down in practice. Her disequilibrium contributed to her sense that she was not being help-ful, and only after reading students' comments in their journals and evaluations about her role in the research process did she understand that she had indeed met their needs. The main criticism this tutor made of the program overall was with regard to the initial training session, which concentrated on enhancing the tutors' understanding of academic research concepts and experience with library resources. The tutor felt that because she already had significant experience with research and library use, she did not need the in-depth training in library tools. Her feedback on training led to some changes in train-ing. Therefore, although the instructor's goals for the class were met, the tutor's dissatisfaction with her own experience suggests that the learning center director's goals, which focused on enhancing class-linked tutors' research, critical thinking, and problem-solving skills, were not realized for this tutor.

Outcomes for Freshman Composition

Although the developmental English instructor and her students saw the peer-tutoring project as a success, evaluations completed by the freshman composition instructor, tutors, and students presented mixed views on the program's overall effectiveness. What became very clear as we analyzed the assessment data is that students' views on the usefulness of the peer tutors varied significantly with the extent to which the students were engaged with the course and the assignments. The students who made full use of the opportunity to work with their peers one-on-one to achieve their research goals expressed satisfaction with the experience; one student commented that the program "is an extremely beneficial resource for students doing academic research"; another praised them for being "there when you needed assistance, a great tool." However, many of the students elected not to consult the peer tutors for research assistance; like the library skills tutors in other programs, the class-link tutors were underutilized for the research.[35] As the instructor observed, "Students do not always take advantage of what is offered to them."[36]

According to the instructor, student attrition in her freshman English classes was high for reasons unrelated to the tutoring program.[37] Based solely on this assertion, the project was unsuccessful. However, the library skills tutors must be seen as resources available for students who choose to make use of them. For these students, the tutors made a difference, particularly in the resources the students chose; according to the instructor, during the pilot semester "there seemed to be fewer students with clearly inadequate sources."[38] The instructor saw the students' choices as an indication of their "ability to engage in the critical thinking necessary to develop and support a cogent argument."[39] The instructor viewed this improvement as a result of the students having a team of people—librarian, classroom instructor, and tutor—supporting them in their library research. Most important, she felt that students knew that help was available, if needed or desired, from a variety of quarters. Ultimately, she does not believe that the impact of the program on student success is "a measurable thing" because student learning is developmental and takes place with a variety of people in a variety of settings.[40] The program met the instructor's goals of providing students with additional help in selecting resources, helping students to think critically, and connecting students with people who can help them succeed academically.

The students' increased capacity to think critically about resources obtained through library research suggests that some of the librarian's goals were met as well. The presence of peer tutors in the freshman English classrooms gave the librarian the ability to focus her instruction sessions on critical thinking and source evaluation, using active learning techniques to enhance these skills. Furthermore, the classroom instructor's assertion that her students were more selective about library resources suggests that the students had internalized the critical thinking skills necessary to become information-literate individuals. Such an improvement in the information literacy of students was the librarian's major goal. In addition, the peer tutors were able to assist students one-on-one with basic research skills, freeing the librarian to use reference interactions for higher-level research concepts. Although it is impossible to ascertain from reference statistics whether the peer tutors alleviated the workload at the reference desk, the public services librarian did personally observe that the peer tutors devoted significant amounts of time and attention to individual students, referring them to the reference librarian only for in-depth research questions.

Unlike the developmental English tutor, the two freshman composition tutors expressed enthusiasm for the program overall and their participation in it. One tutor said that assisting students with library skills "took tutoring to a new level,"[41] and the other indicated that helping students with research is "a natural extension of tutoring writing: it just makes sense."[42] These tutors felt they were underutilized, but we suspect they had unrealistic expectations for the number of students who would seek assistance. They felt that more students would have sought them out if they had been more visible and if there had been more publicity about the tutors' expanded roles. Both tutors saw a need to expand the program in the future by having more trained library skills tutors available to help students, providing drop-in hours at the library, "recommending library mentors to all disciplines,"[43] and publicizing the expanded program to all writing-intensive classes. Indeed, some of the tutors' comments indicated that they had arrived at the same conclusions as the information literacy movement: they expressed their desire to see library skills taught throughout the curriculum and to have research integrated more fully into course content. One tutor summed up her experience with the program by praising the collaboration: "The combination of staff for this program was excellent. It is the perfect 'marriage' between the learning center and the library. I feel that combining these faculty members and departments really makes effective use of the resources available at UNHM."[44]

Although praising the program overall, the freshman composition tutors had the same comments about the initial library skills training session as did the developmental English tutor. Both tutors felt that the training was largely a review of information they already knew as experienced researchers. Follow-up discussion sessions, which prepared them for the in-class presentations and allowed them to talk about actual tutoring sessions with each other and with the librarian, were considered more beneficial. Rather than focusing on library resources, they suggested that the training focus on real-life reference strategy and problem-solving techniques and address specific issues that arise during a library reference interaction. They also saw a need to expand the role of the classroom instructor in the training sessions.

Although the freshman composition tutors met their own personal goals through the program and saw their experiences as tutors enriched accordingly, certain comments they made on session evaluation forms indicate that they did not transfer some tutoring skills, especially asking questions, from their training as tutors into the library setting. While conducting sessions with students, the tutors came to feel responsible for the students' research processes. For example, one tutor expressed the need to come to terms with the fact that she "can't always provide successful results for the student,"[45] and another described having to take a "bulldozer approach"[46] with a student in order to get adequate results. The learning center director saw these remarks as evidence that the blend of theories and the blend of roles did not go as smoothly as we had hoped. The learning center stresses the need for tutors to guide student learning through questioning; such questioning is also a key element in library reference interaction. Because the technique was not practiced in library skills training, the tutors did not shift their questioning skills into the new learning environment. Such a transfer of communication skills was an important learning center goal for the program; indeed, the librarians also had hoped to encourage parallel problem solving between tutors and students. The tutors' comments suggest that these goals were not met. Furthermore, because we had no way to measure whether the peer tutors' critical thinking and problem-solving skills were enhanced by their participation in the program, it is impossible to assess whether these learning center goals were realized. Therefore, although the tutors expressed personal satisfaction with the program and their experiences in it, evidence suggests that some of the learning center director's and the librarian's goals for the tutors were not achieved.

In summary, we can see that some goals were achieved and others were not; overall, however, the results were inconclusive. All of the program's participants were asked to evaluate the program, but we lacked a quantitative measurement tool to assess the effects of the peer-tutoring program on student academic achievement. As one instructor pointed out, students were exposed to a diverse range of people and resources, making it impossible to measure what specific factors contributed most to student success. Indeed, the most significant outcome may be that the project "allowed students to see that, in learning, we are part of a large social fabric."[47] A significant outcome is that the pilot semester has provided insight into the nature of our work together. We have been able to see what elements of our collaboration have proved successful and to reflect on ways that we can improve the collaboration—and the program—in the future.

Improving the Program

The major insight gained from our analysis of the program's outcomes is that the collaboration has to be strengthened in order for the library skills tutoring program to be improved. Greater communication among all the stakeholders is necessary to solve the problems we encountered while implementing the program, and all the collaboration's partners need to become more directly involved in the solutions. The semester has been a learning experience for us and has led us to a more reflective practice. Indeed, the greatest outcome of the pilot is that we have identified several key areas where we can together begin to make positive changes in the project.

Training

At the outset of the pilot project, the collaboration's partners decided that because all class-linked tutors received intensive training in basic tutoring, interpersonal, and communication skills at the learning center, training for their new role as research mentors should focus specifically on library skills. However, comments made by tutors and instructors suggest that this model was not effective. Based on tutor feedback, we plan to change library skills tutor training in the following ways:

- Future training will shift its focus from the use of specific library tools to practical exercises that stress reference technique.
- Training will stress more clearly when tutors should refer students to a reference librarian.
- The new training curriculum will include all of the collaboration's partners—librarian, learning center director, and instructors—more directly in the training of the tutors.
- Instructors will attend all the tutors' training sessions at the library and will assist in the development of training exercises.
- The librarian will attend tutor training at the learning center to learn more about tutoring theory and technique and its potential application in the library environment.

Oversight

Just as training must incorporate the skills and knowledge of all of the collaboration's partners in order to be effective, tutor oversight should involve more of the partners to ensure that the tutors are using appropriate methods to assist students with library research. We propose to:

- Oversee the tutors as a joint effort of the librarian, the learning venter director, and the instructor with all parties providing feedback on tutor/ student interactions in their respective settings
- Supervise tutors more directly, shadowing and/or videotaping certain research tutoring sessions to provide comments and analysis during training sessions

- Hold regular meetings throughout the semester to discuss tutor progress and development
- Ask tutors to meet on a regular basis with classroom instructors to discuss assignments and expectations

Library Instruction

Student comments on questionnaires indicate they prefer instruction sessions to be short and interactive. The freshman English instructor and the librarian need to develop an instruction session that meets the instructor's need for a general library overview early in the class while also providing students with the interactive format that they prefer. The librarian hopes to introduce a problem-based instruction model to replace the traditional lecture/demonstration format, asking students to work together to solve a problem or formulate an argument by using library resources. In addition, the librarian plans to ask students in freshman composition to reflect on their experiences as student researchers and to teach peer tutors to do the same. Using self-reflection as a learning tool has proved effective in the developmental English classroom and may encourage students in freshman English to engage more fully with the research process.

Publicity

Because the freshman composition class-link tutors were underutilized for library skills assistance, the librarian and the instructor need to work together to develop a plan to increase student use of this valuable resource. The instructor plans to refer all students to the class-link tutor specifically for library skills assistance. Shifting the focus of this meeting from being a "tutorial" to a "conference" may encourage students to take full advantage of the tutors' expertise and also encourage the tutor to place emphasis on dialogue during the interaction.

Assessment Tools

In reviewing and analyzing the student questionnaires, the learning center director and the librarian have found that many of the questions were unclear or too open-ended. As a result, we did not garner the kind of student feedback we had hoped for the project. Although it may be impossible to develop a quantitative tool to assess the effect of the library skills tutors on student academic success, we need to work together to design an evaluation form that elicits student feedback more effectively than does the current questionnaire.

Expanding the Program

Our collaboration has had definite advantages for all involved in the project. As the tutors pointed out, library skills are a fundamental component of writing about research; therefore, it makes sense for writing tutors to be trained in library skills. The tutors benefited from adding library mentoring to their tutoring toolkit, and students gained an additional resource to assist them with the task of conducting academic research. It is unlikely that without the collaboration, the library skills peer-tutoring program would have happened. The library would have needed to hire its own tutors and train them in both library skills and basic tutoring, or the learning center would have needed to train the tutors in library skills. Together, we have been able to lay the foundation for an effective program that incorporates the expertise of librarians, learning center staff, and classroom instructors.

All the participants in the pilot semester of the library skills peer-tutoring program at UNHM look forward to working together to improve the program and are pleased to see the project expand. As the program enters its second semester, additional faculty and tutors have been recruited to participate in the program. All the partners in the collaboration are interested in following the tutors' advice by exploring new ways to provide students at UNHM with an opportunity to benefit from the library expertise of a trained peer. Our experiences during the pilot semester have led us to realize that for the program be successful in the long run, we must collaborate closely to ensure that its expansion is implemented thoughtfully and with input from all possible stakeholders.

As one instructor commented, our program broadens that community and "constructs a team of people who can more frequently engage with students at the various points in their learning process."[48] Furthermore, it provides instruction incrementally and in context. Perhaps most important, the model is flexible; it can be changed to fit the goals and needs of individual instructors and course goals. Our collaboration on the library skills peer-tutoring project provided students with a network of people dedicated to helping them achieve their academic goals; together, we introduced students not only to the research process, but also to the intellectual community of the college.

Notes

1. Barbara Rogoff, *The Apprenticeship of Thinking: Cognitive Development in Social Context* (New York: Oxford University Pr., 1990), 8.
2. Alan Reiman and Lois Thies-Sprinthall, *Mentoring and Supervision for Teacher Development* (Reading, Mass.: Longman, 1998).
3. Ethel Auster, Rea Devakos, and Sian Meikle, "Individualized Instruction for Undergraduates: Term Paper Clinic Staffed by MLS Students," *College & Research Libraries* 55 (1994): 550–61; John Culshaw and Ellen Robertson, "Using Active Learning to Support a Peer Term Paper Counseling Service," in *The Impact of Technology on Library Instruction: Papers and Session*

Materials Presented at the Twenty-First National LOEX Library Instruction Conference Held in Racine, Wisconsin, 14 to 15 May 1993, ed. Linda Sherato (Ann Arbor, Mich.: Pieran, 1995), 193–201.

4. Catherine Cardwell and Stephanie Dennis, "Life after Death: Revitalizing Your Term Paper Clinics," *LOEX News* 26 (1999): 3–eoa; Ann M. Klevano and Eleanor R. Kulleseid, "Bibliographic Instruction: Renewal and Transformation in One Academic Library," *Reference Librarian* 51/52 (1995): 359–83.

5. Susan Deese-Roberts and Kathleen Keating, "Integrating a Library Strategies Peer Tutoring Program," *Research Strategies* 17 (2000): 223–29; Prue Stelling, "Student to Student: Training Peer Advisors to Provide BI," *Research Strategies* 14 (1996): 50–55.

6. Nicole Auer, Nancy H. Seamans, and Laura Pelletier, "Peer Advising in the Research Process: A Year of Student Success," in *Managing Library Instruction Programs in Academic Libraries*, ed. Julia K. Nims and Eric Owens (Ann Arbor, Mich.: Pieran, 2003), 25–30; Elizabeth Blakesley Lindsay, "Undergraduate Students as Peer Instructors: One Way to Expand Library Instruction and Reference Service," *LOEX News* 27, no. 4 (2000): 7–eoa.

7. Culshaw and Robertson, "Using Active Learning to Support a Peer Term Paper Counseling Service," 196.

8. Kathleen Bergen and Barbara MacAdam, "One-on-One: Term Paper Assistance Programs," *RQ* 24 (1985): 333–40.

9. Klavano and Kulleseid, "Bibliographic Instruction," 370.

10. Kenneth A. Bruffee, *Collaborative Learning: Higher Education, Interdependence, and the Authority of Knowledge* (Baltimore: Johns Hopkins University Pr., 1993).

11. Rogoff, *The Apprenticeship of Thinking*, 8.

12. Bettina A. Lankard, *New Ways of Learning in the Workplace. ERIC Digest No. 161* (Columbus, Ohio: ERIC Clearinghouse on Adult, Career, and Vocation Education, 1995). (ED 385 778) Available online at http://search.epnet. com [accessed 6 January 2004]. David Stein, *Situated Learning in Adult Education, ERIC Digest No. 194* (Columbus, Ohio: ERIC Clearinghouse on Adult, Career, and Vocation Education, 1998). (ED 418 250) Available online at http://search.epnet.com [accessed 6 January 2004].

13. *American Library Association Presidential Committee on Information Literacy: Final Report (Chicago: ALA, 1989).*

14. K. J. Topping, "The Effectiveness of Peer Tutoring in Further and Higher Education: A Typology and Review of the Literature," *Higher Education* 32, no. 3 (1996): 321–45.

15. Bruffee, *Collaborative Learning*, 81.

16. Ibid., 82.

17. D. Saunders, "Peer Tutoring in Higher Education," *Studies in Higher Education* 17, no. 2 (1992): 211–18. See also Topping, "The Effectiveness of Peer Tutoring in Further and Higher Education."

18. Bruffee, *Collaborative Learning*, 92.

19. Ibid., 85.

20. ALA. *Presidential Committee on Information Literacy*, 1.

21. Association of College and Research Libraries, *Information Literacy Com-*

petency Standards for Higher Education (Chicago: ACRL, 2000), 3.

22. Zhiang, Wenxian. "Building Partnerships in Liberal Arts Education: Library Team Teaching," *Reference Services Review* 29, no. 2 (2001): 147.

23. ALA. *Presidential Committee on Information Literacy*, 7.

24. Stein, *Situated Learning in Adult Education*, under "The Concept of Situated Learning."

25. Lankard, *New Ways of Learning in the Workplace*, under "Situated Learning."

26. Regina McCarthy, note to author, Dec. 22, 2003.

27. Gail Fensom, e-mail to author, Jan. 7, 2004.

28. ACRL, *Information Literacy Competency Standards for Higher Education*, 5.

29. Bergen and MacAdam, "One-on-One," 334.

30. McCarthy, note to author, Dec. 22, 2003.

31. Ibid.

32. Ibid.

33. Ibid.

34. Emily Madison, interview with author, Dec. 22, 2003.

35. Klevano and Kulleseid, "Bibliographic Instruction."

36. Fensom, note to author, Jan. 7, 2004.

37. Several students in that section of freshman English had been advised to take the developmental English class and chose not to do so. Consequently, they were underprepared for the class. In addition, some students were dealing with personal issues that prevented their finishing the class.

38. Fensom, Instructor Evaluation of Library Skills Peer Tutor Program, Jan. 7, 2004.

39. Ibid.

40. Ibid.

41. Dorothy Sherman, interview with author, Dec. 22, 2003.

42. Kirsten Rundquist, Tutor Evaluation of Library Skills Peer Tutor Program, Dec. 22, 2003.

43. Sherman, Tutor Evaluation of Library Skills Peer Tutor Program, Dec. 22, 2003.

44. Ibid.

45. Sherman, Peer Tutor Session Evaluation, n.d.

46. Rundquist, Peer Tutor Session Evaluation, n.d.

47. Fensom, e-mail to author, Jan. 7, 2004.

48. Ibid.

Appendix 1
Library Instruction/Peer Tutor Questionnaire

General Library Use
1. How often did you use the library in your English 401/English 301 class? (*Circle the number on the scale that most nearly describes your experience.*)

1————2————3————4————5
Not at all   Very often

2. Did you ask a reference librarian for assistance? (Reference librarians are the people who are available at the library's main desk to help people find the information they are looking for.) ___ Yes ___ No
If yes, what kind of help did you need?

3. How would you rate the help you received from the librarian?

1————2————3————4————5
Poor   Excellent

4. Please check all of the library tools you used for your English 401/English 301 research project:
___ Print reference sources   ___ UNH online databases
___ The UNH online catalog   ___ WWW sites

5. Please rate your level of comfort using these tools.

1————2————3————4————5
Not comfortable   Very comfortable

In-class Instruction
1. How would you rate the peer tutor's in-class library skills presentation? (*Circle the number on the scale that most nearly describes your experience.*)

1————2————3————4————5
Poor   Excellent

2. How would you rate the librarian's in-class library skills presentation?

1————2————3————4————5
Poor   Excellent

3. How would you rate the usefulness of the librarian's library skills exercises?

1————2————3————4————5
Poor   Excellent

Library Peer Tutor

1. How often did you use the class-link peer tutor for library research skills? (*Circle the number on the scale that most nearly describes your experience.*)

$$1\text{———}2\text{———}3\text{———}4\text{———}5$$

Never   Very often

2. In what ways did the tutor help you? (*Please check all that apply.*)

___ Choosing a topic
___ Focusing the topic
___ Selecting appropriate resources for the project
___ Using library reference sources such as encyclopedias and dictionaries
___ Using the online catalog to find books, videos, and/or other materials
___ Using the online databases to find articles
___ Finding materials on the shelves
___ Using the WWW to find appropriate Web sites
___ Other_____

3. How would you rate the help you received from the peer tutor?

$$1\text{———}2\text{———}3\text{———}4\text{———}5$$

Poor   Excellent

4. Did the assistance of the peer tutor help you to research your topic?

$$1\text{———}2\text{———}3\text{———}4\text{———}5$$

No, not at all   Yes, definitely

5. To what extent did the peer tutor increase your level of comfort in the library?

$$1\text{———}2\text{———}3\text{———}4\text{———}5$$

Not at all   Very much

6. Whom are you more comfortable asking for assistance, the peer tutor or the reference librarian?

___ More comfortable asking the peer tutor
___ More comfortable asking the reference librarian
___ Equally comfortable asking peer tutor and librarian
___ Don't know/undecided

Please answer the following questions as completely as possible. We appreciate your honest feedback! (Please use additional pages if necessary.) Thank you.

1. What library instruction presentations and/or exercises were most useful and why?

2. What library instruction presentations and/or exercises were least useful and why?

3. What changes would you make in library instruction?

4. What are your thoughts about using a peer library tutor for research assistance?

5. What advice do you have for the peer library tutors so that they can better help you with your research projects?

6. What advice do you have for the librarians so that they can better help you with your research projects?

7. Please add any comments you wish to make.

Appendix 2
Evaluation Of Library Skills Peer Tutor Program By Instructors

Please answer the following questions as completely as possible. We appreciate your honest feedback! Thank you.

In-class Library Instruction
1. How would you rate the peer tutor's in-class library skills presentation? (*Circle the number on the scale that most nearly describes your experience.*)
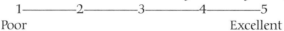
       Poor   Excellent

2. How would you rate the librarian's in-class library skills presentation?
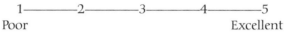
       Poor   Excellent

3. How would you rate the usefulness of the librarian's library skills exercises?
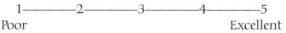
       Poor   Excellent

4. What changes would you make in library instruction?

Peer Tutoring
1. How often did you refer students to the class-link peer tutor for library research skills?
          1————2————3————4————5
       Never   Very often

2. How did the student work reflect your participation in the library skills peer tutor program?

3. What advice do you have for the library supervisor so that (s)he can improve the library skills tutoring program?

4. What advice to you have for the tutor so that (s)he can improve library tutoring skills?

5. What ideas do you have for improving the library skills tutoring program?

6. Please add any additional comments you wish to make.

Appendix 3
Peer Tutor Session Evaluation

1. What was the purpose of the session?

2. What was accomplished?

3. What was unanswered?

4. What resources were used?

5. How would you rate this student's prior knowledge of library skills?

1————2————3————4————5
Minimal   Very thorough

6. How would you rate the student's reliance on the library peer tutor?

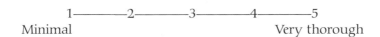

1————2————3————4————5
Minimal reliance   Very reliant

7. How would you rate the student's library anxiety level at the beginning of the session?

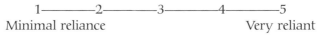

1————2————3————4————5
Minimal anxiety   High anxiety

8. How would you rate the student's library anxiety level at the end of the session?

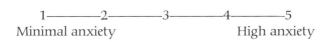

1————2————3————4————5
Minimal anxiety   High anxiety

9. Please record your impressions of how the session went overall.

10. What would you change about your approach to the session?

Appendix 4
Evaluation of Library Skills Peer Tutor Program by Tutors

Please answer the following questions as completely as possible. We appreciate your honest feedback! Thank you.

Training
1. How would you rate the initial library skills training session? (*Circle the number on the scale that most nearly describes your experience.*)

1————2————3————4————5
Poor   Excellent

2. How would you rate the follow-up training session/discussions?

1————2————3————4————5
Poor   Excellent

3. What library instruction training presentations and exercises were most useful and why?

4. What library instruction training presentations were least useful and why?

5. Did the training sessions prepare you for your in-class library instruction presentation? Please explain why or why not.

6. Did the training sessions prepare you for your one-on-one tutoring with students? Please explain why or why not.

7. Are there any topics that were not covered in the training sessions that you would like to see addressed in future training sessions?

8. What changes would you make in the training for the library skills peer tutor program?

Tutoring Sessions

1. How often did you work with students one-on-one as the class-link peer tutor for library research skills? (*Circle the number on the scale that most nearly describes your experience.*)

1————2————3————4————5
Never   Very often

2. In what ways did you assist students during library skills tutoring sessions? (*Please check all that apply.*)
___ Choosing a topic
___ Focusing the topic
___ Selecting appropriate resources for the project
___ Using library reference sources such as encyclopedias and dictionaries
___ Using the online catalog to find books, videos, and/or other materials
___ Using the online databases to find articles
___ Finding materials on the shelves
___ Using the WWW to find appropriate web sites
___ Other_____

3. Please describe a "typical" library skills tutoring session.

4. Please record your impressions of how the sessions went overall.

Program Overall

1. What advice do you have for the library supervisor so that (s)he can better prepare you for library skills tutoring?

2. What advice to you have for the instructor so that (s)he can better prepare you for library skills tutoring?

3. What ideas do you have for improving the library skills tutoring program?

4. What are your thoughts about working as a library skills peer tutor?

5. Please add any additional comments you wish to make.

Chapter twelve
Off-center Collaborations

Nathalie Singh-Corcoran and Thomas P. Miller

Writing makes learning visible, for when we write up our thoughts, we have a means to hold them up to critical scrutiny and rethink them. This power of writing becomes evident whenever we collect a set of papers and discover that what we taught is not what students learned. We also can see how writing documents learning in tutorial or faculty workshops when the discussion shifts from what was learned to how writing shaped that learning. At such junctures, we witness how writing makes learning available for critical reflection in ways that challenge writers and teachers to think through their learning process. Similarly, critical junctures arise in collaborations on library research when faculty come to recognize that research is not the transparent process they have perceived it to be. As faculty learn to attend to what students have to know to be able to do what they do, they are presented with opportunities to reflect upon the assumptions and purposes that shape their scholarly work. The pressures to reflect upon such assumptions have intensified as the attention to writing has spread across the curriculum. Teaching writing has ceased to be the sole responsibility of English departments as literacy has ceased to be defined in universal terms with concrete references to books and papers. A concern for literacy has become dispersed into discussions of *information literacy* or *computer, cultural,* and *visual literacy*. In the course of those discussions, our sense of what is involved in literacy has expanded beyond the individual writer or reader to include the institutional contexts that shape how knowledge is constructed and circulated. As we have become more broadly attuned to how writing documents the workings of disciplines and institutions, writing has become central to interdisciplinary collaborations on instructional technologies, outcomes assessment, peer tutoring, and faculty development. Such student-support networks tend to cluster around writing precisely because it documents learning processes and outcomes and thus makes them more available for assessment and intervention. The power of writing to make learning visible to institutions as well as individuals provides a baseline for assessing how librarians and writing center professionals can work together to raise the visibility of their shared concerns.

Such visibility is clearly part of what this book is about. Readers have been invited to reflect upon the shared interests of librarians and writing center professionals in the initial chapters that set out theoretical frames for increased collaborations and also in the subsequent case studies of how contributors have collaborated on varied projects in different sorts of institutions. Such collaborations between librarians and others who work with literacy have expanded as literacy has become more complexly mediated than it was when students went to the library to sign out a book to write a paper. As several contributors have noted, the genre of the research paper is ceasing to make sense of the challenges of documenting information that circulates through virtual networks where reference points tend to be nodes rather than sources. The complexities of networked literacies have made it impossible for faculty to assume that research is a transparent process or for librarians to rely on what Sheril Hook characterized in chapter 2 as a "tool-based approach" that treated finding a source as simply a matter of locating a book. As literacy has become less concretely defined and more networked, the power of writing to make learning visible has become more diffused, but also more critical. Close reading and sustained analysis are losing their currency to click-and-go forms of interactive literacy that can leave readers unsure of where they are in texts that often lack visible authors, boundaries, or purposes. The values of these highly commercialized information economies are not those traditionally shared by English professors and librarians. If collaborations between literacy specialists are to be redefined and expanded, as called for by the contributors to this collection, we would be well advised to reflect upon whose purposes and needs we profess to serve. That is what we hope to do in this concluding chapter.

This book documents the institutional changes that confront us and provides an opportunity for us to reflect upon how the work of teaching librarians and writing center professionals has gained increased professional visibility. Critical reflections on the professionalization process can help us to take a hard look at the pragmatic forces we face. Historically, one can see how groups become professionally established by identifying their purposes with service to clients and the public in order to set out an apparently disinterested justification for a group's efforts to consolidate its area of expertise and thereby gain control of its work. When a group of practitioners gains professional standing, more onerous and less prestigious service duties are often pushed onto paraprofessionals such as paralegals, nurses, or lecturers. In higher education, this professionalization process culminated with the establishment of the hierarchy that we use to define and assess academic work: research, teaching, and service. This hierarchy has positioned the services provided by librarians and writing centers at the peripheries of disciplines. Service generally has been defined differently in disciplines that include powerful practitioners who are not researchers (such as engineers or architects), in disciplines that have engendered a strong service ethos (as in the case of nurses and librarians), and in subdisciplines identified with applied service work (for example, social work or composition). To claim the standing of a research discipline, librarians have often identified themselves as scientists, as noted by James Elmborg. In reaction to the same sorts of forces that have defined library science, English professors have located composition courses and writing centers at the periphery of their higher concerns. Charting the geography of service in writing center scholarship can help us to set our bearings for reflecting on the collaborations set out in this book. After positioning some of the concerns of this collection in that scholarship, we want to explore the pragmatic purposes that could be achieved if writing center professionals and teaching librarians worked more closely together. Exploring the pragmatics of these issues may provide a useful conclusion for this collection by setting up points of reference that complement the theoretical and practical frames set out in the introductory chapters. Our purpose is not to be conclusive, but suggestive. Toward that end, we will offer heuristics that can help readers to reflect upon their own situations and consider how librarians and writing center professionals might want to collaborate in their institutions to address shared needs and purposes.

The Professional Reaction against the Service Ethos in Writing Center Scholarship

To provide benchmarks for thinking about how scholarly publications such as this collection might contribute to expanded collaborations between librarians and writing center professionals, we will review the history of writing centers as a site of scholarly discourse. The journals of a discipline document how it positions its concerns and articulates its expertise. According to Robert Connors, one of the leading commentators on rhetoric and composition, journals are "powerful institutions" because they distinguish insiders from outsiders, articulate emerging agendas, and thereby create "implicit criteria" for assessing future work.[1] Maureen Goggin has already examined the history of the major journals in rhetoric and composition in *Authoring a Discipline: Scholarly Journals and the Post-World War II Emergence of Rhetoric and Composition*, but she does not examine subdisciplinary journals such as *The Writing Center Journal* and *The Writing Lab News Letter*.[2] According to Goggin, the major journals in rhetoric and composition moved away from practical pedagogical concerns as scholars worked to claim increased professional standing. As the discipline gained professional legitimacy by distancing itself from teaching introductory composition courses, writing center journals remained more closely concerned with practical matters. The rise of composition studies to assume the form of a scholarly discipline has been problematic, for as Charles Schuster has discussed, "composition studies is grounded in practice, in the ways that oral and written language are produced, reproduced, learned, taught, shaped, modified—that is, in the variety of practices that anchor rhetoric and composition within our classrooms and our cultures."[3] Precisely because it sets out the problematics that shaped the disciplinary development of composition studies, Goggin's account provides a useful background for considering the professional standing of those who work in writing centers, for their scholarship is marked by a persistent ambivalence about the peripheral position allotted to those identified with the marginal work of collaborating with students. This ambivalence is reflected in writing center professionals' continuing investment in practical theorizing and in their refusal to repudiate a service ethos in the way that Goggin and others have suggested is fundamental to gaining scholarly credibility.

The professional anxieties of writing center practitioners provide a benchmark for considering the trends at issue in the increasing collaborations of librarians and others who work with literacy because writing centers have been central to that work since their emergence out of peer learning centers in the progressive era a century ago. Writing centers expanded markedly in the open-admissions era of the late sixties and early seventies. As in previous decades, centers were often founded to remediate literacy, but the forces at issue arose from broader changes in learning and the learned. According to Elizabeth Boquet, during the open-admissions era, centers were created to "fix problems that university officials had difficulty even naming, things like increasing enrollment, larger minority populations, and declining (according to the public) literacy skills."[4] Writing centers were crucial to mediating the proliferation of academic discourses that occurred with the diversification of the student body. That diversity prompted leaders such as Muriel Harris to set up writing centers, as evident in her account of the establishment of the Purdue Writing Lab in the mid-1970s to help teachers faced with large classes of students who wrote in ways that did not make sense:

> There were murmurings of starting up a writing lab at Purdue which, like other post secondary institutions around the country, was beginning to find that the literacy crisis was not a media invention or a fiction *Newsweek* made up for a juicy cover story.[5] Something was needed to cure the problem, and a 'lab' sounded like a distinct possibility.

The literacy crisis that Harris set out to "cure" had been heralded by the 1974 National Assessment of Educational Progress (NAEP) report of a broad decline in students' reading and writing. The NAEP report helped to justify the rise of the scholarly journals and graduate programs that established rhetoric and composition as an area of specialized research, rather than simply a staffing problem for English departments. The rise of theories and research on writing created tensions between instructors who were looking for classroom materials and "those who were turning to more speculative projects to create, preserve, and use knowledge about writing, reading, and teaching."[6]

To meet the needs of practitioners, Harris began *The Writing Lab Newsletter* in 1977 after jotting down sixty names at the Conference on College Composition and Communication. In the span of four years, the newsletter's mailing list grew to over a thousand. By 1978, a College English Association survey indicated that several hundred colleges and universities had officially recognized writing centers.[7] Special interest groups and conferences were founded, and the following year the Writing Centers Association met for the first time. The year after that, Stephen North and Lil Brannon began *The Writing Center Journal*. Although North and Brannon set high scholarly aspirations for work in the area, both writing center journals were really rather rudimentary attempts to mediate the isolation of people who worked in writing centers. The articles in both journals have continued to mirror writing center practitioners' daily work, and *WLN* is one of the only publications in composition and rhetoric to give serious scholarly consideration to all of its practitioners, including peer tutors, who are usually undergraduates. This inclusion challenges traditional conceptions of what it means to be an academic professional by bringing a cohort of contributors into the scholarly discussion who perform increasingly important intellectual work, but who themselves do not have professional standing as teachers, let alone researchers. The inclusion of such collaborators documents how writing centers can expand their power base by giving scholarly recognition to contributors who routinely work with the power of writing to make learning visible but have not themselves been visibly recognized as contributors to the scholarly work of disciplines.

In the mid-1980s as graduate programs were spreading across the country, *The Writing Center Journal* attempted to raise the standing of writing centers to garner the sort of professional credibility that rhetoric and composition was achieving at the time. North and Brannon attempted to direct writing center scholarship along the same lines that their own careers were following as they became leading scholars in rhetoric and composition. In the editor's statement of the journal's 1980 inaugural edition, North and Brannon provide a rationale for its establishment as a scholarly medium of exchange. They argue that they began *WCJ* for pragmatic political concerns as well as to foster scholarly inquiry. They identify writing centers as "the absolute frontier" of composition and rhetoric because they are positioned on two disciplinary points of reference—a "student-centered curriculum, and a central concern for composing as a process."[8] According to North and Brannon, writing centers nonetheless remain disempowered by the prevailing perception that they are "correction places, fix-it shops," and "the last bastions of bonehead English."[9] "If writing centers do not mature, do not establish themselves as part of the academic establishment, (even as, perhaps, they maintain their antiestablishment posture), they will surely, deservedly wither away."[10] This passage is marked by a notable ambivalence. Only a few paragraphs after North and Brannon had declared writing centers' independence from the powers that be, they here seem to accept a subordination to the hierarchies that structure the academic establishment. The tensions in this position provide an important point of reference for reflecting on the contradictions that face people who struggle to fit into institutions whose hierarchical assumptions do not fit their collaborative purposes.

These challenges confront all of us who teach in writing centers, libraries, and other collaborative spaces outside recognized disciplinary venues. Alternative collaborative spaces are often located on the downside of the distinction between academic and student services, for student services have limited professional standing when evaluated in terms of the traditional academic hierarchy of research, teaching, and service. On this and related points, writing centers and libraries have developed along parallel historical trajectories, as Elmborg notes in chapter 1. Both writing centers and libraries must contend with larger forces that dilute the impact of their work by pressing it to conform to the subordination of teaching and the marginalization of service. As the analyses of Elmborg and other contributors indicate, research and teaching are not static categories. Intensifying and expanding changes are challenging the subordination of teaching to research and the marginalization of service. Highly commercialized information economies are encroaching on areas of scholarly expertise; disciplines are being pressed to account for the values of their work; and those accountability pressures are being compounded by institutions' rising recognition that they depend on tuition revenues. As research has ceased to be seen as an autonomous enterprise, research libraries have been "redefining themselves, moving away from the warehousing definition of the past and toward instruction models" that are more critically engaged with the interactive dynamics of composing knowledge. (See chapter 1.) These efforts parallel those of writing centers to gain visibility in a changing institutional landscape. Writing center journals have played an important part in repositioning writing center work by challenging institutional conceptions that define that work as peripheral and remedial. While wrestling with the ambivalences of those who want to fit into institutions that do not fit their values, scholar/practitioners in writing centers have established publications to create professional networks to articulate and legitimize their values.

Through these venues, writing centers and libraries have worked to achieve professional standing, a standing that uncertainly bridges the gaps between student services and academic disciplines. Such gaps also are being spanned by technology initiatives, recruitment and retention programs, assessment and learning support programs, and faculty development networks. Like many of these efforts, writing centers and information literacy programs resist traditional definitions, for their values cannot be easily compartmentalized. They occupy the spaces between, not just between disciplines, but also the strategic spaces between the work done within disciplines. Collaborations on writing and information literacy are not confined to demarcated spaces, distinct bodies of knowledge, or departmentalized disciplines. Such collaborations do not provide seat time, nor do they grade students on performances to certify their progress through credentialed programs of study. Because writing center tutorial services and teaching librarians do not fit within traditional academic schema, it has been easiest for institutions to define them according to their most basic service function: tutoring writers on papers and helping them find books. As evident in many contributions to this volume, writing center and librarian scholar/practitioner/professionals are now confronting the truth of Audre Lorde's warning: "If we do not define ourselves for ourselves, we will be defined by others—for their use and to our detriment."[11] As this volume makes clear, if people who work in writing centers and libraries do not articulate identities that highlight their essential contributions to the teaching of critical competencies, they—we—will be defined by faculty and administrators who may be unfamiliar or unresponsive to the potentials and purposes of what we do.

Writing centers and libraries cannot exist in isolation. They are integrally connected to disciplines across the campus. Because of their connection to multiple disciplines, writing centers are classified as service units. They generally do not see anything wrong in being defined as service providers when that service role applies to their relationship with students. Writing centers see themselves as resources for students who want to talk about their writing. As evident in their published scholarship, writing center professionals become markedly ambivalent about being defined as service providers when they are identified with serving faculty in departmentalized disciplines. Stephen North's "Idea of a Writing Center" has been one of the most visible pieces of scholarship on writing centers, and this article straightforwardly repudiates pressures to define writing centers as service stations: "[W]e are not here to serve, back up complement, reinforce, or otherwise be defined by any external curriculum. We are here to talk to writers."[12] According to this "idea," another purpose of the writing center is to educate—and reeducate—faculty and administrators who assume that writing centers provide supplemental instruction. North's piece, and others that make similar arguments, have often appeared in publications aimed at writing center practitioners, though the pressures at issue can be more widely discerned in the ambivalence of composition studies to being defined by a service ethos. These writings have helped writing center professionals develop a shared language to reclassify and reposition their work within the academy. These writings exemplify how writing can make learning visible in ways that can empower isolated individuals by enabling them to make common cause with others in similar situations. In the pages of their journals, writing center professionals can find resources for articulating their centers' institutional currency. Despite their occasional ambivalences about their purposes, these publications (and this collection) show that although writing center professionals and librarians face distinct challenges in negotiating their positions within particular institutions, those challenges arise from broader changes that are opening up interdisciplinary opportunities to intervene in the historical development of higher education. For our writings to have such an impact, they need to be read against the broader dynamics of writing to make learning visible to institutions as well as individuals, for it is that power that gives writing centers and libraries collaborative potential of considerable value.

Intervening in the Pragmatics of Professionalism

The ambivalent aspirations of writing center scholars/practitioners provide a case in point for considering the institutional need for more integrated models of applied research, reflective service, and collaborative learning to guide our work with literacy. We must confront the need for what Elmborg terms "practice-based theory" if we are to raise critical questions about our collaborative purposes because professionalism functions most conservatively where it functions most tacitly. When a discipline operates normally, questions are rarely raised about why it does what it does. Researchers simply write up results, research inevitably advances to serve public needs, and students naturally acquire its modes of thought and behavior by mastering its content. Under normal conditions, little attention is paid to the discipline's rhetorical conventions, its modes of initiation, or its political functions within prevailing economies. When things are operating smoothly, professionals can unproblematically presume that their modes of research are transparent, as David Russell has discussed in his historical account of writing across the curriculum programs.

Although disciplinary specialists depend on writing to produce and convey their expertise, they tend to assume what Russell characterizes as a "rhetoric of transparent disciplinarity" that makes the potentially contested process of composing expertise all but invisible.[13] Normal operating systems can be critically overloaded by the power of writing to make learning visible and so, too, can hands-on collaborations with students on research methods. When an expert is confronted with initiates who do not know the conventions of the discipline, he or she is pressed to account for why the issue is articulated in this or that way. Such questions can be preempted by pedagogies that stupefy students with a stultifying concentration on the mechanics of established conventions, or such questions can open out into critical reflections on the purposes that are served by defining a problem in a given way. Although the composition of disciplinary conventions is part of the power wielded by practitioners, it cannot be contained by them, even under normal conditions, and these are not normal times for work with literacy. "May you live in interesting times" is often cited as an ancient Chinese curse, but it can be a blessing to live in such a time—if one is interested in being an agent of change. To advance change, we need to understand the pragmatics of institutional reform in higher education.

The literate conventions of academic disciplines have been destabilized by technological innovations and political pressures that are generally seen to be working to make information economies more transparent and efficient. Related market forces are functioning to undermine traditional enclaves of professional expertise (with the most-cited case in point being medicine). The spread of vocationalism through the arts and sciences is making many literate conventions seem outmoded, and the conventions of researched writing also are being called into question by the diversification of the student body and intensifying accountability pressures. These trends have opened up spaces within and between disciplines that teaching librarians and writing center professionals have moved into, but the historical forces that are converging on these spaces need to be carefully scrutinized if librarians and writing center workers are to be agents of change for the better. Historically, writing centers have resisted mechanistic pedagogies by focusing on producing not simply better writing, but better writers—writers who can question how assignments are set up to reflect upon the purposes that are served by defining them in that way. Similarly, librarians who oppose prevailing efficiencies have resisted pressures to treat scholarly inquiry as information processing. Many librarians have come out from behind the help desk to teach student writers how to ask better questions. A concern for writing as a mode inquiry can be a converging concern of teaching librarians and writing center professionals, but we need to be as precise as possible on such guiding purposes because we confront tacitly operating forces that press us to serve the interests of efficiency by treating writing and researching as modes of information processing. Attending to the provisional, contingent and transactional dynamics of literacy is critical, and as Sheril Hook has discussed, rhetoric provides categories that can be useful in thinking about authority, audiences, and purposes that can help us intervene in these dynamics.

The power of writing to make learning visible in the research process is a critical resource for teaching librarians and writing center professionals who want to do more than help students fit into prevailing hierarchies. This collection provides several case studies in how to harness that power. Chapter 7 provides an interesting example of how the archival functions of libraries can be expanded to make the histories of student writing a visible part of the development of institutions of public learning. Although the efforts of these contributors are distinctive, if not unique, they provide a powerful case in point for considering how work with student writing can deepen and expand institutionalized understandings of how writing contributes to higher learning. To help faculty and public constituencies understand students' writing as integral to the preservation and advancement of knowledge, teaching librarians and writing center professionals need to be ethnographers of literacy as well as institutional activists. As Elmborg discusses in chapter 1, we need to be "more like anthropologists or sociologists" in studying how academic disciplines compose knowledge in situated transactions with students and other outsiders who call experts to account for what they do and how it relates to other modes of interpreting shared assumptions against changing needs. Work with information literacy has interesting institutional continuities with writing across the curriculum initiatives that often infuse writing centers with broader purposes, as Arzt discusses in chapter 6. Histories of writing across the curriculum, such as Russell's *Writing in the Academic Disciplines: A Curricular History*, can help us think more broadly about our programs and our work with individual students.

When situated in such contexts, the institutional initiatives of libraries and writing centers can be seen as outgrowths of changes that give broad significance for our work with students. These changes have been noted in several chapters in this collection. For example, when Currie and Eodice established joint workshops and a shared space for tutoring in writing and information literacy, they "realized that our university was entering a rich period of change, one that will involve collaborations in number and scope that have never been tried before." (See chapter 3.) Other contributors recount how such collaborations have ranged from recruitment and retention programs through new learning centers to interdisciplinary inquiry courses that are often basic to broader technology, curricular, and assessment initiatives. These programs harness the powers of collaborative learning by creating occasions for students to teach. Such collaborations can help to demystify academic discourse in ways that realize the critical potentials of writing's power to make learning visible. The writings collected here document that power. The authors have opened up the situated and recursive process of finding one's self at work in the play of language. The interactive dynamics of that process are compellingly represented in chapter 10. At the center of Rabuck and Hook's descriptions of their programs, we find writers working to make sense of the potentials of their inquiry together. As in the other accounts, we can see how the recursive dynamics of work with writing empower tutors and students to think critically about how received conventions relate to their own needs and purposes, as Youngdahl reflects upon against theories of critical pedagogy. Such opportunities to rethink prevailing assumptions begin to emerge when students come to us "thinking they know what they want, but not really knowing what they need." (See chapter 3.) Those possibilities deepen as we realize that what students need cannot be prescribed but, rather, must be discovered through our inquiries with them. The critical potentials of those inquiries are realized when we turn back to reflect upon the purposes that have been set for them.

The collaborations of teaching librarians and writing center professionals may be at such a turning point. To realize the potentials of the changes we face, we need to think through our differences. For example, the two of us who have authored this chapter are a graduate student who is in the process of seeking her first job as a professor and a full professor who began publishing more than twenty years ago. Most of the contributors to this volume occupy positions between these extremes. As Elmborg notes in chapter 1, "librarians and writing center staff deal with an anomalous status in their institutions, often lacking full faculty status or full faculty prestige." People working from such ill-defined positions can have disorienting responses from research faculty, who tend to see themselves as "autonomous,"independent researchers who work in, but not for, an institution. (See chapter 2.) Faculty often identify their professional standing with a discipline that is positioned above their local responsibilities. This perspective has positioned service as a peripheral responsibility and teaching as a distraction from the real work of the discipline. The power of writing to make learning visible raises disconcerting questions about such assumptions because it is hard to maintain the assumption that the process of writing up research is transparent when one has to explain it to someone who does not know its conventions. On an institutional level, the power to make learning visible also raises challenges to the assumptions of departmentalized disciplines because expanding changes in literacy have made it impossible for "content" faculty to dismiss writing instruction to skills courses and simply send students to the library to find a book. As faculty have been pressured to attend to and account for how students learn to write in their areas of expertise, we have come to recognize that curricular reforms and instructional needs are subjects of research and not distractions from the real work of higher education.

In our own institution, this recognition has led to changes in tenure guidelines and in the establishment of career alternatives to tenure. At the University of Arizona, we have imitated the position of teaching librarians to create the category of writing specialists who can be promoted from assistant to associate and granted continuing contracts for doing institutional research rather than just traditional scholarly publications. Writing specialists (including the director of the writing center) have been promoted, granted continuing status, and received sabbaticals through the same channels used to review faculty for tenure. Using those channels to articulate the values of their work, writing specialists have composed accounts of their contributions to assessment, curricular reforms, and instructional support. Our university's efforts in these areas have been improved by treating them as subjects of scholarship that include detailed assessments of our students' needs and research on national models. These research studies have helped us to move beyond the common custom of basing major institutional reforms on anecdotal observations that would never be as credible in scholarly inquiries. This custom has been sustained by the failure of professors to recognize the collaborative work of institutional reform as part of their professional responsibilities. Tenure guidelines for teachers of language in the College of Humanities at the University of Arizona also have been revised to recognize research on teaching as a form of scholarship, with textbooks and articles on teaching being an acceptable alternative to traditional scholarly monographs in considering professors for promotion.[14] These changes in job categories and career ladders are not isolated examples. Leading scholarly organizations in English studies have recognized that service is an integral part of the work of the profession,[15] and writing program administrators have organized themselves into a scholarly organization that has put forward administrative service as a type of scholarly activity.[16] These efforts provide major benchmarks for assessing the contributions of writing center professionals and teaching librarians, but we need to think through our differences to learn from the sources of our ambivalences about traditional conceptions of service.

And Where Do We Go from Here?

Such institutional and professional innovations cannot in themselves redress the prevailing tendency to treat research as the higher calling of higher education, but they do provide concrete examples of the sort of hierarchies that need to be renegotiated to intervene in the pragmatics of institutional change. The forces at work in our institutions are daunting. The positions of writing centers have been undermined by the common tendency to temp out writing courses to part-time teachers who are often invisible in the profession because they are not seen as contributing to its scholarly mission. The numbers of such instructors have increased to the point where most college English courses are now taught by part-time and non-tenure-track faculty.[17] Insofar as such teachers have little professional standing, their efforts are not recognized by the profession as part of what it is about. Adjunct lecturers and part-timers are largely invisible to the departments who depend on their work, and as a result of this lack of visibility, the discipline loses the possibility of learning from what they do. As the reliance on non-tenure-track faculty has risen to levels that can no longer be ignored by scholarly organizations, English professors have begun to come to terms with the fact that the very perpetuation of their discipline is endangered by its dependence on the work of those whom they have failed to recognize as coworkers.[18] When the lack of professional positions for doctoral students called the purposes of graduate studies into question, doctoral programs were expanded to recognize scholarship on rhetoric and composition. Such programs have produced faculty to administer writing programs and writing centers, and as those faculty have become organized, they have begun to position administrative work as more than a marginal responsibility.[19] How much impact such position statements will have on the working conditions of most teachers of writing remains an open question.

The historical forces converging on instruction in literacy also are evident in initiatives that are integrally involved with the expanding collaborations of writing centers and libraries. The teaching-with-technology initiatives that are helping to expand work with literacy are a particularly prominent example of the centers of change that are redefining higher learning. As in more established areas of work with literacy such as writing programs and writing centers, such initiatives are often managed by administrators who lack the benefits of tenure, and few tenure-track faculty are involved in the day-to-day work of such initiatives. In many such extracurricular areas, managerial professionals oversee the work of what Gary Rhoades has characterized as "managed professionals." The numbers of such paraprofessionals have increased as "instructional delivery" systems have become diversified beyond the professor at the podium model to include highly mediated forms of instruction that reach out to populations who were generally ignored by institutions of higher education.[20] Distance-learning and teaching-with-technology initiatives are integrally involved with the emergence of information literacy programs, and as such initiatives have proliferated, online tutoring has become an increasingly common part of the services provided by writing centers. We need to reflect upon how the institutional forces at work in such innovations are converging on the work we do if we mean to intervene in the historical changes that confront us. As Rhoades discusses, "academic capitalism" is redefining the nature of academic work as the professoriate ages, loses some of its public credibility, and is not renewed by bringing in a new generation of tenure faculty. Control of the curriculum is being dispersed beyond the departmentalized disciplines that have been centers of faculty governance. As with writing centers and information literacy initiatives, teaching with technology and outcomes assessment programs have been centers for the emergence of "new occupational groupings" that are rising up to challenge their subservient service roles and openly compete with faculty for professional influence.[21] Such competition can be mediated by building the sort of coalitions that this collection calls for. Such coalitions of tenured faculty, administrative professionals, and graduate student teachers and undergraduate tutors can advance changes that address our shared needs, if "we" include redressing prevailing professional hierarchies as part of what we need to change.

As in the daily collaborations with students that are an elemental part of our work with writing and information literacy, such coalitions can be better understood by thinking through the power of writing to make learning visible. As Hook discusses in detail, our understanding of the processes of writing and researching can be enriched if we develop models that do not make the latter subordinate or subsequent to the former. As suggested by Hook and Elmborg, established models of the process of writing up research can be criticized for reducing inquiry to procedures for information processing. Such routinized thinking has been widely criticized in composition studies for divorcing individual writers from the ideological and political forces that shape how problems get posed. Research on the social construction of knowledge has expanded our frame of reference beyond the isolated writer researching a problem to consider how problems are socially constructed. As Elmborg discussed in chapter 1, with the move beyond isolated skills instruction, those who work with information literacy have come to explore "the role of information in the larger learning process of students" in order to help "them make the shift from a world where mastering content constituted education to one in which navigating information systems and making new personal and public knowledge constitutes education." Such collaborative concerns call on us to think of researching and writing as a process of inquiry that advances in a recursive fashion that calls into question the assumptions we began with, and even perhaps the purposes toward which we thought we were moving. This recursive process is a model for much of what we value in our work, including not just our collaborations with students and faculty, but also our collaborations here, on this page, in the process of making meaning by composing our thoughts as we read and write about what we do. The recursive process of collaborative inquiry also provides a powerful counterpoint to the professionalization process, which may be undertaken to gain individual advancement, but which, upon reflection, may enable us to rethink our needs in broader political terms that expand our sense of the services we provide and the purposes they serve. The process of composing and interpreting research such as this collection are transactional. We have not simply written up our research, but we have composed a better sense of what we do by drawing on perceived concerns of readers to try to explain how we can best respond to shared challenges. Insofar as this collection contributes to such collective deliberations by making shared resources and needs visible, it will have served its purposes and, we hope, yours as well.

Notes

1. Robert J. Connors, *Composition-Rhetoric: Backgrounds, Theory, and Pedagogy* (Pittsburgh, Pa: U of Pittsburgh Pr., 1997), 351, 353.
2. Maureen Daly Goggin, *Authoring a Discipline: Scholarly Journals and The Post-World War II Emergence of Rhetoric and Composition* (Mahwah, N.J.: Erlbaum, 2000).
3. Charles Schuster, "Theory and Practice," on *An Introduction to Composition Studies*, ed. Erika Lindemann and Gary Tate (New York: Oxford University Pr., 1991), 33.
4. Elizabeth Boquet, "Our Little Secret: A History of Writing Centers, Pre- to Post-Open Admissions," *College Composition and Communication* 50, no. 3 (1999): 463–82. Reprinted in *The Allyn and Bacon Guide to Writing Center Theory and Practice*, ed. Robert W. Barnett and Jacob S. Blumner (Needham Heights, Mass.: Allyn and Bacon, 2001), 41–60.
5. Muriel Harris, "Growing Pains: The Coming of Age of Writing Centers," *Writing Center Journal* 2, no. 1 (1982): 1.
6. Goggin, *Authoring a Discipline*, 76.
7. Kinkead, Joyce. "The National Writing Centers Association as Mooring: A Personal History of the First Decade." *The Writing Center Journal* 16.2 (1996): 131-43. Reprinted in The Allyn and Bacon Guide to Writing Center Theory and Practice. Ed. Robert W. Barnett and Jacob S. Blumner. Needham Heights, MA: Allyn and Bacon, 2001. 29-39.

8. Stephen North and Lil Brannon, "From the Editors," *Writing Center Journal* 1, no. 1 (1980): 1.

9. Ibid.

10. Ibid., 2.

11. Audre Lorde, *Sister Outsider* (Freedom, Calif.: Crossing Pr., 1984), 45.

12. Stephen North, "The Idea of a Writing Center," *College English* 46 (1984): 433–46. Rpt. in *The Allyn and Bacon Guide to Writing Center Theory and Practice*, ed. Robert W. Barnett and Jacob S. Blumner (Needham Heights, Mass.: Allyn and Bacon, 2001), 63–78.

13. David Russell, *Writing in the Academic Disciplines: A Curricular History*, 2nd ed. (Carbondale: Southern Illinois University Pr., 2002).

14. See College of Humanities, University of Arizona, "Promotion and Tenure: Criteria" (1995, rev. 2000). Available online at http://www.coh.arizona. edu/COH/facinfo/pandtcriteria2000/pandtcriteria2000.htm [accessed 17 December 2004].

15. See Modern Language Association Committee on Professional Service, "Making Faculty Work Visible: Reinterpreting Professional Service, Teaching, and Research in the Fields of Language and Literature" (1996). Available online at http://www.mla.org/resources/documents/rep_facultyvis [accessed 17 December 2004].

16. See Council of Writing Program Administrators, "Evaluating the Intellectual Work of Writing Administration" (1998). Available online at http://www.wpacouncil.org/positions/intellectualwork.html [accessed 17 December 2004].

17. See Coalition on the Academic Workforce, "Who Is Teaching in American Classrooms? A Collaborative Study of Undergraduate Faculty, Fall 1999." American Historical Association. Available online at http://www.historians.org/caw/index.htm [accessed 20 December 2004].

18. See Modern Language Association Committee on Professional Employment, "Final Report" (July 2003). Available online at http://www.mla. org/resources/documents/rep_employment/prof_employment [accessed 20 December 2004].

19. See Council of Writing Program Administrators.

20. Gary Rhoades, *Managed Professionals: Unionized Faculty and Restructuring Academic Labor* (Albany: State University of New York Pr., 1998), 272.

21. Ibid., 89.

Additional Reference

Association of Departments of English Ad Hoc Committee on Staffing. 1999. "Report of the ADE Ad Hoc Committee on Staffing." *ADE Bulletin* 122 (spring): 1–24.

Centers for Learning: Writing Centers and Libraries in Collaboration

Contributors

Judy Arzt is director of the Academic Resources Center at Saint Joseph College, Conn.

Colleen Boff, the "R" in our RWPC pilot, is associate professor and first-year experience librarian at Bowling Green State University, in Bowling Green, Ohio. She holds an MA in library science.

John C. Brereton, historian and consultant to the UNH writing archives project, is director of university writing and professor of English at Brandeis University.

Lea Currie is coordinator of instruction and education subject specialist for the University of Kansas Libraries. She has been with KU since 1999. She has an MLIS from the University of Texas and a BA in history from Texas A&M University. Her special interests include training peer reference consultants, promoting information literacy across the curriculum, and collaboration among faculty, student services, and libraries to provide useful services to students at the university.

James K. Elmborg is an assistant professor in the School of Library and Information Science at The University of Iowa. He taught composition and literature for twenty years before becoming a librarian in 1996. He has authored one book, a literary study of the poetry of Edward Dorn, and several articles on library instruction. He received the Publication of the Year award in 2003 for "Teaching at the Desk: Toward a Reference Pedagogy."

Michele Eodice, Ph.D., is director of the writing center at the University of Kansas, where she also teaches a course in writing center theory and practice and a technical writing course. She is the associate editor of development for the Writing Center Journal and coauthor of the book *(First Person)²: A study of Co-authoring in the Academy*. In addition, she has published work in the areas of plagiarism, writing center administration, and writing groups. Finally, she is an active member of the International Writing Centers Association, the Midwest Writing Centers Association, and the National Conference on Peer Tutoring in Writing.

Cinthia Gannett, formerly director of Writing-across-the-Curriculum Center at the University of New Hampshire, is currently director, Writing across the Curriculum and Writing Center, and associate professor of communication at Loyola College, in Maryland.

Michele Giglio, M.A. IRLS, University of Arizona, is Systems Librarian and Instructor at Wesley College.

Sheril Hook is coordinator of instructional services in Mississauga Library at the University of Toronto. She has been teaching writing and research for twelve years. During the writing and editing of this book, she was the English and theatre arts librarian at the University of Arizona.

Sarah Leadley is head of reference and instruction services in the Campus Library at the University of Washington, Bothell, and Cascadia Community College.

Thomas P. Miller directs the writing program at the University of Arizona, where he has taught for more than fifteen years. He received the Administrator of the Year award from the Council of Graduate and Professional Students in 1999, and he won the Mina Shaughnessy Award in 1998 for the first volume of his history of college English studies, *The Formation of College English: Rhetoric and Belles Lettres in the British Cultural Provinces.* He is currently working on the second part of that study, "The Formation of College English: From the American Republic of Letters to the Information Economy."

Kamolthip Phonlabutra (Pla), MA, has been on the faculty of the Humanities and Social Sciences Department at Rajabhat University Phetchaburi, in Thailand since 1998. She is on leave to pursue her Ph.D. at the University of Arizona.

Margaret Pobywajlo has been training peer tutors for fifteen years in her role as director of the learning center at UNH-Manchester. Her prior professional experience at the college level was in teaching freshman composition. She holds a BA from Notre Dame de Namur University, an MA in English from California State University at Sacramento, and is currently completing her Ph.D. in education at the University of New Hampshire.

Becky Reed Rosenberg is the director of the writing center at the University of Washington, Bothell.

Donna Fontanarose Rabuck, Ph.D., is the assistant director of the University of Arizona's Writing Skills Improvement Program and director of the Graduate Writing Institute.

Casey Reid is co-assistant director of the SMSU writing center.

Nathalie Singh-Corcoran is Writing Center Coordinator at West Virginia University where she also teaches courses in the composition program. Her research interests include Writing Program Administration and community/university partnerships. She has recently completed a dissertation entitled: "Connections and Fissures: Reconsidering the Writing Center in Composition and Rhetoric and the Academy."

Elizabeth Slomba is the university archivist and an assistant professor at the University of New Hampshire.

Connie Strickland, M.A. Education, University of Denver, is Writing Center Director and Instructor of English at Wesley College.

Katherine E. Tirabassi is a doctoral student in composition at University of New Hampshire and assistant director of the Robert J. Connors Writing Center (spring 2002–spring 2003).

Barbara Toth, the "W" in our pilot, is coordinator of the writing center and assistant director of academic enhancement at Bowling Green State University, in Bowling Green, Ohio. She holds a Ph.D. in rhetoric and composition.

Carolyn White is an assistant professor/library specialist at the UNH-Manchester Library, where she specializes in library instruction and reference services. Before becoming a librarian, she taught freshman composition and introductory literature courses at the college level. She holds a BA in English from the College of the Holy Cross; an MA in English from Indiana University, Bloomington; and an MLIS from the University of Rhode Island.

Pat Youngdahl, Ph.D., an activist scholar and writer, teaches in the Writing Skills Improvement Program at the University of Arizona in Tucson. Most recently, she is the author of *Subversive Devotions: A Journey into Divine Pleasure and Power*.

Amy A. Zenger is a doctoral student in composition at University of New Hampshire and assistant director of the writing-across-the-curriculum (fall 2001–spring 2003).

Index